The Organizational Complex

Reinhold Martin

The Organizational Complex

Architecture, Media, and Corporate Space

The MIT Press

Cambridge, Massachusetts

London, England

This book was set in Myriad by Graphic Composition,
Inc., and was printed and bound in the United States
of America.

Library of Congress Cataloging-in-Publication Data

Martin, Reinhold, 1964–
The organizational complex : architecture, media, and
corporate space / Reinhold Martin.
    p. cm.
Includes index.
ISBN 0-262-13426-8 (alk. paper)
1. Architecture and society—United States—
History—20th century. 2. Commercial buildings—
United States. 3. Commercial buildings—
Communication systems. 4. Corporate image—
United States. I. Title.

NA2543.S6 M36 2003
725'.2'097309045—dc21

                                    2002035585

For my parents

Contents

Acknowledgments

This book is a product of discourse. As such, it owes an enormous debt to those with whom I have had the opportunity to discuss its content as it has developed, beginning with its first incarnation as a dissertation at the School of Architecture at Princeton University. At Princeton and thereafter I have had the benefit of readings, criticism, conversation, and insight from Georges Teyssot, Beatriz Colomina, Alan Colquhoun, Robert Gutman, Alessandra Ponte, Anson Rabinbach, and Mark Wigley, all of whom have my most sincere gratitude. I am also most grateful to Kenneth Frampton, Mary McLeod, Anthony Vidler, and Gwendolyn Wright for their readings and advice on the text. Peter Papademetriou has likewise been of great assistance with the Saarinen material in particular. Any lingering errors, omissions, or other indiscretions are purely my own.

In addition, I am indebted to my colleagues at *Grey Room,* Branden Joseph and Felicity Scott, who have offered an intellectual context that has been central in developing many of the ideas in this book. Many others have also provided friendship, insight, and support along the way: Mark Cousins, Laurie Hawkinson, Tom Keenan, Laura Kurgan, Duncan McCorquodale, Detlef Mertins, the late Ernest Pascucci, and Henry Urbach. At the Graduate School of Architecture, Planning, and Preservation at Columbia University, I am grateful to Dean Bernard Tschumi for his generous support for this project. I have also benefited immensely from the input of many students who have participated in seminars based on this research at Columbia, and earlier at the School of Architecture at Yale University.

The late Gyorgy Kepes, Juliet Kepes, Julie Kepes Stone, Jim La Due, Kevin Roche, and Phil Summers were all kind enough to share with me their thoughts and experiences regarding this material. Chris Barker has been heroic in his assistance with image research. Numerous individuals at the various institutions at which this research has been carried out have also been most helpful. I am grateful to Roger Conover of the MIT Press for his interest in and support for this project, to Matthew Abbate for his guidance, to Alice Falk for her precision and thoughtfulness in editing the manuscript, and to Emily Gutheinz for her elegant design.

While I was at Princeton, a portion of this research was carried out with the support of the Mrs. Giles Whiting Foundation. The publication itself has been supported by a grant from the Graham Foundation for Advanced Studies in the Fine Arts.

Earlier versions of two chapters have appeared elsewhere: chapter 1 as "The Organizational Complex: Cybernetics, Space, Discourse," in *Assemblage,* no. 37 (1998), and chapter 5 as "Computer Architectures: Saarinen's Patterns, IBM's Brains" in Sarah Williams Goldhagen and Réjean Legault, eds., *Anxious Modernisms: Experiments in Postwar Architectural Culture* (Montreal: Canadian Centre for Architecture; Cambridge, Mass.: MIT Press, 2000).

This work is dedicated to my parents, Josephine Martin and Reinhold Martin. And my last thanks are reserved for Kadambari Baxi, who has been my companion on this space odyssey from the beginning, and to whose "new vision" I owe more than I can say.

New York, August 2002

The Organizational Complex

Introduction

If there is something comforting—religious, if you want—about paranoia, there is still also anti-paranoia, where nothing is connected to anything, a condition not many of us can bear for long.

Thomas Pynchon, *Gravity's Rainbow*

We're told businesses have souls, which is surely the most terrifying news in the world.

Gilles Deleuze, "Postscript on Control Societies"

What follows is a map, intended as a guide to thinking differently about the corporate architecture that rose in the United States in the immediate aftermath of the Second World War. This map cannot be taken up as though the historical space it describes is now visible in its totality. Nor does it provide access to some mythic uncharted territory waiting to be absorbed into the academic or professional canon. Nor, finally, should the reader assume that its primary referent, the architecture of the corporations, is or ever was simply transparent to the imperatives of capital—or indeed, of remote corporate power. Instead, this map charts architecture's immanence within a network of networks that I am calling an "organizational complex."

The organizational complex can be described as the aesthetic and technological extension of what has been known since the early 1960s as the "military-industrial complex." Its defining epistemologies coalesce into an organicism that operates on the model of a total, if pliant, system. Within this system architecture acts as a conduit for organizational patterns passing through the networks of communication that constitute the system's infrastructure. The system's phantasmagorias—with built architecture also counted prominently among these—likewise constitute an indelibly real system of images, with indelibly real consequences. Far from simply staging a spectacle that screens out the structural logic of corporate power by coaxing the spectator-user into a state of passive distraction, architecture works here actively to integrate spaces and subjects into naturalized organizations, specifically to the degree that it is "reduced" to corporate image.

In excerpting case studies for analysis, I have concentrated on corporate architecture in the United States, in the technological, aesthetic, and social context of the late 1940s, 1950s, and early 1960s. Although this focus may appear to limit the conclusions that can be drawn here with regard to the postwar trajectory of modern architecture in general, it marks a specific site that, during the period of McCarthyism and the cold war, must always be understood implicitly to harbor its geopolitical exterior. The architectural developments examined should likewise be seen against the implicit backdrop of a multifarious international modernism that often took contradictory forms during the immediate postwar period. This was a period of accelerated commercialization, of decolonization, and—in the context of advanced aesthetic practice and thought—of considered reassessment of the effects and legacies of the modernist avant-gardes. It was also a period when, owing in large part (but not exclusively) to wartime techno-scientific developments, the fabric of modernity itself underwent substantial transformation.

Thus, while the corporate architecture of the postwar United States may appear at first to mark the apotheosis of the alienated, modernized "mass," in its historical specificity it extends a new and different vector. Not simply the vector of standardization or of the assembly line as projected in the seriality of the ubiquitous metal-and-glass curtain wall, this was the historical vector that redirected such processes and their artifacts toward a reconditioning of the modern subject. Such a tendency was already visible in the United States by the early 1930s, in a fusion of aesthetic and technological practices that presented commodities such as automobiles as an ever-evolving system of choices addressed to the perceived individuality of the new subject, who was understood fundamentally as a *consumer*. The construction of an individualized consumer was, in that sense, a technocratic response to the alienating effects of the encroaching "mass ornament" so vividly described by Siegfried Kracauer in the late 1920s in Europe.[1] This new subject effectively regained an organic connection to the functional whole of society by virtue of his or her own "individual" choices, made within a system that was designed to offer variety by providing interchangeable elements in standardized formats. Architects would call these elements *modules.*

In certain exemplary office buildings of the 1950s, earlier modernist experiments with spatial flexibility through modular assembly were exhaustively reworked and redeployed. The universal space associated with the steel frame and the planning grid was assimilated into a finely modulated field. This modularity, and the flexibility that it implied, became the very image—and the instrument—of the organizational complex. A comparable module likewise appeared in the social life of the postwar corporations, in the form of the figure designated by William H. Whyte as the "organization man." As a cultural stereotype, this figure was hopelessly and even comically conformist. But as an instrument of that complex (which uses images such as stereotypes as if they were machines), the organization man brought together the twin imperatives of variety and standardization in a newfound humanity. No alienated cog in an indifferent mechanism, the organization man identified with the corporation as though it were his family. The corporate doctrine of "human relations" encouraged this identification under the thesis that it would increase productivity. But Whyte, like many other critics of corporate culture then and now, failed to recognize that such conformism did not merely overrun a more thoroughgoing individuality, thought to insulate the consumer from metropolitan anomie. Rather, like capitalism in general, it broke down the modern subject from within by encouraging consumerist differentiation *as itself a norm,* thus dividing the individual into an ever-finer set of indefinitely variable (yet enumerable) regulating codes that Gilles Deleuze was to identify, in the early 1990s, as constitutive of an emergent "control society."[2]

In exploring architecture's imbrication within such processes, I have sought out the proximity of what Max Horkheimer and Theodor Adorno have called the "culture industry" to Deleuze's control society, while suspending the dialectical role played by the reflective interiority of the Enlightenment subject in Horkheimer and Adorno's analysis.[3] If there is an apparent contradiction here, it is that such an interiority functions for them as the pivot point for a negative dialectics that prevents their account from collapsing into the totalizing perspective they attribute to the culture industry itself. For Deleuze, in contrast, following to a large extent Michel Foucault, the control society emerges out of an epistemological rupture that transforms the very terms on which discourse, including critical discourse, is organized. Thus the inside-outside relation of reflective subject to society is itself reformulated. I retain such a reformulation as central to my hypothesis, in order to test architecture against it and vice versa.

Absent dialectical negation, however, this approach may seem to attribute an a priori seamlessness to the organizational complex that cannot help but be confirmed in the details of the analysis. My characterization of architecture as one among many media might seem to secure such a reading, since it positions architecture firmly within the culture industry without offering any leverage for resistance, thus potentially reinforcing the very forces it sets out to challenge. Indeed, communications media play a central role in the epistemological modulation I am exploring here. And perhaps no single building has served more effectively as a totem for thinking about the relation of architecture and mass media in the context of the North American culture industry than Ludwig Mies van der Rohe's Seagram Building, completed in 1957. Its supposed "silence"—in the face of what Kracauer once called the "pictorial deluge" of mass communications—has, in one eloquent analysis, granted this object the privileged status of a mute witness withdrawing in dignified horror from the debased urban scene of New York's new commercial center, Park Avenue.[4] Or, more dialectically still, Seagram has been characterized as a "handmade readymade," confronting architecture-as-mass-reproducible-commodity (in the form of the curtain wall) with the provisional, waning aura of the singular artwork, in an indeterminate oscillation.[5] But such readings, while making effective use of the critical tools supplied by the Frankfurt School and by Adorno in particular, are prevented by their dialectical commitments from engaging the historical transformation of the subject as anything other than a loss.

For is it not the case that Seagram's own reproducibility, both in the form of the much-lamented "copies" that rapidly infiltrated the New York skyline and in the form of the many "lesser" curtain-walled variations in Mies's own work, marks even that building as a mere module, a unit of exchange passing through invisible circuits while providing a silent circuitry of its own? And is it not perhaps the case that the building thereby bears paradoxical witness not so much to the withering away of the aura as to the collapse of the architectural object into a field of modulated patterns visible at every scale, from the urban to the interior? Is it not possible, then, that the apparent seamlessness of the culture industry figured in these patterns may be confronted critically not with profound silences, but with the noise in its own channels? That is: Can we not imagine an architectural analysis in which repetition replaces opposition as a critical tool, relentlessly articulating the circuitries of control implied by the modular, patterned cascade, as well as the networks of power and knowledge that make it possible? And might not such an analysis also provide access to the holes embedded *within* those networks, holes that were and are the modern media, including buildings like Seagram?

A response to such questions requires attention to media specificities. And like network television—its historical contemporary—the architecture of the curtain wall is a medium to be *watched* in passing rather than looked at like an artwork.[6] That is, it channels flows, patterns of patterns. Hence, in treating Seagram (in passing) as only one among many curtain-walled office buildings of the period rather than as a singular exception, I have attempted to watch the curtain wall as it switches architectural channels, from one corporation to another, one city to another, one module to another. This is the logic of organization. Where the skyscraper monuments of the postwar period may appear to assimilate corporate authority into the symbolic locus of the church and the state (and the mythic power these embody), in actuality these buildings harbor a new, horizontal network of open circuits to which Mies was relatively indifferent. This network reaches outside the city and ultimately across the globe, proliferating in lines of transportation and communication that also constitute the space of a new symbolic.

Still, even today these buildings are often treated as though they were and remain brute, mechanical force incarnate, rather than what they are: empty skins full of individualized consumer-subjects that, like giant television sets, organize through the agency of an auratic delirium. Revisionist debates concerning their preservation (and secure entombment), as well as quaint vanguardist maneuvers designed to overcome their apparently authoritarian rigidity (the formalist critique of the modernist "box"), converge on the assumption that these buildings mark the culmination—the end— of something. But these buildings are not merely the tombstones of the modern avant-gardes. Like the ubiquitous monoliths of the 1960s—the primary objects of minimal art, the black boxes of communications theory, the black space-slab of *2001: A Space Odyssey,* and the World Trade Center—they are ciphers in which past and future are scrambled into a continuous, modulated hum: an endless feedback loop. These fragments of circuitry, these weightless patterns, these shadows, are ghosts that cannot and must not be chased away.

I have therefore attempted in successive chapters to summon up certain of these ghosts, beginning with that of the organizational complex itself as seen through the medium of an emergent cybernetics and, in particular, through the application of redundant feedback loops to an urban context in which the city was understood as a primary cold war target. In this cybernetic sense, decentralization, or the dispersal of urban infrastructures into an increasingly horizontal network of communication and transportation lines, was an instrument not merely of civil defense against an external enemy but of defense against an internal one: the disorder that was anticipated with the demise of centralized governmental and civic authority in the immediate aftermath of a nuclear strike. And so technocratic and aesthetic research accelerated in the direction of ever more efficient mechanisms of *self*-regulation, *self*-organization. These in turn helped invent new kinds of cities, new kinds of architectures, and with them a new "self," none of which could be said to possess the traditional spatial properties that divided inside from outside in any meaningful sense.

This dissolution of the inside via its potentially infinite, external replication is also indicative of a historical transformation affecting the nature of networks in general as spatial, technological, and social instruments. Within the organizational complex itself, such a transformation was already characterized typologically and chronologically by the early 1960s, with "centralized" systems seen as manifesting rigorous hierarchies, newer "decentralized" systems regulated through local, more dispersed centers, and emergent "distributed" systems fully self-regulating and without hierarchy or center in any sense.[7] Though these network types represent idealized and rather formalistic models, they are useful diagrams that describe potentially distinct configurations of power and knowledge. Within the organizational complex, for example, decentralization is pursued (and realized) at a variety of levels, even as corporate hegemony is consolidated in what was called at the time a "power elite." But this consolidation actually serves a pervasive systematicity whose ultimate horizon is the capillary distribution of power into microphysical protocols. Such a high degree of personalization is among the distinguishing characteristics of Deleuze's "control society," in which even businesses are said to have "souls."

At the source of this reenchantment is an organicism that I am therefore describing as "organizational." Networked, systems-based, feedback-driven—this organicism, and the circuits of power that it serves, sustains myths of dynamic deregulation, corporate benevolence, and dispersed, de-hierarchized interactivity. In architecture, it must be distinguished from the organicist premises of any number of earlier modernisms, including Mies's "skin and bones" transparencies and Le Corbusier's cellular preoccupations, all of which nevertheless constitute a matrix out of which the new formation emerged.[8] Thus, the historical *discontinuity* marked by the development of a systems-based notion of organization in architecture takes the form of a manifest *continuity* with specific modernist practices that preceded it. The grandiosity of this disturbance in the epistemic field is measured by the fact that that it occurred quietly, surreptitiously. Earth-shattering yet nearly invisible, it was the result of a covert operation carried out under the rubric of "modernism," with even its agents and its managers caught unawares.

Though at certain moments it may even seem that the terms *architecture* and *organization* have been converted into synonyms here, their meanings are not identical. They are to be understood, rather, as partial and uneven functions of one another. As it becomes one among many media, architecture also becomes one among many technologies of organization. Organization, on the other hand, is not merely the inverse, some root function of architecture, or a sophisticated means of carrying out architecture's age-old assignment of imposing order. Organization belongs, in this instance, to the project of naturalization as carried out through the medium of architecture. As the theoretical basis for understanding the formation of organisms since the nineteenth century, organization has been called up repeatedly as compensation for the loss of nature and the crisis of mimetic representation that occurred at the onset of modernity. In the context I examine here, organization thus becomes the basis for the production of a new, architectural and technological nature that, after the war, promises not a return to the mythic *Gemeinschaft* (or organic community) of pre-metropolitan subjectivity but an advance into a new kind of organic integration, of which we likely have yet to experience the final chapter.

Articulating such a shift in epistemological terms exemplified by cybernetics, I pursue the emergence of the new organizational model in case studies passing through a variety of channels. These include passages through the writings of the visual theorist Gyorgy Kepes that track the translation of Bauhaus principles into the cybernetic milieu; through the curtain wall and its internal histories; and through a series of corporate works by Eero Saarinen, the architect who, along with his contemporary Gordon Bunshaft, perhaps best understood the imperatives of business in relation to those of modern architecture.

Though the works of such figures as Saarinen and Bunshaft have proven largely resistant to interpretation in canonical terms, it has been suggested often enough and in various ways that the modernisms they practiced in the corporate context monumentalize the withering of the visionary ideals of the European avant-gardes into the cynical instrumentality of capital: from tragedy to farce.[9] We will see, however, how certain avant-gardist gestures, built on a technological organicism from the start, are in fact realized—rather than betrayed—as modern architecture is brought into the service of the corporate mythos. At this level, the "glass architecture" of the postwar curtain wall has little in common with the vitreous utopian fantasies of the 1920s, despite genealogical ties that span the intervening decades. Glass architecture had from the start been a vessel for the organicist myth but, paradoxically, its realization in the curtain wall also transformed it beyond recognition, as it materialized a substantially *different* organicism—though an organicism nonetheless.

In treating architecture as one among many media regulating the organizational nexus, I have also sought to account for its capacity to "build" corporate images. In each instance, these images certainly possess semantic content. However, as with the patterns punched into the cards that drove the so-called IBM machines, I have not characterized the messages they carry primarily in semantic terms, although the construction a new visual "language" was a key aspect of the organizational project. More significantly, these images constituted a kind of operating system designed to regulate the performance of the emergent human-machine assemblage. In their production, transmission, and reception as what the cyberneticist Norbert Wiener called "pure patterns in a natural world," they were representations that declared victory over representation itself. That is, in the lexicon of cybernetics and information theory, they were informatic in that they were negentropic. They resisted disorder by transmitting abstract, organized patterns of visual data as input into a complex whose output would consist of more organized patterns of data. In turn, the human subject as constituted through these flows came to be understood as nothing more—or less—than an organized, informatic pattern.

The entropic specter against which the organizational complex gathered its resources in defense of this subject appears most vividly in the atomic cloud, whose image was recorded in tests with the same photographic rigor that informed the most advanced speculation about architecture. Yet what was most threatening was not the flash of light or the rising of the great plume, but rather the interruption in the flow of data that it signaled. Similarly, architecture was not at all threatened by the fact that its surfaces had been reduced to thicknesses measured in fractions of an inch, as its affect approached the glare of the photographic plate or of the television screen. It was perfectly possible to conceive an organic architecture of images, or of organized patterns. What was intolerable was the emptiness of its surfaces, relentless patterns evacuated of any residual interiority that might have been previously accorded to architectural spaces and their inhabitants. These surfaces were the instruments of organization. But they were also the agents of entropy, since the corporate organicity they sought was to be obtained under the sign of an impossible transparency that, through one of the many topological inversions we will witness, converged onto an undifferentiated blankness.

In positioning architecture within this field, I borrow the notion of a "discourse network" from Friedrich Kittler, who in turn borrows it from the paranoid musings of *Senatspräsident* Daniel Paul Schreber.[10] My use of Kittler's rich and complex concept is, however, decidedly literal. It is simply that architecture, including buildings, asserts its irreducibly discursive aspect as a node in a communications network within and between disciplines and regimes of knowledge and production. But architecture and architects can also lay claim to a specific function within this web, relating to the spatial articulation of the "network" as such. What is a network? What does it look like? These are the kinds of questions that many architects ask. And many were already asking them speculatively in their efforts to redirect modernism in those years. Such efforts are visible in, for example, the work of the Team X group—Jaap Bakema; Candilis, Josic, and Woods; Alison and Peter Smithson, and others. They are also to be found slightly later in the reinvention of the Bauhaus concept at Ulm under Max Bill and after him Tomás Maldonado, and in the technological speculations of Cedric Price and of the Archigram group, among others.[11]

But the architecture that will occupy our attention here is a network architecture that quite rigorously *does not look like a network*. In addition to taking up the corporate architecture of Skidmore, Owings & Merrill, I have excerpted the case of Saarinen from within a vast array of works and practitioners since, in carrying out yet redirecting his father's legacy, he elicits the apparent contradictions of the modern/antimodern currents that course through the twentieth century, spanning its wars and continuing to this day. But he also brings to the surface the half-conscious encounter between architecture and the corporate ethos that lies hidden in the work of others. Saarinen's willingness to broker a merger between architectural experimentation and the imperatives of the military-industrial complex is most visible in a succession of projects that he undertook during the 1950s for those very corporations that have come to summarize the drift toward a postindustrial techno-economic milieu: General Motors, International Business Machines, Bell Telephone. These institutions and their histories will in turn be seen as inseparable from architectural analysis, not merely as context or client but rather as technical interface.

In still another sense, this study begins and ends with the discourse of Gyorgy Kepes. Purveyor of a "language of vision" adequate to what he called a "new landscape" of scientific and aesthetic principles that he tirelessly inventoried, Kepes offers a lens through which architecture takes on a different aspect. The set of visual techniques he termed "pattern-seeing" enables us to recognize the curtain wall and its topological innovations as modulations of a continuous, dynamic field pulsing up and down in scale. It also enables us to see the utopianism of this vision, as well as its complicity with the scaleless, open circuitry of control. Kepes may have been aware of this complicity, but his irrepressible optimism, modern to the core, drove him away from its ultimate implications. I have therefore sought to inhabit his insight, if only to subject it to a reversal that cannot be seen as anything other than a betrayal. With Kepes, organicism is given new life, which is what compels me to revisit his work in the context of an enigmatically organicist architecture to which he made infrequent reference, and vice versa. And so we are given these two, Saarinen and Kepes (whose own biographies included only occasional encounters): not as mutual influences, or as representatives of a generalized *Kunstwollen* or *Zeitgeist,* but as vectors of communication. That is how discourse networks work. They transmit information, patterns that in turn give rise to more patterns. We must, with Kepes, learn to see these patterns, which also means learning to see them precisely where none, apparently, exist.

The degree to which this map succeeds in inducing a certain vision can thus be taken as one measure of its value as an instrument with which the empirical realities to which it refers may be grasped with greater lucidity, their scope measured, their gaps identified, their overdeterminations exploited. Among other things, its objects and characters may be counted as late entries into the roster of pharmacological agents that organize Thomas Pynchon's map, in *Gravity's Rainbow* (1973), of a universe parallel to that which I am exploring here. The difference—that in this case we are dealing with the world of historical facts rather than historically based fiction—is secondary. Such resources as Pynchon's novel work to supplement and thereby mediate a naturalized historical vision. Here, I have attempted to telescope together the two states named and explored by Pynchon: paranoia and anti-paranoia, a situation in which everything is connected to everything, and yet within each connection there remains an unbridgeable, intolerable gap. The scope of the ensuing endgame—paranoid organicism on the one hand, entropic dissipation on the other—designates the ethico-political horizon of my project.

Though I characterize the effects of this endgame in terms of the emergence of what might be called a "postindustrial" or even "posthuman" subject, a subject immersed in and constructed by data flows and patterns, I have also endeavored to displace any residual totalizations that remain detectable in such figurations. Indeed, an overdetermined quest for an integrated totality dedicated to the maintenance of "dynamic equilibrium" is discernible in each historical instance I examine. The restoration of an equilibrated, organized complexity, whether in terms of the perceptual field, the social system, a unified science, or even a unity of art and science, became the rallying cry of those most sensitive to techno-scientific interference in the processes of gestalt formation, or the processes of identification with perceived unities that assured the subject of its own coherence. Calls on the part of architects, designers, and their apologists for organic integration were thus evidence of a deep anxiety in the face of the formlessness, disintegration, and entropic overload that were the pathological constituents of an aesthetically and technologically produced normality.

Finally, as I develop the claim that the midcentury rupture of the war and the conditions that underlay it left in their wake a new and qualitatively different aesthetico-technological formation, many relevant issues and counterexamples may appear unjustly ignored. I do not, for example, locate architecture in the context of ideological struggles per se. My focus instead is on the complex intertwinings of discourse—that is, on the intertwinings of words, images, and things. Nor do I take up explicitly the constructions of gender, class, or race within the enforced normalcy associated with the corporations. I thus risk encouraging the misunderstanding that the "organization man"—white, middle-class, male—is invoked here as an authoritative prototype. On the contrary, as a technologically mediated module circulating within the organizational complex, the organization man should be understood as one of many "cyborgs" (or cybernetic organisms) produced by postwar technocracy.[12] And just as the actual, lived alienation of such figures prevents their full assimilation into the corporate whole, their very artificiality is a potential instrument for an emancipatory politics that resists naturalization and seeks out new collectivities ungrounded in organicist pieties.

I note this here because my primary effort has been to show that architecture has never for one minute been exempted from the historical transformations that shaped the latter half of the twentieth century and continue to shape our present. That today this assertion cannot simply be dismissed as a mere truism is registered in the fact that the 1960s and early 1970s—the years during which the World Trade Center was being designed and built—saw the definitive withdrawal of the architectural avant-gardes in the United States and elsewhere from confrontation with the geo-political actualities of their era, into pseudo-oppositions such as that of formal autonomy versus populist historicism. Significantly, these safe new homes in which so-called debates could continue unimpeded by historical disturbances were constructed against the background of the curtain wall and of corporate modernism in general.[13] In turn, the set of architectural techniques developed during the postwar period to consolidate corporate imagery offered a technical basis—the manipulation of the "skin"—through which that imagery was reinvented in the name of "history" by the postmodernisms that followed.

Similarly the architecture of the curtain wall and of patterned modularities haunts all debates in today's digital age, which is to say today's globalized age, an age that began in both senses in the wartime cauldron of technological innovation and market realignment. Half a century later, under the regime of a millennial "new economy," the corporate pathos by then condensed into a paper-thin historicism was reborn in the new networks of finance capital in the form of a Silicon Valley-style futurism. Along the lost highways of the postindustrial landscape, the digital age has thus found its architectural expression as a routinized amalgam of historical pastiche and technological triumphalism. Such a triumphalism has been echoed in the academic design laboratories by a digital neo-avant-garde in an organicist repression of its own technologically accelerated entropy. This avant-garde has unproblematically identified itself and its nostalgic products with the softwares and hardwares marketed by a new generation of corporations. These corporations have in turn marketed *themselves* as models of casual sociability and neatly packaged novelty, symptoms of an enforced togetherness under the sign of a consumerist "global village."

In that sense, the map that follows here must always be understood to harbor its architectural futures, if only as a prehistory condemned to compulsive repetition. Locked in such repetitions, we might do well to follow the command that, at IBM, applied equally to humans and to machines: "Think." At Apple Computer, IBM's one-time challenger, this command was to be converted in the 1990s into the coyly insipid "Think different." Thus with each repetition, the organizational complex extends itself further—not only into the interiors of thought but into difference itself. Yet each repetition also offers an opportunity for productive misuse, and for recursion and redirection, in which thinking differently can also mean issuing a challenge by raising the stakes, which is what I have attempted here. Though each subsequent stage in the development of the organizational complex has been shot through with countertrends, resistances, innovations, and critical rearticulations, in each is still discernible the remnants of the postwar constellation, like the delayed light emanating from a not-so-distant galaxy.

1

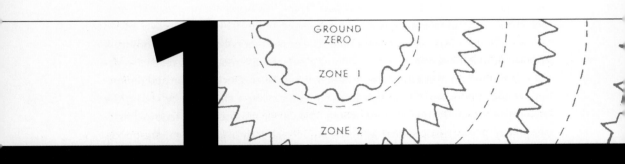

The Organizational Complex

Media organize. To be sure, they also communicate; they transmit messages, circulate signs. But to leave it at that is to fail to grasp the significance—for architecture—of Marshall McLuhan's dictum "The medium is the message." For in the cybernetically organized universe in which McLuhan made his home, it was precisely *organization* that was communicated—as both message and medium, image and effect, form and function—through the multimedia channels that never ceased to fascinate him. There, where architecture was both humbled and enchanted by its own status as one among many media, is where we begin, by reconstructing a small fragment of that tangled network I am calling the *organizational complex.*

In 1948 mathematician Norbert Wiener chose the subtitle *Control and Communication in the Animal and the Machine* for *Cybernetics,* a text that launched the interdisciplinary research program of the same name. The book itself is alternately limited and far-reaching in scope, evidencing Wiener's reluctance to generalize his scientific research into other domains, even as he acknowledges the possibility of such an undertaking and its pursuit by many of his colleagues. But Wiener's reluctance to translate scientific hypotheses concerning natural or technological processes into an operative social theory stemmed from a practical rather than a theoretical problem: the difficulty of obtaining social data of sufficient breadth, depth, and objectivity. He does not hesitate to diagnose social imbalances as symptoms of communicative imbalances. Nor does he hesitate to suggest that the informatic devices constructed and studied by cybernetics—such as the hypothetical chess-playing machine he describes in his concluding comments—are capable of approximating the communicative intelligence of humans. Wiener merely notes that any endeavors to treat society as if it were such a machine would inevitably be confronted with insufficient, incomplete, or tainted data. Accordingly, "there is much we must leave, whether we like it or not, to the un-'scientific,' narrative method of the professional historian."[1]

The *theoretical* basis on which any "scientific" extensions of cybernetics might be undertaken is marked in Wiener's subtitle and implicit throughout the book as a common ground of "communication" regulating the behavior of both organisms and the new information-processing machines. In theory, the means by which social imbalances might be regulated—if that were practically possible—is what Wiener's subtitle identifies as "control." Symptomatically, in defining his terms here, Wiener himself has recourse to something resembling what he calls the "narrative method of the professional historian." Having declared that "the thought of every age is reflected in its technique," he goes on to suggest that "if the seventeenth and early eighteenth centuries are the age of clocks, and the later eighteenth and nineteenth centuries constitute the age of steam engines, the present time is the age of communication and control." And so he observes of the study of automata ("whether in the metal or in the flesh") that "scarcely a month passes but a new book appears on these so-called control mechanisms, or servomechanisms, and the present age is as truly the age of servomechanisms as the nineteenth century was the age of the steam engine or the eighteenth century the age of the clock."[2]

Forty years later, and in the wake of numerous studies of an emergent, technologically differentiated epoch,[3] Gilles Deleuze made a similar historical observation, with at least one important difference. For Deleuze, as for his colleague Michel Foucault, observable parallels between technological and social processes were based not on the instrumental application of scientific techniques or social theory but on their mutual imbrication in relations of *power* and *knowledge*:

One can of course see how each kind of society corresponds to a
particular kind of machine—with simple mechanical machines

corresponding to sovereign societies, thermodynamic machines to disciplinary societies, cybernetic machines and computers to control societies. But the machines don't explain anything, you have to analyze the collective apparatuses of which the machines are just one component. Compared with the approaching forms of ceaseless control in open sites, we may come to see the harshest confinement as part of a wonderful happy past. The quest for "universals of communication" ought to make us shudder.[4]

1.1

Machines based on the conversion of energy to motor power occupied a privileged position within the nineteenth-century constellation that begat modern subjectivities and modern forms of collective experience, configuring relations of force around processes of displacement and aligning their trajectories in the railroad, the assembly line, and, eventually, the automobile. As Anson Rabinbach has shown, an energetics informed by the second law of thermodynamics provided the framework through which the bodies moving along these trajectories could be theorized as fields of force, and diagrammed by scientists like Etienne-Jules Marey, in what Rabinbach calls a "physiognomy of labor power."[5] These developments in turn flowed from the emergence of biology as a fully codified science, rearranging the terms of the earlier debate between mechanism and vitalism into a new and multifaceted organicism. Indeed, by the early part of the nineteenth century, *organization,* or the pattern of relationships binding the organs together and integrating their individual functions into a coordinated whole, was a privileged term, designating at least one condition of possibility for life itself. Such an attentiveness to the integration of structure and function within the organism was subsequently extended to the organism's relation with what Auguste Comte called its *milieu,* or environment. And with the work of the physiologist Claude Bernard, the notion of the *milieu intérieur,* or interior environment, was introduced to describe the internal space in which the regulatory functions of organisms are performed. The resulting tripartite assemblage—structure, function, environment—came to define the regulatory processes of organized (and thereby organic) bodies conceived as internal combustion engines.[6]

The field of comparative anatomy saw a related shift when Georges Cuvier broke down the totality of known organisms into four mutually exclusive branches on the basis of their organizational "plan," according to which each organ was seen to

perform a specific function in the service of the whole.[7] It is to this taxonomic fragmentation of life itself, in which the great continuous chain of being ramified into the
unbridgeable discontinuities separating Cuvier's branches, that Deleuze refers when
he reminds us (in his book-length essay on Foucault) that in the nineteenth century
"the co-ordination and subordination of characteristics in a plant or animal—in brief,
an organizing force—imposes a division of organisms which can no longer be aligned
but tends to develop on its own."[8] A distributional imperative that proves constitutive of the postclassical *episteme* mapped by Foucault, this shift in the organism's status is coordinated around what we can call its spatiality. As the historian of science
François Jacob puts it:

> What was radically transformed at the beginning of the nine-
> teenth century, was, therefore, the way in which living beings were
> arranged in space: not only the space in which all beings were dis-
> posed, broken into separate islands and carved into indepen-
> dent series—but also the space in which the organism took up
> its abode, coiled round a nucleus, formed by successive layers
> that extended beyond the living being, linking it to its surround-
> ings. It was both the relations established between the parts of
> an organism and those uniting all living bodies that were en-
> tirely redistributed.[9]

From cell to milieu, and notwithstanding the manifest distinctions between these various approaches, the organism was thus integrated into a bounded whole in which, as
in the panoptic machines through which Foucault articulated the disciplinary epoch,
everything was in its place.

      This effort to think about the organism on its own terms—as an organic total-
ity—thus yielded what Jacob calls a spatialization of organic bodies "in depth."
Holding it all together was an invisible "secret architecture" (Jacob) or "hidden architecture" (Foucault)—what Jacob terms a "second-order structure" (organization) in
which the parts are distributed and their individual functions coordinated. But this architecture also brings with it a degree of epistemological confusion. With Bernard and
others, the biological notion of organic integration, particularly in the form of the cell
theory, was initially articulated through an economic and political model that compared the integration of the unit (the cell) into the whole of the organism to the integration of the individual into society. While enabling biologists to accord priority to
integration over simple mechanical assembly, this comparison was eventually challenged by a physiologically based project in which, in the words of Georges Canguilhem, "the organism is its own model," since "[f]or an organism, organization is a fact;
for a society, organization is a goal."[10]

All of this was subject to revision with the emergence of cybernetics, communications theory, and systems theory during the middle of the twentieth century. The confusion remains, however. Social, biological, technological, and aesthetic space are networked together in Norbert Wiener's "age of communication and control." And architecture is right there with them, in more ways than one.

Returning to the "control society," we find that Deleuze also distinguishes control from the techniques of spatial confinement characteristic of disciplinary regimes, on the basis of a networklike spatiality: "Confinements are *molds,* different moldings, while controls are a *modulation* [e.g., the modulation of signals], like a self-transmuting molding continually changing from one moment to the next, or like a sieve whose mesh varies from one point to another."[11]

The irreducibility of this "control society" to its *technē*—even as certain network-based technologies are decisively implicated in it—or to its modulated structure suggests that along with cybernetic machines, certain aesthetic techniques might also belong to that collective apparatus dedicated to what Deleuze calls "the approaching forms of ceaseless control in open sites." Architecture's own *technē*, suspended between art and science in the discourse of the period, thus forms multiple, complex links with this apparatus. But in what way does a cybernetic regime modify what Jacob describes as "the way in which living beings [are] arranged in space"—the organicist integration of components in a milieu ranging from interior to exterior? And with respect to feedback loops that bring the outside back in, how do we confront the history and theory of communications networks from *within* the logic of these same networks? Unlike the confined, molded institutional spaces of disciplines (e.g., architecture), these are systems of modulation with no absolute inside or outside, interminably "open sites" where we perpetually traverse domains ("outside" architecture—e.g., cybernetics) in which we appear to have no business operating in the first place. In this supposedly postdisciplinary epoch, has not the discipline from which we write become itself merely a modulation of interconnected networks and knowledge banks?

1.2

In a letter dated 28 March 1951, a young Herbert Marshall McLuhan introduces himself to Wiener by declaring that "as a friend and student of Sigfried Giedion's I have paid special attention to your *Cybernetics* and *The Human Use of Human Beings,*"[12] Wiener's two most widely read books. Given the free use McLuhan would later make of cybernetic principles like feedback in his own work, it is not surprising that he contacts Wiener at this early date. Slightly more surprising, perhaps, is his use of Giedion's name as a reference. Yet a year before McLuhan's letter, Giedion, too, corresponded with Wiener, thanking him for the opportunity to attend a meeting of the Inter-science Committee at the Massachusetts Institute of Technology (where Wiener taught), before which he was later invited to speak. In less than perfect English, he expresses solidarity: "I felt reconforted, because thoughts & ideas, which I had to work out lonely for many years are growing in your circle by the force of similar circumstances."[13]

By the time he wrote those words, Giedion had already conducted his own series of case histories of everyday mechanical objects and systems in *Mechanization Takes Command: A Contribution to Anonymous History* (1948), researched and written in the United States from 1941 to 1945. The book is an allegory that needs little decoding. It is unnecessary for Giedion even to name Hiroshima or Auschwitz, which, in the book as in history, actualized the mechanized death for which modernity had been preparing itself for an entire century.[14] For Giedion, ghostwriter of modern architecture's dreams, runaway mechanization could be controlled only by subordinating it to what he calls "human needs." Under such conditions, mechanization is forced to double back on itself—first by responding to rudimentary biological needs, such as the need for food and shelter, and second by recalibrating the human body to withstand the destabilizing effects of its own prosthetic supplementarity, in an adaptation to the constant change resulting from scientific and technological progress. This feedback loop is the basis for what Giedion calls "dynamic equilibrium," a balanced state of flux and interchange between individual and environment. Its prime agent, according to Giedion, is to be a new human type, a "man in equipoise," capable of balancing irreconcilable forces.

Cryptically, Giedion adds the caveat that "we should not have dared to suggest the new type of man our period calls for if physiology had not discovered astonishingly parallel trends," listing as evidence the work of a variety of scientists, including Claude Bernard and Walter B. Cannon.[15] Half a century after Bernard's studies of physiological self-regulation, Cannon had developed the notion of *homeostasis* to describe the body's ability to maintain certain functions (such as temperature) in a steady state and to restore its internal processes to equilibrium following moments of excitement or disruption. In doing so, he took up once again the analogy between biological and social processes, concluding his 1932 classic, *The Wisdom of the Body,* with an epilogue titled "Relations of Biological and Social Homeostasis."[16] Extrapolating from the biological to the technological domain, with the stage set by the biosocial hypotheses of figures like Cannon, Giedion thus (implicitly) uses "dynamic equilibrium" to invoke organic homeostasis as a model for the restoration of balance in an environment overrun with machines.

Dedicated to the neurophysiologist Arturo Rosenblueth, Wiener's collaborator and Cannon's colleague, *Cybernetics* is the first systematic exposition of the research conducted by Wiener, Rosenblueth, and others on parallels between communications networks and the human nervous system. Cannon's work represents an important precedent for this hypothesis, which explains in part Giedion's recognition of an affinity between his own work and that of Wiener. *Cybernetics* takes its title from *kybernētēs,* the Greek term for "steersman"; *kybernētēs* is also the root of the English term "governor," which is applied to devices that regulate the performance of machines (as in the governor of a steam engine). Extending concepts originating in nineteenth-century thermodynamics into systems of information measurement and management, Wiener defines information in relation to its opposite: entropy. The second law of thermodynamics holds that the overall level of entropy, or disorder, tends probabilistically to increase in any closed system. Wiener proposes that like energy, the amount of information, or "negentropy," within a system is subject to a similar process of breaking down and leveling off, also measurable as entropy.

Conversely, the degree of antientropic, informational *organization* in cybernetic systems is regulated through feedback, a continuous cycling of information (obtained by artificial "sense organs") back into a system to correct its course, consolidate its form, or modify its output. Wiener developed his theory of feedback through wartime research on electromechanical systems designed, in his words, "to usurp a specifically human function."[17] In an early project for an antiaircraft firing mechanism, for example, Wiener proposed a device, called an antiaircraft predictor, capable of obtaining information on the position and velocity of the aircraft and making the necessary calculations regarding its trajectory—a task previously performed by an individual known as a "computer"—as well as anticipating and factoring in the pilot's future behavior.[18] Although Wiener's proposal was never fully realized, the notion of machine-to-human and machine-to-machine feedback contained therein is central to his science of communication.

More generally, *Cybernetics* postulates morphological and functional parallels between the human nervous system and early information-processing devices by, among other things, comparing nerve synapses to vacuum tubes.[19] Thus the feedback loops and servomechanisms on which Wiener had begun working at the same time that Giedion was writing *Mechanization Takes Command* represented both the diagrams and the material components from which the "new type of man" announced by Giedion could potentially be assembled. There are no surprises here: since the 1920s, the "new man" and his organs had been appearing in avant-gardist discourse, including that of Giedion's friend László Moholy-Nagy (whose advice Giedion acknowledges in his preface). Moholy-Nagy, who died two years before *Mechanization Takes Command* appeared, had long been advocating conscious self-adaptation to technological advances in the form of a "new vision," and his mark is visible throughout

Giedion's book. Moholy-Nagy argued that the ubiquity of rapid movement in all aspects of modern life necessitated a biological adaptation of the human visual apparatus, aided by experimental photography, in order to process visual information received at greater speed than ever before (very much like Wiener's antiaircraft apparatus, with its proposed replacement of the human "computer" with a technological device).[20] Consequently, Marey's chronophotography was one point of departure for photographic work, such as that done by Harold Edgerton at MIT, that informed Moholy-Nagy's own aesthetic experiments with the human sensorium. Giedion, for his part, identifies Marey's documentation of the body as an integrated assemblage of functional vectors working in harmony as a basis for the links among science, social organization, and aesthetics forged in his chapter on the time and motion studies of Frank and Lillian Gilbreth and Frederick Winslow Taylor, and their counterparts in modern art.[21]

While in the United States researching *Mechanization Takes Command,* Giedion also wrote prefatory remarks for *Language of Vision,* a landmark effort to codify a new syntax for optical communication that was published in 1944 by Moholy-Nagy's friend and colleague at the Institute of Design in Chicago, the artist and visual theorist Gyorgy Kepes. In his comments Giedion commends Kepes, who utilizes numerous examples from contemporary graphic design and advertising, for attempting to introduce principles of formal coherence into the images saturating everyday life. In his own introduction, Kepes sounds many of the themes that Giedion would later reiterate in *Mechanization Takes Command.* Most notably, he laments the chaotic disorganization and formlessness of modern life, which he attributes to "our failure in the organization of that new equipment with which we must function if we are to maintain our equilibrium in a dynamic world."[22]

Giedion and McLuhan had met in St. Louis a few years earlier, in 1939. McLuhan later acknowledged his intellectual debt to Giedion, indicating that after the encounter "I naturally studied him more intensely and used his methods in my own work."[23] So when *Mechanization Takes Command* appeared, it became an important reference for McLuhan in his own research into the technologically generated by-products of modernity. This research was published in 1951 as *The Mechanical Bride: Folklore of Industrial Man,* a series of commentaries on advertisements found in newspapers and popular magazines. Like Kepes, McLuhan felt himself confronted with a visual landscape out of control, an entropic "maelstrom" of mechanically produced images used to manipulate an unsuspecting public rather than to communicate openly with them. In his words, such a "whirling phantasmagoria can be grasped only when arrested for contemplation. And this very arrest is also a release from the usual participation."[24]

It was at this time—upon the publication of *The Mechanical Bride*—that McLuhan first approached Wiener to solicit his opinion of the book, which had already been marked by McLuhan's encounter with Giedion, whose own earlier correspondence with Wiener was noted above. Wiener had just published *The Human Use of Human Beings: Cybernetics and Society,* dedicated to elaborating to a nonspecialist audience his thesis that "the physical functioning of the living individual and the operation of some of the newer communication machines are precisely parallel in their analogous attempts to control entropy through feedback."[25] Here Wiener speculates on the capacity of the new machines, which he refers to as "communicative organisms," to regulate social relations by supplementing human intelligence. In doing so, he repeatedly invokes the well-worn analogy between biological organization and social organization, except that the organizational systems in question have now changed. The epistemological status of the two categories underwriting the comparison—the organism and the machine—has also changed. At both levels, the change is registered in specifically spatial terms.

Discussing what he calls "communicative behavior," Wiener argues that a community of ants is characterized by rigid, protofascistic social organization. He observes that the ant's lack of a respiratory system limits it to a certain size, beyond which it could not function with any degree of efficiency. He illustrates this constraint by comparing a cottage and a skyscraper. Whereas a cottage requires no specialized ventilation system, a skyscraper, with its rooms within rooms, is habitable only if equipped with a sophisticated means for circulating and exchanging air. The same goes for the nervous system. Wiener argues that what counts is not the size of the basic components (such as neurons, which are similar in humans and ants) but their organization, which determines the "absolute size" of an organism's nervous system—its upper limit of growth and index of social advancement. An organism's social potential, conceived in terms of its ability to organize into complex communications networks, is thus measured as a function of the size of its internal circulatory and communications systems, which is a function, in turn, of their own organizational complexity. The original analogy between the social and biological organism is thus collapsed, as the two become directly linked as part of the same network.

The organism's previous depth is also flattened out, as the distribution of the body's organs, or compartments (like the rooms within rooms of a skyscraper), becomes a function of the networks that service and regulate them. A relational logic of flexible connection replaces a mechanical logic of rigid compartmentalization, and the decisive organizational factor is no longer the vertical subordination of parts to whole but rather the degree to which the connections permit, regulate, and respond to informational flows in all directions. Furthermore, in a technologically mediated social environment, machines capable of performing such regulatory functions begin to assume a human character. According to Wiener (in the significantly revised second edition of *The Human Use of Human Beings*), if the ant's inability to learn and the relative perfection of its performance from birth make it comparable to a "computing machine whose instructions are all set forth in advance on the tapes," then the human being is comparable to an information system able to learn and thus adapt to its environment based on feedback: "Theoretically, if we could build a machine whose mechanical structure duplicated human physiology, then we could have a machine whose intellectual capacities would duplicate those of human beings."[26]

"Organization as Message" is the title of the book's fifth chapter, in which Wiener proposes what he misleadingly calls a "metaphor" wherein "the organism is seen as message."[27] He begins the chapter by characterizing *homeostatic* processes as those by which an organism maintains its level of organization in an otherwise entropic environment. For Wiener,

It is the pattern maintained by this homeostasis which is the touchstone of our personal identity. Our tissues change as we live: the food we eat and the air we breathe become flesh of our flesh and bone of our bone, and the momentary elements of our flesh and bone pass out of our body every day with our excreta. We are but whirlpools in a river of ever-flowing water. We are not stuff that abides, but patterns that perpetuate themselves. A pattern is a message, and may be transported as a message.[28]

What differentiates this cybernetic notion of the organism from its nineteenth-century predecessors is not so much the idea of the pattern as such, nor the flux of matter passing incessantly through this pattern, but rather the pattern's newly acquired status as "message." Ultimately, the organism's identity—its resistance to the entropic flood of de-differentiation, whereby it maintains a difference with everything that is not itself—is based not on its flesh, its material body, but on a materially transmissible body of information.

Wiener sees the physical body as nothing but pattern; moreover it is a pattern that can be transported (hypothetically) over telephone lines. To illustrate this point, he chooses the example of an architect:

To see the greater importance of the transportation of information as compared with mere physical transportation, let us suppose that we have an architect in Europe supervising the construction of a building in the United States. I am assuming, of course, an adequate working staff of constructors, clerks of the works, etc., on the site of the construction. Under these conditions, even without transmitting or receiving any material commodities, the architect may take an active part in the construction of the building. Let him draw up plans and specifications as usual. Even at present, there is no reason why the working copies of these plans and specifications must be transmitted to the construction site on the same paper on which they have been drawn up in the drafting room. Ultrafax gives a means by which a facsimile of all the documents concerned may be transmitted in a fraction of a second, and the received copies are quite as good working plans as the originals. The architect may be kept up to date with the progress of the work by photographic records taken every day or several times a day; and these may be forwarded back to him by Ultrafax, or teletypewriter. In short, the bodily transmission of the architect and his documents may be replaced very effectively by the message-transmission of communications which do not entail the moving of a particle of matter from one end of the line to the other.[29]

This illustration is only a prelude for speculation on the telephonic transmissibility of the human body itself as an organizational pattern, speculation that Wiener readily admits contains heavy doses of fantasy but nevertheless sets a defining limit for his version of the organism as information system. It relies on a notion of embodiment grounded in patterned integrity rather than in spatial extension. The body as "communicative organism" is, for Wiener, to be understood as a vortex of data whose integrity is maintained homeostatically by virtue of its linkages to physical communications networks. Its materiality, and the materiality of all bodies, has *not* been superseded but has rather been reformulated.

Wiener's reformulation of the body's organizational logics as "message" also bears traces of a reflexivity—in the form of *feedback*—related to that of the "control society." For if the organism is fundamentally pattern (like the architect's design in Wiener's example), the instantiation and maintenance of this pattern depend not only on the availability of raw materials but also on the preexistence of a material substrate of communications systems (like the "Ultrafax" and the telephone lines). To the extent that bodies are understood as a function of their internal communications systems, which are in turn connected into social and technological networks to which they respond through feedback, the outer limits of the organism begin to erode even further than they did in the earlier *milieu intérieur*–external environment assemblage. The terms *interior* and *exterior* ultimately lose their meaning, since each point in the network is engaged in a two-way relationship with every other point, in what Deleuze calls a "modulation." This system, as well as any point within it, is reflexive to the degree that it is *self*-regulating and not merely acting in reciprocity with an external environment, having already incorporated the "environment" into itself through feedback.

For Deleuze, "the digital language of control is made up of codes indicating whether access to some information should be allowed or denied. We're no longer dealing with a duality of mass and individual. Individuals become *'dividuals'* and masses become samples, data, markets, or 'banks.'"[30] Consequently, the mark of identity is transferred from the signature, the trace of the physical body, to the password—a code that connects the subject with its own externalized databanks. Progressive individualization, in the form of personalized codes through which the subject interfaces with the market, is really progressive "dividualization," or the internal splitting of subjectivity into subsets of data. And the "self"—what Wiener calls the human organism's "personal identity"—is constituted through the exchange of codes (in the form of organizational patterns circulating across the network), while the network *it*-self that supports the circulation is constituted reflexively through those very patterns. There is no outside, or inside.

At this point, we are reminded of Foucault's comments before the Parisian Architectural Studies Circle in 1967, when, having identified a new spatiality he calls "emplacement," he takes up a cybernetic idiom:

Further, we are aware of the importance of problems of emplacement in contemporary engineering: the storage of information or of the partial results of a calculation in the memory of a machine, the circulation of discrete elements, with a random output (such as, quite simply, automobiles or in fact the tones on a telephone line), the identification of tagged or coded elements in an ensemble that is either distributed haphazardly or sorted in a univocal classification, or sorted according to a plurivocal classification, and so on.[31]

The text in which Foucault made these comments also articulated his notion of "heterotopia" in concretely spatial terms that would prove influential to the subsequent architectural reception of his thought. Central to this reception has been Foucault's later interpretation (in *Discipline and Punish,* 1975) of Jeremy Bentham's Panopticon as a diagram of spatial relations characteristic of nineteenth-century discipline. But already here, in Foucault's early comments to architects, we see another diagram emerging that, by the second half of the twentieth century, marks the dispersal of the panoptic model into diffuse networks of control.[32]

Like Wiener, Foucault does not differentiate between the circulation of physical bodies (automobiles) and the movement of information ("tones on a telephone line"). Both are submitted to a regime of coding that tracks and manages their movements through infrastructural networks whose dynamics are reducible to what he calls "the problem of knowing what relations of proximity, what type of storage, of circulation, of identification, of classification of human elements are to be preferentially retained in this or that situation to obtain this or that result."[33]

As is also implied by Foucault's choice of examples, the conversion of the organic domain into a problem of coding renders the boundary separating organisms from machines, and especially Deleuze's "cybernetic machines and computers," increasingly permeable. One effect of this permeability is to further destabilize distinctions between scientific, technological, and sociological knowledge, despite Wiener's reservations.[34] In describing the human organism as a node in an information system, cybernetics does not distinguish between human-to-human and human-to-machine communication. It also raises the possibility that humans could be left out of the loop altogether—a new version of the paranoid fantasy of machines dominating humans to which both McLuhan and Wiener allude. Moreover, cybernetics becomes the basis for renewed comparisons between organic bodies and social structures, in which technologically mediated social relations develop under the shadow of a pathological tendency toward entropy. Thus cybernetics is not just one more instance of a correlation between machines and the societies in which they exist. Despite its vaguely humanistic overtones, it *actively theorizes* the dissolution of the human organism's "humanity." It links up bodies, machines, and societies into one vast network, at precisely the same moment that the very existence of humanity is also threatened by its own scientific and technological development. This linking of organism, machine, and socius is so radically destabilizing that "organization" is called in to integrate the entire matrix into a self-regulating totality and to restore its homeostatic organicity. Unfortunately, the force of this organizational imperative leaves little room for an alternate, more volatile "body," for which Deleuze has another name: "If I call it the body without organs, it is because it is opposed to all the strata of organization—those of the organism, but also the organization of power. It is the totality of the organizations of the body that will break apart the plane or the field of immanence and impose another type of 'plane' on desire, in each case stratifying the body without organs."[35]

What is more, for Wiener as for Giedion—both writing in the context of the cold war and the arms race—not only had mechanization taken command, but there was a need to appeal to science for a defense against itself and the weapons it had produced. In Wiener's words, it mattered little "whether we entrust our decisions to machines of metal, or to those machines of flesh and blood which are bureaus and vast laboratories and armies and corporations."[36] Here emerge the full implications of Wiener's "human use of human beings," a title that further encodes the reflexivity of the entire situation. This is not about preserving the "human" by restricting its contact with machines. It is about steering the organized human-machines named by Wiener back toward something like "humanity." This "humanity," characterized by total communicational transparency, is to be reconstituted as a biosocial organism protected by its organizational robustness from weapons that are themselves produced and deployed by highly organized "machines of metal" and "machines of flesh and blood," since for Wiener, "the effect of these weapons must be to increase the entropy of this planet, until all distinction of hot and cold, good and bad, man and matter have vanished in the formation of the white furnace of a new star."[37]

1.3

With the above concerns in mind, we can now consider the peculiar moment when urbanism makes an appearance in Wiener's public career. In the 18 December 1950 issue of *Life* magazine, an article under the title "How U.S. Cities Can Prepare for Atomic War" outlined a proposal by Wiener and two of his colleagues at the Massachusetts Institute of Technology, political theorist Karl Deutsch and historian of science Giorgio de Santillana, for the decentralization of urban infrastructures to mitigate the aftermath of a nuclear strike.[38] Arguing that the panic and chaos caused by the breakdown of transportation and communication lines would potentially be far more devastating than the direct effects of the explosion itself, the plan called for the construction of exurban "life belts"—infrastructural networks in radial patterns around every major American city. These networks were designed to control and direct the flow of traffic toward safe areas at the urban periphery during the hours immediately following a nuclear detonation aimed at the concentration of people, goods, and services in the city centers, while also providing bypass routes for major railroads and highways.

Wiener was the primary author of the plan, which appeared soon after *The Human Use of Human Beings* as a strategic deployment of that work's organizational principles. Indeed, a draft version of the explanatory text written partly in Wiener's hand declares: "We have conceived the city as a net of communications and of traffic. The danger of blocked communications in a city subject to emergency conditions is analogous to the danger of blocked communications in the human body."[39] It follows, then, that just as a skyscraper is a more developed organism than a cottage, and humans are socially more advanced (in principle) than ants, so too this proposed city is to be understood as a giant "communicative organism." The city extends the human nervous system in the name of what Giedion would have called "equipoise," reaching outward to maintain equilibrium and to overcome the entropic effects of traffic jams and communications breakdowns in the wake of nuclear bombardment by providing multiple, redundant pathways.

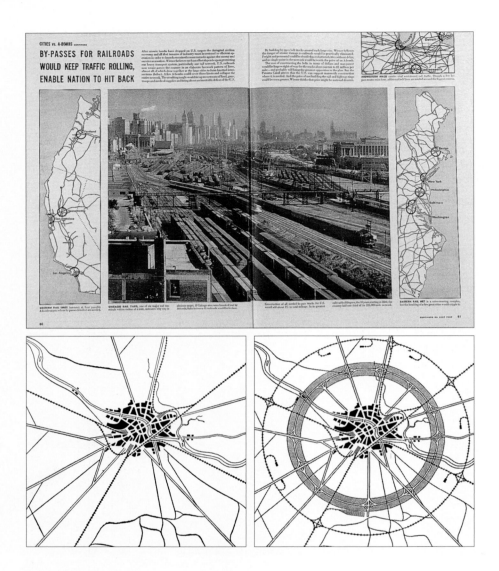

1.3

Norbert Wiener, Karl Deutsch, and Giorgio de Santillana, existing urban hubs. From "How U.S. Cities Can Prepare for Atomic War," *Life,* 18 December 1950, 80–81.

1.4

(bottom left) Norbert Wiener, Karl Deutsch, and Giorgio de Santillana, typical city. From "How U.S. Cities Can Prepare for Atomic War," *Life,* 18 December 1950, 78.

1.5

(bottom right) Norbert Wiener, Karl Deutsch, and Giorgio de Santillana, proposed city. From "How U.S. Cities Can Prepare for Atomic War," *Life,* 18 December 1950, 79.

What the plan's authors call "defense-by-communications" is also what distinguishes this project's schematic urbanism from other postwar civil defense planning strategies advocating decentralization.[40] As Wiener's revised notion of entropy indicates, the focus is not on the direct effects produced by the energy expended in a nuclear detonation but rather on the ensuing interference in communicational flows. Proposals such as the physicist Ralph Lapp's diagrams for linear or satellite cities or Ludwig Hilberseimer's decentralization plans, vividly illustrated with diagrams showing the geographic extent of an atomic blast, all defend against the thermodynamic effects of the bomb.[41] In contrast, the strategy proposed by Wiener and his colleagues defends primarily against the breakdown of the information and transportation systems regulating the city's equilibrium.

For Wiener, the nuclear arms race was also the very figure of a science out of control, a runaway technological juggernaut riding a wave of mistrust and deceit. Like many scientists, he was shocked by Hiroshima; after the bomb was dropped he actively resisted involvement in military projects. Though somewhat fatalistic about the complicity of science in domination, Wiener continued to insist that science use its own knowledge and techniques to regulate itself and the society in which it exists. In *The Human Use of Human Beings,* he quotes from a critical French review of *Cybernetics:*

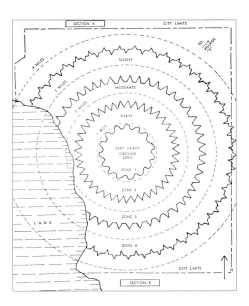

1.6

City "X" diagram. From Ralph E. Lapp, "Atomic Bomb Explosions—Effects on an American City," *Bulletin of the Atomic Scientists* 4, no. 2 (February 1948): 51.

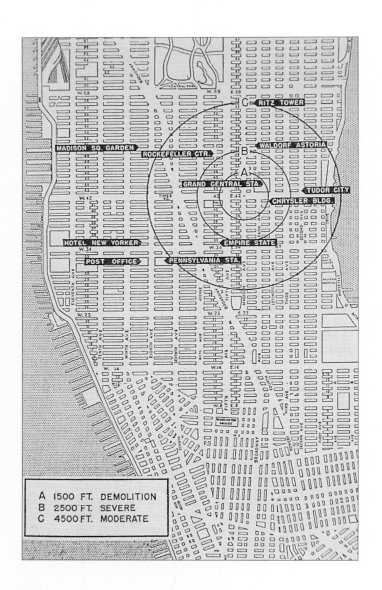

1.7

Ralph Lapp, New York City diagram. From *Must We Hide?*
(1949), 83.

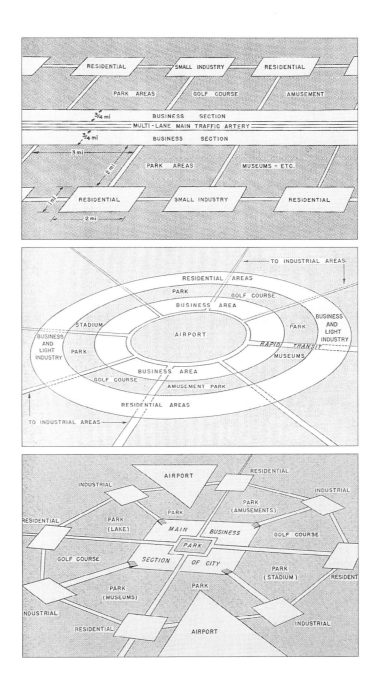

1.8

Ralph Lapp, "rodlike" city, "doughnut" city, and "satellite" city (top to bottom). From *Must We Hide?* (1949), 162–164.

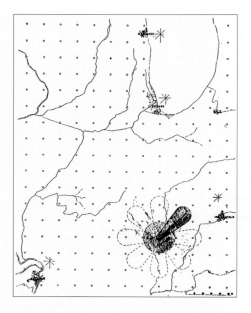

Can't one even conceive a State apparatus covering all systems of political decisions, either under a regime of many states distributed over the earth, or under the apparently much more simple regime of a human government of this planet? At present nothing prevents our thinking of this. We may dream of the time when the *machine à gouverner* [the cybernetic machine] may come to supply—whether for good or evil—the present inadequacy of the brain when the latter is concerned with the customary machinery of politics.[42]

In citing this reviewer, Wiener evokes the same communicative transparency between science and society promoted by groups such as that formed immediately after the war around the *Bulletin of the Atomic Scientists*.[43] But in the United States, there exists a more familiar marker for the realignment of power within the "state apparatus" that followed the technological, logistical, and economic rupture of the Second World War.

On 17 January 1961, in his farewell speech to the American people, President Dwight D. Eisenhower warned against the "unwarranted influence" of the "conjunction of an immense military establishment and a large arms industry," becoming the first in a long line of theorists of what he called the "military-industrial complex." As Eisenhower put it, "the potential for the disastrous rise of misplaced power exists and will persist."[44] The irony of these remarks is not confined to Eisenhower's biography as

1.9

Ludwig Hilberseimer, radius of hydrogen bomb blast.

From *The Nature of Cities* (1955), 283.

both an agent and a symptom of the very forces he identifies, including his early support for a national science foundation that would formalize the close ties developed among science, business, and the military during the war.[45] What is more significant is the way in which Eisenhower's formulation brought together institutions, technology, and power.

Inscribed in the expression "unwarranted influence" is a relation wherein power works instrumentally in the interest of a shadowy elite operating outside the parameters of everyday civil society. But as is demonstrated by the extensive scholarship that has arisen on the topic, the membership of the military-industrial complex is, if anything, characterized by a certain brazen visibility.[46] It was Eisenhower's own secretary of defense, former General Motors president Charles E. Wilson, who flatly declared that what was good for General Motors was good for the country. Even more, the corporations vying for defense contracts during the 1950s, and the various government agencies distributing them, relied heavily on public relations to construct the sense of self-evident necessity that legitimized their very existence. The instrumentality of "unwarranted influence" conceals a mutation in which cross-disciplinary knowledge banks and interinstitutional transmission systems—systems existing precisely *between* institutions like the military and the corporations—become the locus and the test site for the new forms of sociopolitical regulation that both Wiener and Deleuze call "control." In this sense, Eisenhower's spectacularization of the military-industrial complex, by resorting to the oddly reassuring terminology of central command, serves to obscure rather than reveal the relevant power-knowledge dynamic.

Among those most often credited with contributing to the critical resonance of such terminology is the sociologist C. Wright Mills, who, in *The Power Elite* (1956), announced (and denounced) the existence of an increasingly centralized concentration of power at what he called "command posts" within that stratum of American society occupied by corporate executives, military "warlords," and political leaders.[47] One of Mills's harshest critics was his fellow sociologist Talcott Parsons, who viewed Mills's assessment of an uneven distribution of power as exceedingly conspiratorial. Moreover, Parsons found Mills indifferent to the possibility that even should such a nexus exist, nothing prevents it from integrating its goals into those of society as a whole.[48] This organicist subordination of the individual will to the imperatives of the whole underlies the bulk of Parsons's own theory of social organization, of which his critique of Mills constitutes a part. By 1960 Parsons's neo-Weberian studies of integrated organizational systems had also absorbed the cybernetic lexicon. For example, he lists a "communicative complex," saturated with "feedback" and "noise," as one of four components in the "principle structures of community," reflecting "a sense in which human personality and society must be fitted into the ancient concept pair of biological theory: organism and environment."[49] Nevertheless, it was Karl Deutsch, Wiener's collaborator on the *Life* project, who most explicitly extended cybernetic principles into a theory of sociopolitical regulation.

In *The Nerves of Government: Models of Political Communication and Control* (1963), Deutsch outlines a political theory based on what he calls a "limited structural correspondence" between a cybernetic command-control nexus and "political communication," proposing a state steered by the "nerves" of the body politic rather than governed by "muscular" power relations.[50] He characterizes his approach as transforming the static "ideal types" of Max Weber into "relatively full-fledged models of communication and control," or as adding "search criteria," in the form of "particular patterns of goal-seeking and goal-setting, self-steering and feedback," to the structural-functional approach of Parsons and his contemporary Robert K. Merton.[51] Furthermore, Deutsch extends the "general interchange model" of Parsons, in which a social system is made up of four functional subsystems—internal pattern maintenance, adaptation to environmental conditions, goal attainment, and integration of functions into a coordinated whole—to a theory of political power. As a result, power quantifiable as "force" is converted into a kind of "currency" merely flowing through the system, thereby reducing its claim on what Deutsch calls the "essence of politics." The new essential that replaces it, which for the most part Deutsch *also* designates as "control," is underwritten by a cybernetic organicism: "the dependable coordination of human efforts and expectations for the attainment of the goals of the society."[52]

Thus the hierarchical power structure identified by Mills and absorbed into the discourse on the military-industrial complex is overlaid with a systemic notion of power—as control—theorized by figures such as Parsons and Deutsch.[53] Control, naturalized by the organism, becomes the linchpin of a technocratic program of diagnosing and correcting societal imbalances through an organizational dynamics. But the totalizing imperatives of organization, and the attendant project of optimizing performativity through a feedback-based responsiveness, remain untouched.[54] As an externalization of the homeostatic apparatus of the human nervous system, the antinuclear city appearing in *Life* can thus be said to correspond to the state apparatus foreseen by Wiener (and his critics) and celebrated by Deutsch, as it attempts to supplement human intelligence during a moment of profound disorientation and to steer society out of its scientifically induced confusion. But this urban planning project also represents an early convergence of cybernetic spatial and technological strategies that would work to supplement the institutions of the state with the more diffuse organizational protocols of the control society.

By the time the project was published in 1950, the existing state apparatus was already conditioned by the networks organizing the military-industrial complex named by Eisenhower a decade later. For example, in 1949 the Soviet Union—to the surprise of the American military establishment—tested its first nuclear device, and by 1950 it was rumored that the Soviets had overtaken the United States in the arms race. Concerned that its preemptive policy of "prompt use" of nuclear weapons would be ineffective against a strengthened enemy, the United States began to explore early warning defense options. The result was a comprehensive, computer-controlled air defense network called the Semi-Automatic Ground Environment, or SAGE. Implementing this system required the combined efforts of the U.S. military, International Business Machines, Western Electric, Bell Laboratories, MIT's Lincoln Laboratories, the Rand Corporation, and many other organizations, with numerous technical innovations in the areas of computer hardware, software, interface, and networking, including digital transmission over telephone lines. SAGE was described by one Air Force colonel as "a servomechanism spread over an area comparable to the whole American continent."[55]

In this sense, the infrastructure of weapons systems like SAGE materialized many of the key components in the communications networks that Wiener saw as theoretically necessary to realize the full organizational potential of cybernetics. Conversely, Wiener's own "defense-by-communications" proposal must also be counted among these weapons systems, at two levels. First, it uses many of the same techniques—decentralization, redundancy, information management, feedback—to defend against and regulate the entropic effects of imminent atomic catastrophe that constitute the primary justification for the collaboration of science, industry, and the state embodied in the very idea of the military-industrial complex. But second, in a kind of cybernetic feedback loop, it also uses scientific concepts, developed in the laboratories and testing grounds of the complex, to defend against science itself. The project's dream of communicative transparency maintained by a network of roads, highways, train lines, and telephone wires constitutes a "defense-by-communications" not only against the bomb but against the specialized, incommunicative discursive environment that created it. Through the fissures of a bipolar cold war there thus emerged a logic of control so encompassing that it aspired to the status of both material *and* discursive regulator, an organizational "pattern" encoded in images circulating through the same mass-media networks (including *Life* magazine) that McLuhan analyzed in *The Mechanical Bride*.

Thus, while Wiener himself was often skeptical about the possibility of applying cybernetic principles to other domains, especially to the so-called human sciences, his urban planning project—with its sociopolitical overtones—is nevertheless representative of large-scale efforts on the part of cyberneticists to forge an interdisciplinary research program designed to overcome the isolating loss of perspective that they attribute to such highly specialized realms as atomic science. This dream of communicative transparency, including what Deleuze calls the quest for "universals of communication," in fact presides over nearly all of cybernetics' early adventures. Numbered among these is its institutionalization as an interdisciplinary science in the conferences sponsored by the Josiah R. Macy, Jr. Foundation that were held regularly between 1946 and 1953 and attended by leading representatives in diverse fields, from Wiener to such figures as anthropologist Margaret Mead, ethnologist Gregory Bateson, sociologist Paul Lazarsfeld, mathematician John von Neumann, and linguist Roman Jakobson.[56]

As always, architects and theorists of architecture were noticeably unwilling to be left out of such enterprises. Thus, writing to Wiener in early 1954, Richard Neutra lines up behind the others, declaring himself "a grateful reader and owner of your two books."[57] That same year, Neutra published *Survival through Design,* his own guide to the nuclear age, in which he cites both Wiener and Walter Cannon;[58] he also sent Wiener a copy. In 1956 an article by Neutra titled "Inner and Outer Landscape" appeared in *The New Landscape in Art and Science,* edited with commentary by Gyorgy Kepes; in it, the architect announces that the continuity between microcosm and macrocosm celebrated by Kepes in his compilation of scientific images reaches "right into our own innermost physiology, the processes within our skin, within our organism, our nervous system," and must be served by a designer who "switches on currents and cross-currents which continuously flow through the individual, the group, the physical surroundings."[59] Included in the same volume are texts by Giedion and by Walter Gropius, with Giedion again deploring the chaos and lack of coordination in modern life, Gropius adopting Giedion's terms—"equipoise" and "dynamic equilibrium"—to call on architecture as a means of reorienting the bewildered postwar subject, and Kepes quoting from transcripts of the Macy conferences in his commentary.[60]

The New Landscape in Art and Science also includes an essay by Norbert Wiener titled "Pure Patterns in a Natural World." In this brief reflection on the mathematical elegance of the patterns embodied in a number of the photographs published by Kepes, Wiener insists—again, despite his own initial hesitancy to pursue such comparisons—that "the significance of the processes of breakdown is great not only in physics, but even in the study of sociological processes."[61] Upon receiving this text in mid-1951, Kepes wrote back to Wiener enthusiastically requesting that he elaborate further. Wiener refused, and Kepes apologetically tried again, declaring, to no avail, that "after reading your essay I saw that your contribution could be the focal point of my book."[62]

But although Kepes never succeeded in extracting from Wiener more details on the correlation between aesthetic form (patterns) and resistance to social entropy, the infrastructure of the military-industrial complex around which the entire discussion was coiled makes a pointed appearance in aesthetic discourse here, when Kepes compares the human sensorium, navigating through feedback, to intelligent weaponry: "We ourselves are self-regulating systems; when we put out our hand for an apple, our movement sends back to us a continuous indication of where we are; similarly to the

1.10
(following page) Illustrations provided by Gyorgy Kepes
for Norbert Wiener's "Pure Patterns in a Natural World." In
Kepes, *The New Landscape in Art and Science* (1956), 276.

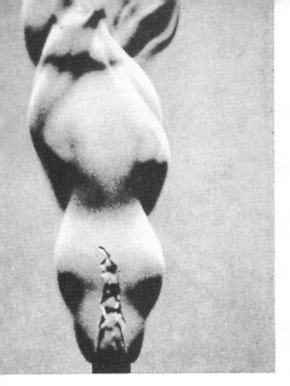

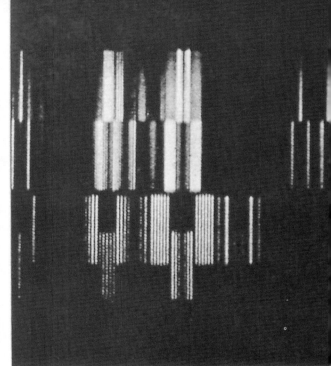

341 Fig. 4   343 Fig. 7

342 Fig. 5

guided missile, we continuously correct for error as we seek our destination."[63] Just as McLuhan observes that the delirious overproduction of advertisements unfolds into a "single landscape" possessed of its own internal logic, so Kepes sees the new landscape made visible by scientific imaging as a communicative topography made up of relational patterns whose naturally occurring equilibrium can be incorporated into art and architecture. The images themselves are used as a kind of feedback mechanism, in another effort to deploy the techniques of the "control society" to regulate its own militarism, by converting the output of science into organizational input fed back into the guided missile of the human sensorium to correct its course. This new landscape also belongs to what Kepes calls a shift from "thing-seeing" to "pattern-seeing," where the body into which this sensorium is embedded is decisively flattened. What was once a "thing" in space, an organism made up of carefully arranged functional organs, has become, for Wiener as well as for many biologists, a communications network linked to other networks in all directions, a "pattern."[64]

This reduction to the degree zero of organized patterns also seeks to resolve the conflict implied by the conjunction of art and science in Kepes's title. If Foucault succeeded in extending the epistemological hypotheses of historians of science such as Gaston Bachelard and Canguilhem into multiple aspects of human endeavor, including the production of "man" in the "human sciences," aesthetic questions still seem to resist formulation in epistemological terms so rooted in scientific discourse. In a sense, this resistence could impose an immediate limit on our effort to explore the implications of Foucault's theses, and those of Deleuze, in an interdisciplinary network capable of including architecture. Conversely, it could cause us to limit our architectural inquiry to questions of technique. But here we find Kepes seeking precisely to unify art and science on the common ground of control and communication, with architecture represented as an agent of homeostatic regulation, maintaining what Giedion called "dynamic equilibrium."

It is exactly a new, aesthetically advanced biomechanical, sociotechnical "organism" that Kepes is attempting to theorize and to build with his stunning compilation of patterns in *The New Landscape in Art and Science.* For him, these "pure patterns in a natural world" are revealed to art by science, only to be fed back into science by art. Architecture is merely one of many media enabling the exchange. The informatic reduction on which the entire process depends is, in the long run, essentially the reduction of all biological, technological, and aesthetic input and output to patterns of ones and zeroes. It is also constitutive of what we can call the "organizational complex," or the discursive formation from which both the technomilitarism of control systems *and* proposed antidotes to this militarism—including the technocratic prospect in Wiener as well as the aesthetic prospect in Kepes—sprang during the 1950s and early 1960s in response to the tendency toward entropy exhibited by those same systems.

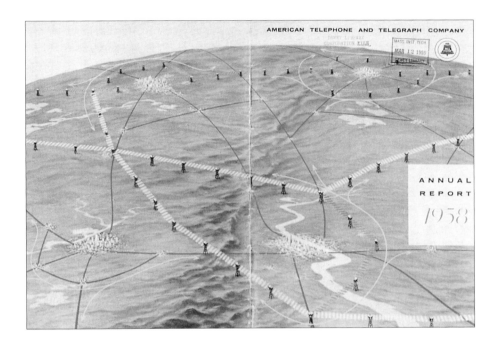

ANNUAL
REPORT
1958

What remains for us to study, then, is the vast patterned network of networks left behind by this complex, an "open site" (Deleuze) wherein scientific knowledge and aesthetic strategies constantly change places in an epistemological blur. Periodically, each node in the network contributes its own modulation to the organization of "control," such as when the American Telephone and Telegraph Corporation proved itself an equally accomplished theorist of antientropic techniques, using the occasion of its 1958 annual report to echo Wiener's doctrine of "defense-by-communications." As part of what the company called "building communications for a strong defense," it revealed a strategy whereby "new telephone routes bypass critical areas to insure that essential nationwide communication will be maintained in case of disaster." A diagram on the cover shows telephone lines being routed around major cities, so that "if these cities are destroyed, communications can bypass them."[65] The basis of this strategy was made clear three years later in another AT&T annual report that contained a manifesto, also titled "Communications for Defense," which declares ominously that "in communications, defense of the nation comes first."[66] Here is confirmed Deleuze's assertion that the quest for universals of communication should make us shudder. The much-advertised resilience and scope of the so-called Bell System is mobilized as a guarantee that the lines will be kept open in the face of all imaginable forms of interference, nuclear or otherwise.

1.11
Cover of the American Telephone and Telegraph Corporation, *AT&T Corporation Annual Report* (1958).

The Organizational Complex

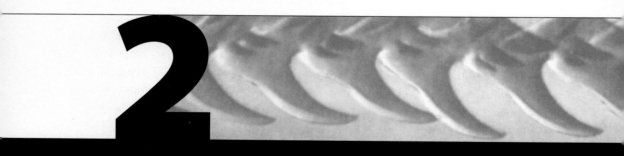

2

Pattern-Seeing

Writing in a section of *The New Landscape in Art and Science* titled "Thing, Structure, Pattern, Process," Gyorgy Kepes observes that "a crystal growth is not a fixed form that emerges from nowhere; it is a space-time boundary of energies in organization."[1] Kepes distinguishes the visual recognition of such emergent, fluctuating boundaries ("pattern-seeing") from the habituated perception of static objects ("thing-seeing"). But the fact that his example actually refers to an image of the growth pattern of silicon carbide crystals generated in the research laboratories of the General Electric Corporation also indicates the proximity of what Kepes calls a "new vision" to the emergent pattern of institutional and technological networks that later became known as the military-industrial complex.

More precisely, the organicism of his pattern-seeing was and is commensurate with the logic of this complex. Henceforth, according to Kepes, everything would be

Pattern-Seeing

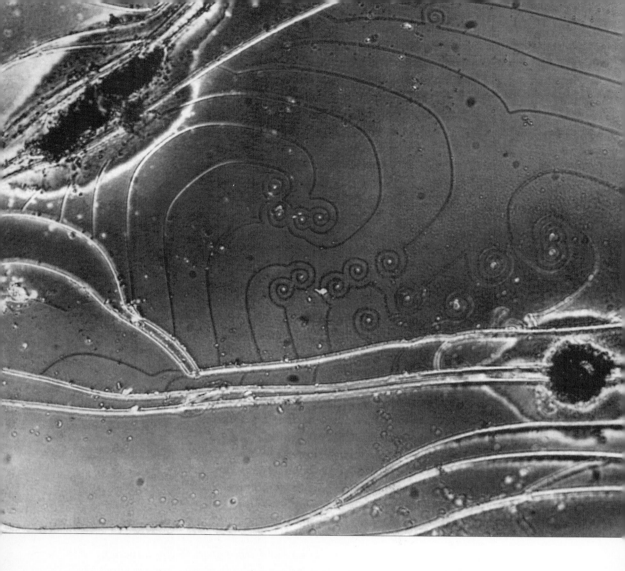

2.1

Growth pattern of silicon carbide crystals, electron micro-

graph, General Electric Research Laboratory. From Gyorgy

Kepes, *The New Landscape in Art and Science* (1956), 208.

connected to everything else through a cascading series of feedback loops. Microcosm and macrocosm, blown apart by the instruments that revealed an unrecognizable new nature in the deep space of the laboratories, would be reunited through what he called "a new common denominator of the extended scale revealed by science and the gross scale of our unaided senses."[2] This avowed modernist named his common denominator "structure," taking care to insist that he was referring to structural patterns as traces of process, or what he called interrelated "patterns of action," rather than as static, isolated objects. Thus the concentration of architectural imagery at the end of the book described a modern architecture at once dynamic and structural—a kind of telos diagrammed in scientific photography. Still, this explanation does not address the epistemological interface that underlay architecture's implied position, as announced in the book's title. For Kepes "structure," expressed morphogenetically in photographic patterns, also represented a key point of contact between two institutions, art and science, whose mutual alienation was blamed by many for the violent effects of modernity's latest convulsions.

Kepes gradually abandons "structure" for "organization" as the book continues, revealing his revisionary ambitions even as he pays ambivalent homage to his own modernist origins. Thus he concludes, "What the new landscape suggests is not static harmony but dynamic continuity; it eludes our comprehension except as a chain of organizational levels." Significantly, this chain of patterns seen only by a new, technologically enhanced vision finds its most prescient articulation not in static scientific photographs but in the instruments of the mass media: "Motion-picture, television and related techniques have now given us the flexibility we need to mark the time flow of images, the growth, succession, rhythm and orderly continuity of vision."[3] So even as architecture is mapped onto the new landscape of natural patterns visualized by science, it is immediately held to the standards of media that imply its potential obsolescence as an instrument of perceptual reorientation. The question, unanswered by Kepes, was whether architecture, too, could manifest the "flexibility" necessary to engage and to manage—to organize, in the manner of film and television—a dynamically changing "new landscape." The corporate ethos of the organizational complex ultimately answered this question in the affirmative. But in order to grasp its scope, we must first explore the details of its meandering genealogical recesses.

Trained not as a writer or theorist but rather as an artist, Kepes throughout his career played the role, alternately, of receiver and transmitter.[4] Just as organized patterns of data flickered across the screens of the human-machine interfaces of the Semi-Automatic Ground Environment (SAGE) positioned strategically within black box–like command centers, so did luminous patterns collected from art and science flicker across the pages—and in the lecture halls and seminar rooms—activated by Kepes. And just as figures like Norbert Wiener supplied a lexicon for the new science of communication, so Kepes synthesized and processed their terminology and their discourse through an aesthetic project with roots sunk deep into earlier modernisms.

Although he never studied there, Kepes retained an abiding allegiance to the German Bauhaus through his friend and Hungarian compatriot, László Moholy-Nagy. This was the Bauhaus that, with the transfer of the foundational *Vorkurs* (or preliminary course) into the custody of Moholy-Nagy and Josef Albers in 1923, Walter Gropius had sought to convert into a laboratory to test the vectors of mechanization as they converged on architecture, formalized in his diagram published that same year that showed the concentric organization of the Bauhaus curriculum.[5] And though the image of architecture harbored at the school until then was most vividly expressed in Lyonel Feininger's woodcut of a radiant, crystalline cathedral on the cover of the Bauhaus manifesto of 1919, the organic luminosity emanating from Bruno Taut and Paul Scheerbart that underlay that image was now being passed through the prism of the machine—not to kill off the organism but to breathe new life into it. What Gropius sought in his functionalism was nothing less than an organic architecture possessed, as he put it, of an inner logic, "radiant and naked, unencumbered by lying facades and trickeries."[6]

This period was also marked by the proliferation of photographic cameras among both Bauhaus students and faculty, although photography was not taught formally at the school until Walter Peterhans entered the Dessau Bauhaus in 1929. Together, Moholy-Nagy and his wife, Lucia Moholy, began to develop photographic techniques and theories that became central to the culture of the image that accompanied the infiltration of the camera into nearly all modes of Bauhaus production.[7] These techniques paradoxically contributed to the primacy of the photographic image over the architectural object itself, while claiming for that object—precisely to the degree that it was transmissible as an image—a renewed organicity, via the discourse from which Kepes was to emerge.

In addition to the multitude of photographic experiments thus performed, one important by-product of this convergence was a series of texts, beginning with *Painting, Photography, Film* (1925), volume 8 in the Bauhausbücher series. Among the brief essays collected in this volume, which were published under Moholy-Nagy's name but for which Lucia Moholy acted variously as coauthor, editor, and "translator" of his rough German, was "Production Reproduction," first published in the Dutch journal *De Stijl* in 1922.[8] Its title summarizes the book's polemic: photography is expected to *produce* new optical relationships, and not merely *reproduce* what already exists. These optical effects were addressed to the biological need of the human organism—described as a "functional mechanism"—to be exposed to ever-new sense impressions. Photography was said to possess an untapped potential for "productive creativity" in this regard, concentrated in the light-sensitivity of the photographic medium.

"Photography is the manipulation of light" was a refrain repeated by Moholy-Nagy throughout his career. It is clear from the beginning that he understood this manipulation of the light falling onto a silver bromide plate to belong, in two senses, to a new but still wholly organic order. First, photography laid claim on the organic in seeking to extend the biological capacity of the human sensory apparatus to its outer limits.[9] To that extent, photographic art would literally contribute to the evolutionary advancement of the species, by retraining human vision. Second, the photograph opens out onto the organic through its subject matter, seen dispassionately by the lens and recorded with precision on film. As evidenced by the book's illustrations, this

2.2

Enlarged photograph of a head louse. From László Moholy-Nagy, *Painting, Photography, Film* (1925), 53.

subject matter was not to be nature as found, but rather a new nature made visible through technological mediation.[10]

What also bears recognizing in *Painting, Photography, Film* is the sequence of media laid out in its title and followed by its texts and imagery. For Moholy-Nagy, this sequence is developmental. Painting, for example, once freed from the task of representation by the naturalistic exactitude of photography and film, can focus itself on the investigation of "pure color composition," thereby in turn pressuring the newer media to slip out of the representational noose by their own means.[11] But this reciprocity is ultimately overturned by the "from-to" structure organizing the entire book—*from* painting *to* photography *to* film—which brings Moholy-Nagy closer still to Marshall McLuhan's observation, four decades later, that the content of a medium is always another medium, and registers the media-driven organicism common to both figures. For Moholy-Nagy, visual media *evolve,* and thus they support the further evolution of the human sensorium. Formal techniques are carried from one medium to the other, in a crescendo of effects that is judged equal to the task of mastering the new, second nature of metropolitan experience. Thus *Painting, Photography, Film* concludes with a layout for an unrealized film, "Dynamic of the Metropolis." The layout's final image is an X-ray photograph of a dead chicken: confirmation that the film's "optical creator" (Moholy-Nagy's term) recognized the disenchantment of metropolitan life, but also evidence of an optical instrument training its lens on a dead nature in order to impart to it a new, artificial life through the kinesthetics of the motion picture.[12]

This logic was crystallized in Moholy-Nagy's second Bauhaus book, *Von Material zu Architektur.* Published in 1929, one year after its author's departure from the Bauhaus, the book is a compendium of the visual experiments carried out in the *Vorkurs,* supplemented by a pedagogy centered on the retraining of the sensorium to adapt to the disjunctive pace of modernity. Its 1932 translation into English, *The New Vision: From Material to Architecture,* contributed significantly to the Anglo-American reception of Bauhaus design theory and pedagogy. The English title makes the book's project explicit. To the "from-to" structure of the original, with architecture as the destination, is added a "new vision" carried by photography and film. In other words, architecture is now positioned at the end of the evolutionary development, with photography and film acting as agents of advancement by providing a new visual apparatus.

Condensed into the "material" named in the title are the artistic techniques taught at the Bauhaus during Moholy-Nagy's tenure and illustrated in the book. These appear in sequence, with each element broken down according to questions of texture, form, and motion. Photography both illustrates the evolutionary development and, together with film, participates in it as it converges toward kinetic spatial construction.[13] By treating each medium in its turn—painting, sculpture, and proto-

architectural construction—as taught at the Bauhaus, Moholy-Nagy again transposes aesthetic principles from one to the next. But taken together with his earlier book, *Von Materiel zu Architektur* also represents a significant revision of the theoretical lines established by the Bauhaus manifesto of 1919, in which Gropius sought a unity of media under a transcendent architecture. In Moholy-Nagy's version, architecture is one medium among many, although its synthetic nature is preserved by virtue of its being last in line and the recipient of lessons learned from all other media. The final illustration in *Von Materiel zu Architektur* is a photomontage by Jan Kamman. Printed in negative and captioned "Architecture," it consists of an image of the iconic Van Nelle factory in Rotterdam superimposed onto an image of a traditional Dutch townhouse. It is Moholy-Nagy's answer to the Feininger woodcut, and its caption suggests that this type of photographically produced illusion of spatial interpenetration awaits actualization with the arrival of "glass architecture," after which "the next generation will perhaps see buildings like this."[14] In *The New Vision* "glass architecture" is thus a late stage in the evolution of media, standing poised on the horizon and close to the "biological needs" of the human organism.

2.3

X-ray photograph of a dead chicken. From László Moholy-Nagy, sketch for *Dynamic of the Metropolis* (1922), in Moholy-Nagy, *Painting, Photography, Film* (1925), 137.

Pattern-Seeing

"Architecture." Photomontage by Jan Kamman in László
Moholy-Nagy, *Von Material zu Architektur* (1929), 236.

In 1935 Moholy-Nagy emigrated to England. The same year he was joined in London by his friend Kepes, and the two started a design business specializing in commercial graphics and displays.[15] But the extension of the evolutionary project of *The New Vision* from Moholy-Nagy to Kepes is not the only line we must follow, for as we enter Kepes's archive, we discover that it has an archive of its own.

In London, Kepes befriended James J. Crowther, the science editor for the *Manchester Guardian,* whom Kepes describes as a "mentor." In 1937 Crowther published a popularization of modern physics, *The Outline of the Universe,* whose cover was designed by Kepes and Moholy-Nagy. Through Crowther Kepes came into contact with a number of important British scientists, including J. D. Bernal, Joseph Needham, Conrad Waddington, and J. B. S. Haldane.[16] Another figure not mentioned by Kepes in his recollections of these years, but one with whom Moholy-Nagy had contact in London, was biologist Julian Huxley, patron of modern architecture at the London Zoo.[17]

Kepes, speaking into a tape recorder several decades later, recalls being struck by the concern these scientists had with annexing a social agenda to their specialized knowledge and scientific lives:

> Again . . . the reason I mention it is because I know that when I begin, confident that there is a task to find links between science and art, it was not my own sudden invention. There is a Greek proverb [that is] supposed to say that everybody has a father. It came from some of this contact with people who were doing, in a certain way, the same thing that I intended to do later, but less concentrated, because their own needs were different. As scientists they didn't emphasize the art, though Waddington was emphasizing it.[18]

But this invocation of scientific fathers does not fully address the question of the scientific *image* that would so thoroughly condition Kepes's discourse. The theories of the Gestalt school of perceptual psychology were also an important source for Kepes's ideas during the 1940s on the organization of the visual field; these eventually led to the notion of "pattern-seeing" developed in *The New Landscape,* which sought to su-persede a perceptual aesthetics based on the recognition of figural *Gestalten.*[19]

The work of the scientists Kepes met in London specifically addressed questions related to those he would explore in his own work, including the question of *organiza-tion,* through related means. Needham and Waddington were among the founding members of the Theoretical Biology Club, a group of leading organicist biologists that had begun meeting at Oxford in 1932.[20] Among its other allegiances, including ties to general systems theory, this discourse also made use of concepts of pattern formation drawn from Gestalt psychology, since the problem of organization in the formation of unified, organic wholes was central to the organicist project.[21] But more significantly, for these biologists the study of organizational processes in life at all scales was largely figured as a problem of *visualization.*[22] Liquid crystals, railway switchyards, and undulat-ing topographies were among the images they utilized to visualize specific biological processes. As Donna Haraway puts it in her study of the group: "All these gross analo-gies grew out of organismic biases; *they were attempts to visualize wholeness* so the ab-straction could be translated into common, scientific, systematic understanding."[23]

The affinity between such imagery and the photographs later exhibited by Kepes was confirmed when Kepes himself published illustrated texts by Conrad Wadding-ton and Paul Weiss in the 1960s.[24] But Kepes, whose first acknowledged exposure to science was to its images, and who would later claim these image-driven scientists as fathers, was not merely subordinating art here to the rigors of science. He was encoun-tering an aporia implicit in the conjunction he would try so hard to effect between these two arenas, an aporia in which the authority of scientific knowledge is undone by the constitutive role played by aesthetic form in its visualization. Haraway, writing as a historian of science unproblematically utilizing aesthetic terms, resolves it by re-ferring to these images as "metaphors."[25] This characterization will shortly be modified here with respect to Kepes, as we take into account the theoretical status accorded to the image in his own discourse.

Soon after moving to Harvard in 1937, Gropius was asked to be the director of a new design school in Chicago inspired by the methods and teachings of the Bauhaus. He recommended Moholy-Nagy instead. The project was backed by a group of Chicago industrialists who told Moholy-Nagy that they wanted to establish a school of industrial design "along Bauhaus lines" but also "along practical and real lines."[26] Moholy-Nagy was hesitant but ultimately accepted the offer, and arrived in Chicago in the summer of 1937. Shortly thereafter he invited Kepes to join him to establish a "light workshop" at the school, which opened in October 1937 as the New Bauhaus. Kepes agreed, and emigrated to the United States in the early fall.

But he was only one link in the network that was emerging. At the University of Chicago were a number of figures associated with the Unity of Science movement, which had developed out of Viennese logical positivism and was committed to formulating a common language enabling communication between the sciences. Among them was the philosopher of language Charles W. Morris, who taught a course called "Intellectual Integration" at the New Bauhaus. Morris believed that art, too, could contribute to this common language, and vice versa.[27] He had begun to study relationships between sign systems and human behavior, dedicating himself to constructing a common ground on which specialists could communicate and integrate their knowledge into an organic totality.[28]

Not coincidentally, then, the New Bauhaus was itself premised on the notion of integration from the start. Its curriculum consisted of one year in preliminary courses and three years in workshops such as wood, metal, plastics, display, exhibition, and theater. Architecture was reserved for a two-year graduate course. This structure thus basically echoed that of the Bauhaus during the period when Moholy-Nagy taught there, except that where Gropius had described the *Vorkurs* as "Elementary Theory of Form; Experiments with Materials," the New Bauhaus advertised three parallel preliminary courses as "Basic Design Workshop," "Analytical and Constructive Drawing," and "Scientific Subjects." The last of these, supplemented by more advanced courses in "Nature Study," "Comparative History of Art," and "Science," marked the inclusion in the curriculum of more traditionally academic courses than had been offered at the German Bauhaus. These courses were accompanied by an apology for the reputation of abstract formalism that had followed the Bauhaus from Europe:

> We have in the past given the function of art a formal importance, which segregates it from our daily existence, whereas art is always present where healthy and unaffected people live. Our task is, therefore, to contrive a new system of education which, along with specialized training in science and technique leads to a thorough awareness of fundamental human needs and a universal outlook. Thus, our concern is to develop a new type of designer, able to face all types of requirements, not because he is a prodigy but because he has the right method of approach. We wish to make him conscious of his own creative power, not afraid of new facts, working independently of recipes.[29]

This doctrine of "everyone is talented" had been present from the beginning in Moholy-Nagy's pedagogy. Now, however, it was focused on the production of what he called a "new type of designer." This projected designer was, in effect, a new social type, bearing a humanistic, universal outlook, an evolutionary adaptation capable of managing the reorganization of vision for the benefit of humanity as a whole.

Measured against such an ambition, the actual influence of the New Bauhaus, its faculty and students, was negligible. Nevertheless, the school formed a key link in a network of discursive practices in which such questions are secondary. What matters more here are the lines of communication that passed through this point, which become visible on closer examination.

One important guide for Moholy-Nagy's attempts to redirect human evolution by inscribing a technologically mediated new vision was the so-called evolutionary humanism of the biologist Julian Huxley. Huxley, whom Moholy-Nagy had met in London in the mid-1930s, argued that humanist principles should be used as criteria in the scientific management of evolutionary development. He believed that human consciousness had evolved to the degree that it could now initiate a second order of evolutionary progress, in which the brutality of natural selection would be replaced by self-conscious, rationally managed population control. One practical consequence of this position was Huxley's involvement with eugenics, which he (with his coauthor H. G. Wells) described in 1929 as "the preferential breeding of the best."[30] Moholy-Nagy thus found in Huxley's ideas the theoretical framework for intervening in the evolution of vision. In Chicago, he adapted these ideas to a specific pedagogical context. Because culture could now be seen as a source of criteria for self-conscious evolutionary selection, there was no contradiction in introducing a humanistic element into the otherwise vocation-oriented Bauhaus curriculum devoted to the logic of the machine.

Nevertheless, the brief life of the New Bauhaus still encapsulates the cliché-ridden conflict between the pragmatism of American industry and the utopianism of the European avant-gardes. Pressure was exerted on Moholy-Nagy to step down after the experimentalism of his approach became evident, and financial support was withdrawn after the school's first year. Apparently, experimental visual research had succumbed to the demands of the marketplace. But these events may be more accurately interpreted as a realignment, in microcosm, of the Bauhaus project toward the model of the research laboratory—an image laboratory—with both industrial and academic affiliations. "This is not a school but a laboratory" were Moholy-Nagy's first words in his opening address to students. This shift already prefigures the "laboratory" for the study of art and technology called the Center for Advanced Visual Studies that Kepes would found at the Massachusetts Institute of Technology in 1967. In addition, it coincides with the beginnings of a realignment within American industry itself toward "pure" research not expected to yield immediate productive gain, a shift that would eventually underwrite what was called the "military-industrial-academic complex" of the mid-1960s, which we will encounter in chapter 6. It was premised on the same duality encountered but not engaged by Haraway in her study of organicist science, the duality between image as representation (or "metaphor") and image as a machine that, like a microscope or an oscilloscope, adapts human vision to new modes of seeing.

Following the closing of the New Bauhaus in 1938, Kepes continued to teach in an improvised setting, while rebuffing offers from the school's sponsors to stay on in an institution restored under new leadership.[31] Instead, again under Moholy-Nagy, he and others who had taught at the New Bauhaus reopened the school independently at another Chicago location in the winter of 1939, as the School of Design. Included in this group was Morris, who was joined at the new school by his University of Chicago colleagues Carl Eckhart and Ralph Gerard as unpaid faculty lecturing on their specialties. Gerard, who was a physiologist and member of the New Bauhaus faculty from the beginning, later played an important role in the dissemination of cybernetics and was a regular participant in the Macy cybernetics conferences. To find him here collaborating with Moholy-Nagy and Kepes to keep their enterprise afloat thus suggests not only the presence of a protocybernetic discourse in this transplanted Bauhaus from the start; it also implies the presence of a commitment to Bauhaus-related principles in the cybernetic discussions that were to come.[32] In keeping with such affinities, Morris's description of the rapprochement between art and science begun at the New Bauhaus was reprinted in the School of Design prospectus in abbreviated form, reinforcing the school's continued orientation toward the academy.[33] Along the same lines, in lieu of the board of directors representing the interests of industry that had been the source of conflict at the New Bauhaus, Moholy-Nagy solicited what he called the "moral support" of a list of important academics and intellectuals: philosopher John Dewey, Gropius, Harvard dean Joseph Hudnut, Julian Huxley, publisher W. W. Norton, educator William Bacharach, and museum director Alfred H. Barr.

In 1938, after the school's inaugural year, W. W. Norton published a revised version of Moholy-Nagy's *The New Vision*, now with the subtitle *Fundamentals of Design, Painting, Sculpture, Architecture*.[34] A "virtual volume" produced by a rotating wire construction, executed in 1937, is among the illustrations of student work from the New Bauhaus that Moholy-Nagy added to this edition.[35] The study and production of such effects at the School of Design, which in 1944 became the Institute of Design, is more fully documented in Moholy-Nagy's last book, *Vision in Motion*, published posthumously in 1947. The book, an amalgam of his writings from the 1940s, is illustrated prolifically with work of New Bauhaus and Institute of Design students, as well as that of his own contemporaries, all placed in a theoretical framework that modifies significantly the propositions found in *The New Vision*. Mirroring the inclusion of humanistic courses at the New Bauhaus taught by University of Chicago faculty, the introduction self-consciously uses quotations in place of images to illustrate its arguments. The focus on "biological" necessity in *The New Vision* is converted to "sociobiological" necessity, accessible only through an education that combines the humanistic and technical spheres. "Art has two faces," Moholy-Nagy writes, "the biological and the social, the one toward the individual and the other toward the group."[36]

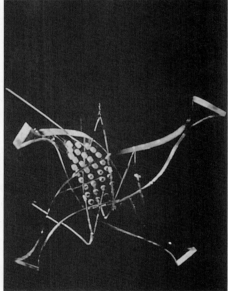

2.5
Richard Koppe, "virtual volume," ca. 1938. From László
Moholy-Nagy, *The New Vision: Fundamentals of Design,
Painting, Sculpture, Architecture* (rev. ed., 1938), 129.

2.6
László Moholy-Nagy, *Space Modulator* (bottom left, 1940)
and its "virtual volume" (bottom right). From *Vision in Motion* (1947), 242–243.

This new emphasis on the integration of the designer into society also contains an overtly primitivist component, reflected in Moholy-Nagy's account of the disintegration of traditional societies into the disorganized modern marketplace.[37] He does not interpret this as a reason to return to premodern forms of artistic expression, asserting instead that "tradition is man-made" and thus demands constant reassessment and refinement, like an industrially produced object. This is to say that the supposedly balanced state of nature represented by premodern cultures can be restored through human intervention, and Moholy-Nagy expects the new subspecies of designer to intervene in human evolution in favor of a stabilizing vision. The framework for such an intervention is again supplied by Huxley—now an advisor to the Institute of Design—whom Moholy-Nagy quotes at the outset of his first chapter: "There are many obvious ways in which the brain's level of performance can be genetically raised—in acuteness of perception, memory, synthetic grasp and intuition, analytic capacity, mental energy, creative power, balance, and judgment."[38]

This notion of human intervention in evolutionary processes is also what enables Moholy-Nagy to write that

> The biological and evolutionary progress of man was possible only through the development and constructive use of all his senses, hands, and brains, through his creative ability and intuition to master his surroundings; through his perceptive power, conceptual thought, and articulated emotional life. But concomitant with the stabilization of the industrial revolution these biological functions were suffocated under the tinsel of an easy-going life full of appliances and amenities, much too overestimated in their value. Man who is by nature able to express himself in different media allowed these most valuable biological potentialities to be amputated or paralyzed.
>
> It is an individual as well as social waste to have eyes and not see; ears and not hear; to destroy the endowment of instincts to create. The result is an atrophy of capabilities, a step-by-step deterioration. Man's strong nature may endure for generations but the end is disintegration.[39]

Thus, for Moholy-Nagy, even as the evolutionary sequence of media leads to the emergence of a "new vision" among designers, industrial success brings with it suffocation under the superficialities of consumerism and fashion. He makes this critique explicit when he counterposes the sense of organic necessity embodied in D'Arcy Wentworth Thompson's description of a swimming fur seal with the fashionable pouring of streamlined styling like "brown gravy in cheap restaurants" over all manner of static, industrially produced objects.[40] Moholy-Nagy thus sought literally to evolve a humanistic visual faculty able to see through these illusions and replace them with what he argued was a biologically necessary "organic design." The means of transmitting this vision were provided by Huxley's revision of Darwinism to favor the intervention of science and culture in nature. This line of thought is developed through the rest of *Vision in Motion,* under chapter headings such as "New Method of Approach—Design for Life," and "New Education—Organic Approach." The emphasis is on the integration of media—"painting, photography, sculpture, space-time problems, motion pictures, literature, group poetry"[41]—into a communicative organicity for the benefit of the species.

2.3

Vision in Motion was dedicated to Elizabeth and Walter Paepcke, original supporters of the New Bauhaus who reemerged as sponsors and advocates of the School of Design. Beginning around 1934, the year in which the "Century of Progress" world's fair in Chicago catalogued the streamlined design overtaking consumer objects, Walter Paepcke, the head of the Container Corporation of America, was urged by his wife to turn his attention to the way in which his company represented itself to the public. Closely connected with Chicago's artistic circles and a collector of modern art, Elizabeth Paepcke suggested that he hire the designer Egbert Jacobson to set up an "art department" at the CCA and to produce a corporate image with a distinctly modern aesthetic. The result was a marketing campaign in which the packaging company repackaged itself by commissioning such artists as Herbert Bayer, A. M. Cassandre, Kepes, Willem de Kooning, Fernand Léger, and Herbert Matter to produce posters and other graphic works for the CCA, which were eventually exhibited in 1945 at the Art Institute of Chicago under the title *Modern Art in Advertising.*[42]

By that time, the Institute of Design had a board of directors under Paepcke that included executives from Marshall Field, United Airlines, Sears Roebuck, the Harris Bank, and the Chicago Association of Commerce. The selection underscored a commitment to make itself useful to industry in order to remain in existence, even as Moholy-Nagy continued to emphasize a broad, humanistic orientation. The school had survived the depressed economic conditions of the war by offering its services to the government, and immediately thereafter these gestures toward a wider public were converted into a renewed emphasis on design as a marketing tool.[43] During this period, Kepes had been developing a curriculum in "visual design" at the school that would eventually be converted into a book of his own.[44] The book, *Language of Vision* (1944), brought Kepes national recognition and became a required text in visual design curricula in architecture and design schools across the country.

In Kepes's *Language of Vision,* advertising takes the place previously accorded to architecture by Moholy-Nagy in *The New Vision:* it is both agent and product of a visual faculty adapted to the dynamism of modern life. Among the "visual fundamentals" with which Kepes concerns himself in the book is what he calls the "organization of optical belonging," or the capacity of a visual unit or pattern of units to integrate itself into a larger field of similar patterns. Kepes illustrates this "law of visual organization" with an image of a snake with a patterned skin blending into the background of a bed of leaves: "a snake camouflaged by nature is not a snake."[45] In 1942 this same illustration accompanied an article in *Civilian Defense* magazine describing a course on camouflage taught at the School of Design by Kepes and Moholy-Nagy.[46] The course began with the "basic problems of visual perception" that would allow the *camoufleur* to deceive the eye of the enemy. Here the "new vision"—already a vision in motion— was brought to bear on the subject, since "the aerial observer for whom camouflage has to be largely considered today is a mobile observer. Every factor involved in his vision is in continuous movement. His eye is moving, the light conditions are changing and the elements of the landscape are moving."[47]

The finding and fixing of a target, isolated from its surroundings after the visual evaluation of tone, color, and texture, are formulated in terms of gestalt recognition strikingly similar to those used by Norbert Wiener in his efforts to track the movements of enemy pilots with his antiaircraft predictor. "This is the reason why at the beginning of camouflage teaching there is a basic investigation of point, line, tone, color, shape, etc.," the course outline continues. Thus it is necessary to study figure-ground relationships, borders, shadows, reflections, and other properties identical to those studied by designers in the same school. In other words, the course was basic training in the *Language of Vision.*

The other, more abstract diagrams illustrating the *Civilian Defense* article are of the same order as those illustrating the opening section of *Language of Vision* titled "Plastic Organization," where Kepes defines his terms:

> The experience of a plastic image is a form evolved through a process of organization. *The plastic image has all the characteristics of a living organism.* It exists through forces in interaction which are acting in their respective fields, and are conditioned by these fields. It has an organic, spatial unity; that is, it is a whole the behavior of which is not determined by that of its individual

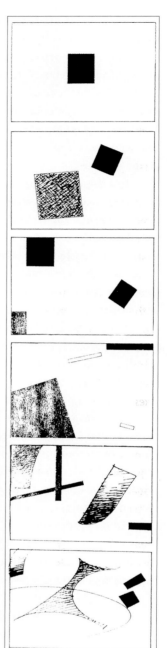

2.7

Gyorgy Kepes, snake on patterned background. From *Language of Vision* (1944), 45.

2.8

Gyorgy Kepes, diagrams illustrating "spatial tension" and "dynamic equilibrium." From *Language of Vision* (1944), 37.

components, but where the parts are themselves determined by the intrinsic nature of the whole. It is, therefore, an enclosed system that reaches its dynamic unity by various levels of integration; by balance, rhythm and harmony.[48]

Here already we find a concise summary of the concepts that would condition Kepes's work for the next two decades: the image as organism, formed through an organizing process in which the individual parts were determined by the dynamics of an encompassing, integrated "system."

The focus on the organization of the visual field throughout the book thus reflects more than simply pattern recognition for the sake of legibility, or (in the case of camouflage) the reverse. The opening lines of his introduction, written during the war, make clear what Kepes believes to be at stake here: "Today we experience chaos. The waste of human and material resources and the canalization of almost all creative effort into blind alleys bear witness to the fact that our common life has lost its coherency. In the focus of this eclipse of a healthy human existence is the individual, torn by the shattered fragments of his formless world, incapable of organizing his physical and psychological needs."[49] It is at this point that he invokes the "tragic formlessness" indicating failure in organizing the new "equipment" provided by science and technology into an "equilibrium" that, as we have already seen, resonates with Sigfried Giedion's call for a "dynamic equilibrium" in the concluding chapter of *Mechanization Takes Command,* published four years later.

Giedion's preface to Kepes's book does little more than interpolate Kepes into a "third generation" of practitioners of the "new spatial conception." But Kepes was doing more than simply extending Giedion's project, so closely tied up with Moholy-Nagy's, into the realm of visual design. He was not mapping the contours of a new spatiality but rather was attempting to formulate the rules of a new *language.* According to Kepes, "the *language of vision,* optical communication, is one of the strongest potential means both to reunite man and his knowledge and to re-form man as an integrated being." But even here there is the potential for confusion, since ultimately the key term in Kepes is not "language" but "communication," and what appears to be a linguistic hypothesis turns out to be a theory of media. As Kepes puts it:

> Visual language can convey facts and ideas in a wider and deeper range than almost any other means of communication. It can reinforce the static verbal concept with the sensory vitality of dynamic imagery. It can interpret the new understanding of the physical world and social events because dynamic interrelationships and interpenetration, which are significant in every

advanced scientific understanding of today, are intrinsic idioms
of the contemporary vehicles of visual communication: photography, motion pictures, and television.[50]

The reappearance of the sequence of media laid out in Moholy-Nagy's writings
of the 1920s, with television taking the place of architecture at the end of the line, suggests that Kepes is far more interested in the structural effects of each medium than
he is in the manifest content of the "message." Or, again to paraphrase McLuhan
(whom Kepes would later befriend and publish),[51] the message being communicated
by the language of vision lies in the properties of the media of optical communication
themselves. This is where "organization" literally enters the picture. The "organized
image" is not the carrier of a message; it *is* the message. Kepes argues, "To perceive a
visual image implies the beholder's participation in a process of organization. The experience of an image is thus a creative act of integration. Its essential characteristic is
that by plastic power an experience is formed into an organic whole. Here is a basic
discipline of forming, that is, thinking in terms of structure, a discipline of utmost importance in the chaos of our formless world."[52] For Kepes, then, organization is nothing
more—or less—than a media effect.

Nevertheless, the second section of *Language of Vision,* titled "Visual Representation," would seem to return us to the problem of linguistic or semantic meaning,
as Kepes takes the reader through an illustrated history of representational techniques. The same could be said of the last section of the book, "Toward a dynamic
iconography," whose subsections include "Laws of organization of meaningful visual signs" and "Disintegration of the fixed system of meaning organization." Indeed,
the book does systematically seek to restore a manifest content, or a "general semantics," to modernist abstraction, a project reinforced by its introduction—written by
S. I. Hayakawa, founder of the General Semantics movement, which was dedicated to
extending the analysis of linguistic meaning into all realms of human endeavor, including science.[53] Here also, McLuhan's guidebook to reading advertisements, *The Mechanical Bride,* which appeared several years later (after his encounter with Giedion), is
relevant to decoding a "dynamic iconography." But the most significant figure for such
a decoding is Charles Morris, who read and commented on Kepes's manuscript during
its preparation.

Two years after the appearance of Kepes's book, Morris published *Signs, Language, and Behavior.* In it, he sought to develop what he called a "science of signs"
reflecting the "biological basis" of a "science of behavior," citing the behavioral psychology of Clark L. Hull on the stimulus-response structure of what Morris refers to as
"sign-behavior."[54] Significantly for the history of the organizational complex, it was

during this same period that Norbert Wiener also began speculating on relations between input-output feedback loops and the stimulus-response circuits of behaviorism.[55] Morris would later note the subsequent assimilation of the terminology of information theory into semiotics by referring to the distinction between "information" and "meaning" made by Claude Shannon, a distinction that was also maintained by Wiener.[56] For Morris, semiotics and the study of "sign-behavior" were concerned with the content and interpretation of signs: in other words, with signification. "Information," in contrast, was required to possess no meaning, only an organization. This is also what Wiener meant when he referred to "organization as message" in *The Human Use of Human Beings* (which appeared after *Language of Vision,* and thus cannot be counted among its subtexts). Both of these notions are present in Kepes's book: the organizational "message" of abstract visual patterns and the semantic instrumentality accorded to visual signs by Morris. The duality is resolved in the purported capacity of both forms of message to regulate human behavior and thus, for Kepes, to restore order to a world out of control. In the sense of both pattern and sign, *organization* as an agent of social equilibrium is the message of *Language of Vision.* It is what is being advertised on every page of the book.

In fact, the book nears its conclusion with a series of advertisements designed by Kepes and others, many of which were commissioned by the Container Corporation of America under Walter Paepcke. Four years earlier, in 1940, Kepes published a small pamphlet on his graphic design work that included some of these same images. At that time he was already at work on *Language of Vision,* whose working title—"The Anatomy of the Created Image"—clearly announced the book's optical organicism. In a brief text included in the pamphlet, "The Task of Visual Advertising," Kepes identifies spatial experience as the theoretical basis for advertising design.[57] Taking a cue from *The New Vision,* this experience is described as one of mobility and speed, with graphic elements (such as advertisements) acting as "traffic signs" guiding the consumer through "this mobile landscape of our environment." Thus while Moholy-Nagy concluded the sequence of media in *The New Vision* with an image of a protocinematic new architecture, Kepes concludes his own extension (and revision) of that project with advertisements intended to regulate the flows of a consumerist landscape—a second nature given over to what he calls the "eye of the customer."

Kepes completed *Language of Vision* after having left the School of Design in 1943, while he was teaching courses on visual fundamentals at North Texas State College and subsequently at Brooklyn College in New York. The book drew immediate attention upon its release, and in 1945 he accepted a full-time appointment as associate professor in the School of Architecture and Planning at the Massachusetts Institute of Technology.[58]

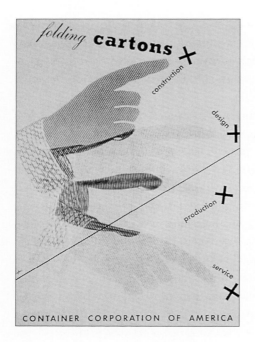

Kepes taught four courses during his early years at MIT: "Visual Fundamentals," "Light and Color," "Graphic Presentation," and "Painting"; the first two were of greatest consequence in the development of his discourse. Here it may seem that we are witnessing nothing more than the ongoing assimilation of Bauhaus pedagogy in the American context.[59] But the difference was significant. As Kepes put it in a 1948 letter to Moholy-Nagy's second wife, Sibyl Moholy-Nagy:

As far as I can generalize, the difference[s] between my approach and that of the old Bauhaus lie in that the Bauhaus emphasized the exploration of new materials, techniques and sensory fields such as the tactile, which was mainly a process of opening up the horizon; whereas I was more interested in *organizing* these new findings, and put the emphasis, as in my book, on the meaning of order in visual experience in its present social context. My approach implied that all exercises introduced in the light and color workshop and in visual fundamentals had their focal points not only in the extensions of the range of visual sensibilities, but also in acquainting the students with the structural laws of plastic experiences. I always tried to refer these structural laws back to their social meaning.[60]

2.9

Gyorgy Kepes, advertisement for the Container Corporation of America, 1938. From *Language of Vision* (1944), 181.

In this way, Kepes sought to absorb Bauhaus fundamentals such as point, line, plane, and texture into a homeostatic organizational matrix seeking dynamic equilibrium. For him, the organized—and thus organic—image was the correlate and catalyst of an organized—and thus organic—society. This was the message he brought to architects during the mid-1940s.

In March 1947, for example, Kepes participated in a conference on "planning man's physical environment," which was held as part of Princeton University's bicentennial celebration.[61] Here he explicitly referred to a "second nature" of commodities in which "images take forms—forms cheat functions—functions are robbed of their natural sources—human needs."[62] For Kepes speaking to architects and planners at Princeton, organism, environment, and "plastic truth" are to be integrated by a retrained visual faculty focused on order and structural unity. In this way, the debased "second nature" of the physical environment would be restored to a "true nature" with new imagery—what he called "a new symbolic form of basic human values."[63]

Another contribution to the conference that even more literally addressed retraining the vision of architects and planners was a series of demonstrations of visual phenomena by the perceptual psychologist Adelbert Ames. Ames and Giedion were on the same panel, and Giedion's impressions of Ames's demonstrations were published three years later in the inaugural issue of the interdisciplinary review *Trans/formation*. These were accompanied by Alfred Barr's report to a committee at the Museum of Modern Art on his visit to the Hanover Institute (formerly the Dartmouth Eye Institute), where Ames was conducting his research. At Princeton, Ames had suspended a series of sticks in space in such a way that when viewed from a particular vantage point they assembled into a recognizable figure, a chair. The effect was, in Giedion's words, the recognition that "[w]hat the 'eye perceives' can be a chair, but it may also turn out that this chair is nothing but a few sticks hovering in mid-air."[64] The significance attributed by Ames to his studies is symmetrical with Kepes's efforts to unify the aesthetic, scientific, and social realms.[65]

One month after attending the Princeton conference, Kepes received from Ames information on the research on which these demonstrations were based.[66] Among the documents sent was "Integration of Recent Developments and Hypotheses in the Sciences of Physics, Biology, and Psychology," a paper in which Ames and his colleagues attempted to theorize their observations on the contingency of vision in relation to the physicist Erwin Schrödinger's landmark effort to integrate the findings of modern biology with those of modern physics, specifically around the question of the production and maintenance of order or, in biological terms, organization.[67] With the addition of Giedion (with his allusions to modern physics), Kepes (with his connections to theoretical biology), and even the Museum of Modern Art to this nexus of discursive relations, we can see how the project of integrating art and science belonged to a larger attempt to integrate diverse forms of knowledge and thereby treat the totality of human experience as a single sociobiological system.

In the late 1940s Kepes compiled a substantial list of texts on different aspects of the synthesis he was attempting to effect. These working bibliographies offer a glimpse of the archive that conditioned both his teaching and his writing. Louis Sullivan's *Kindergarten Chats* (1947) is listed alongside a Cambridge report on the physiology of vision, Sergei Eisenstein's *Film Sense* (1942), and E. M. Stephenson's *Animal Camouflage* (1946). Matila Ghyka's *Geometry of Art and Life* (1946) is followed by D'Arcy Wentworth Thompson's *On Growth and Form* (rev. ed., 1942) and Herbert Read's *Education through Art* (1943). Kepes's command of German allowed him to list Erwin Panofsky's "Die Perspektive als 'Symbolische Form'" (1927) alongside John Dewey's *Art as Experience* (1934) and Gottfried Semper's *Der Stil in den technischen und tektonischen Künsten; oder, Praktische Aesthetik* (2nd ed., 1878). Ames's "Depth in Pictorial Art" (1925) follows a series of "biological references" that include Joseph Needham's *Order and Life* (1936), Conrad Waddington's *Organisms and Genes* (1940), and Paul Weiss's *Principles of Development* (1939), whose authors were mentioned above in the context of image and scientific paradigm. Finally, among the other texts listed are *The Organism* (1939), by the biologist Kurt Goldstein; *The Growth of the Mind* (1928), by the Gestalt psychologist Kurt Koffka; *A Dynamic Theory of Personality* (1935), by the psychologist Kurt Lewin; *Raumaesthetik und geometrisch-optische Tauschungen* (1897), by the empathy theorist Theodor Lipps; and the statement on the activities of the Dartmouth Eye Institute supplied by Ames.[68]

On its own this list may seem eclectic, but its coherence derives from Kepes's solicitation of an organizational imperative from a diverse range of discourses. To a greater or lesser extent they are linked by the affinities he identifies between scientific and psychological research and theories of aesthetic experience that seek, in different ways, to overcome the alienation between observer and object. As he developed his own discourse, Kepes collected quotations and notes from sources that referred to the overall problematics he had set in motion in *Language of Vision* and would elaborate in his later work. For example, such formulations as "visual art is a good seismograph of cultural feedback" indicate his awareness of cybernetic thought. This is made explicit in a page of notes on Wiener's *Cybernetics,* in which, as we saw earlier, "control" is designated as a central category of a new technological epoch. Wiener's words were copied and underlined by Kepes as follows: "If in the XVIIth century and early XVIII century are the age of clocks, and the later XVIII and XIX centuries constitute the age of steam-engines the present time is the age of <u>communication and control</u>."[69]

This citation makes clear that quite early on—at the latest, by the early 1950s—Kepes recognized *and identified himself with* the conditions that underlay the organizational complex. He attempted to make scientific analyses, and especially theories of biological self-regulation (he also refers to Cannon's *Wisdom of the Body,* with its articulation of homeostatic processes), the basis for an aesthetic project. As he puts it to himself elsewhere in his notes, "The importance of pattern increases with the complexity of the things, from simple nuclei, electrons, mesons, crystals—enzymes + hormones, organs, man's body → social unity. In art form the pattern is a common pattern, from the physical arrangement—to the psychological, emotive, perceptual configuration—here is one common patterning."[70]

This notion of the common pattern as a means of aesthetico-social regulation (or control) would reemerge several years later as the central thesis of Kepes's *The New Landscape of Art and Science* (1956), in which appeared Wiener's text "Pure Patterns in a Natural World." In early 1951, Kepes installed *The New Landscape,* an exhibition of scientific photography, in the Hayden Gallery at MIT. These images were among those he collected for the forthcoming book, in which he compared the patterns made visible by science to the organizational matrices of modern art and modern architecture. In the exhibition, the synthetic agenda emerging out of Kepes's reading of science was expressed not only in what the brochure called the "delicate architecture" revealed in these images but also in the status accorded to this architecture within the project of reorganizing and integrating aesthetic experience and scientific knowledge: "This rich new material of the world is often buried in the research laboratories of the different specialists and seen only with the specialist's eye. Here brought into common focus visual features which were formerly too fast or too slow, too large or too small, too dense, too scattered, otherwise concealed from our eyes, could evoke an awareness of the values inherent in the expanding world of knowledge and vision."[71]

Thus had the "new vision" opened onto a "new landscape" of images coming out of the research laboratories of the military-industrial complex, where the alienation of the scientific specialist was to be overcome by the retrained eye of the artist. In order to sustain this effect, the media through which images were transmitted had to be naturalized. It was as though these miraculously organized patterns, the products of the same scientific artifice that had brought about Hiroshima and Nagasaki, were the very materialization of the organic image Kepes had sought in *Language of Vision.* Thus, on 16 July 1945 fifty cameras recorded the first atomic explosion at Alamogordo, New Mexico. And it was Harold Edgerton, whose stroboscopic photograph

of a golfer's swing Giedion had compared to the kinesthetics of Rockefeller Center in *Space, Time and Architecture*—versions of which were also reproduced by Kepes in *Language of Vision* and Moholy-Nagy in *Vision in Motion*—who would photograph the first test of a hydrogen bomb on Eniwetok Atoll while flying in an airplane over the Pacific Ocean on 1 November 1952.[72]

The chronophotography of the physiologist Etienne-Jules Marey, as it was absorbed into the techniques of scientific management practiced by Frank and Lillian Gilbreth in the factories of the early twentieth century, forms a basis for Giedion's own conjunction of modes of visualization—both aesthetic and technical—with the effects of mechanization. In a section that reveals the poignantly allegorical nature of *Mechanization Takes Command*, Giedion says of the slaughterhouses he visited in the United States that given the resistance of organic bodies to the geometric regularity of mechanical processes, "Killing itself then cannot be mechanized. It is upon organization that the burden falls." In the gas chambers, and by extension with atomic weaponry, "organization" thus replaces "mechanization" in Giedion's terminology. According to Giedion, the efficiency and rapidity of this carefully monitored and controlled process, in which death cries and the whirring of gears cannot be distinguished, also induces a certain numbness, or "neutrality": "One does not experience,

2.10

(previous page) Gyorgy Kepes, *The New Landscape* exhibition, Massachusetts Institute of Technology, 1951. From *The New Landscape in Art and Science* (1956), 101.

2.11

Harold Edgerton, *Golfer Multiflash,* n.d. From Gyorgy Kepes, *Language of Vision* (1944), 182.

2.12

Harold E. Edgerton, K. J. Germeshausen, and H. E. Grier, hydrogen bomb explosion photographed from an airplane, Elugelab, Eniwetok Atoll, Marshall Islands, 1 November 1952.

Pattern-Seeing

one does not feel, one merely observes." And to make clear his ultimate reference, he concludes the section: "This neutrality toward death may be lodged deep in the roots of our time. It did not bare itself on a large scale until the War, when whole populations, as defenseless as the animals hooked head downwards on the traveling chain, were obliterated with trained neutrality."[73]

Giedion's reference above is largely to managerial and bureaucratic forms of organization that were developed in the late nineteenth and early twentieth century to implement and regulate Taylorist and Fordist production processes, whose most prominent analyst was Max Weber. But by 1951, three years after the appearance of his friend's book, Kepes had already passed this discourse through the lens of theoretical biology, cybernetics, and a semiotics of communication. It was not mechanization but *organization* that had taken command—or more to the point, taken *control*. This takeover was recorded in the new landscape exhibited by Kepes at MIT. It was also recorded in the command and control centers of the military-industrial complex that produced and photographed the hydrogen bomb and, half a decade later, put in place networked, servomechanical systems like SAGE to regulate its effects.

The utopianism of Kepes's project of integrating art and science through new modes of visualization is thus always already discolored by its own elision of the a priori collaborations practiced by photographers like his MIT colleague Edgerton. In order to extract a benevolent organicity out of such collaborations, Kepes had to suppress the organized dystopias presented with "trained neutrality" by the eye of the camera, to which even Giedion alluded. He therefore appealed to the organizational pattern as a means of overcoming the formlessness of a subjectivity exposed to the conditions of the cold war, a subjectivity whose inner dissolution had already been figured by Herbert Matter—whose work also appears in both *Vision in Motion* and *Language of Vision*—in a photomontage of an atomic explosion occurring inside the mind of a human silhouette that was featured on the cover of *Arts and Architecture* in December 1946. Such inner and outer formlessness was only visible to the camera momentarily, as the mushroom cloud of the hydrogen bomb dissolved into an invisible and unphotographable cloud of radioactive fallout that systematically eliminated all life. This too was a new landscape, the entropic emptiness of what was left after Eniwetok—a dead nature whose reenchantment could be registered only as ideology in pictures.

In the summer of 1951 Giedion, who was vacationing in the Mediterranean, sent a postcard to Kepes indicating that he was unsure what to write about Kepes's images and mentioning as an aside that he was planning to meet Lancelot Law Whyte, "author of Growth + Form," the following day.[74] Gropius, too, apologized for not having sent his own contribution as promised and expressed a similar anxiety, writing that "[i]n order to bring myself in the right spirit, I read Lancelot Whyte's book 'Analysis of

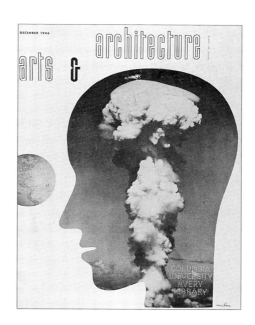

Form,' which I suppose you know as it is so very close to your own. The result was that I felt even less able to venture into an approach of my own, as I found some of my ideas already most ably expressed in that book."[75] The actual title of Whyte's book, misread by both Giedion and Gropius, was *Aspects of Form,* a collection of essays that had grown out of a conference held on the occasion of the exhibition *Growth and Form* at London's Institute for Contemporary Art in 1951; it was inspired by D'Arcy Thompson's *On Growth and Form,* which had been revised and reissued in 1942.[76] Among those scientists contributing to the book were Joseph Needham and Conrad Waddington, the two members of the Theoretical Biology Club whom Kepes had met in London in the 1930s. In this way, those scientists whose ideas had contributed to Kepes's formation of an *aesthetic* project of organic integration were now getting together, in response to further aesthetic initiatives, to pursue what Whyte recognized in retrospect as a shift "from the *discovery of new fundamental laws* to the *progressive identification of natural structures* [or patterns]."[77] Art and science had effectively switched places in this feedback loop. Where Kepes sought an aesthetic response to science, here at the same time was science—the very same science of organicist biology—attempting to respond to the morphogenetic will of art.

Located, then, near the end of the trajectory we have been following is *The New Landscape in Art and Science,* published by Kepes in 1956. Confronted with the book's own archive, described above, we are tempted to read it as the complement to *Aspects*

2.13

Herbert Matter, cover of *Arts and Architecture* 63 (December 1946).

Pattern-Seeing

of Form: a conclusive synthesis of aesthetic and scientific knowledge, or a depiction of a reorganized nature mapped from an aesthetic point of view, as implied by its title. But Kepes himself warns that this is a book of "allusions and not conclusions." He even goes so far as to declare in the opening line of his preface: "This book is meant to be looked at more than read."[78]

Looking at the book, we are overcome by a sense of exhaustion. The pieces eventually contributed by Giedion and Gropius are relatively benign restatements of the homeostatic project. Richard Neutra's essay, as we have already seen in the preceding chapter, ecstatically affiliates itself with Kepes's mission of uniting microcosm and macrocosm, "inner" and "outer," through a quasi-cybernetic collapse of architecture into neurophysiology. And, as we have already noted, Kepes had sought to make Wiener's contribution a centerpiece but had to settle instead for his own presentation of cybernetic material. Also included in the volume are essays by the former New Bauhaus faculty members Ralph Gerard ("Design and Function in the Living") and Charles Morris ("Man-Cosmos Symbols") as well as by the biologist C. F. A. Pantin ("Organic Design") and the crystallographer Kathleen Lonsdale ("Art in Crystallography"). Among others, Karl Deutsch, Wiener's friend and collaborator and Kepes's MIT colleague, is thanked for his advice on the project. Kepes's own texts repeat, in a variety of terms, the exhausted call for the restoration of equilibrium.[79]

The sense of exhaustion permeating the book's words is exacerbated by its profuse imagery. The bulk of these images are collected in a central section devoted to the *New Landscape* exhibition, in which natural patterns are compared with the formal structure of modern and classical artworks. Technical photographs acquired from a variety of scientific laboratories are arranged in four categories: "Magnification of Optical Data," "Expansion and Compression of Events in Time," "Expansion of the Eye's Sensitivity Range," and "Modulation of Signals." Each attempts to illustrate the commonality of naturally occurring organizational patterns, according (respectively) to temporal, spatial, physiological, and informatic continuities. But despite this effort to demonstrate continuities of pattern at all scales and across all modes of visual reception, the overall effect is much more like the proliferation of advertising images that Marshall McLuhan described as a "whirling phantasmagoria." Indeed McLuhan had already written in 1951 (the same year Kepes first exhibited these images) that the advertisements collected in *The Mechanical Bride* are "unfolded by exhibit and commentary as a single landscape."[80] But where he designated these images "the folklore of industrial man," we must insist that the scientific images collected by Kepes belong to another kind of "folklore," albeit one that converges on that of the "global village" later projected by McLuhan in its dependence on cybernetic principles.

If the afterimages of the atomic blast register a world out of control, then the scientific images collected by Kepes are corrective patterns fed into the visual conscious-

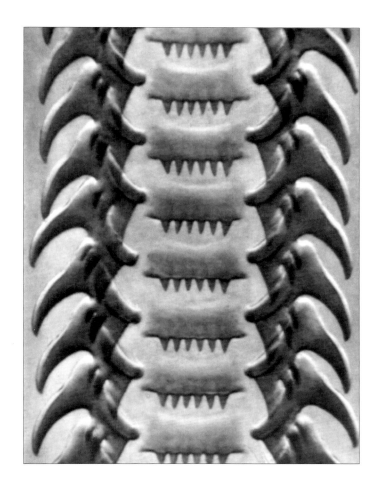

ness of architects (like those he taught at MIT), among others. They are, in that sense, an organizational software written in the patterned code of the images. As an extension of Kepes's efforts in *Language of Vision* to generate a "dynamic iconography," the folkloric function of these scientific patterns is thus necessarily derived from their supposed organicity: software as myth. Therefore, it matters little whether we read the captions provided by Kepes to identify each image, or even the extended captions that constitute the book's text. Ultimately, these will only send us back to the images, since what holds everything together is their operative logic: science has unleashed technological, cognitive, and social processes that have spun out of control even as it has produced new images capable of regulating its own informatic degeneration; art

2.14

Snail's tongue. From section on "magnification of optical data" in Gyorgy Kepes, *The New Landscape in Art and Science* (1956), 115.

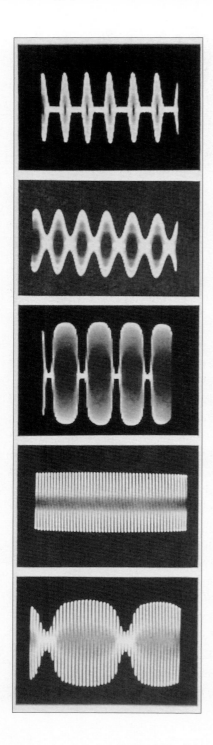

2.15

Cathode-ray oscilloscope patterns. From section on "modulation of signals" in Gyorgy Kepes, *The New Landscape in
Art and Science* (1956), 179.

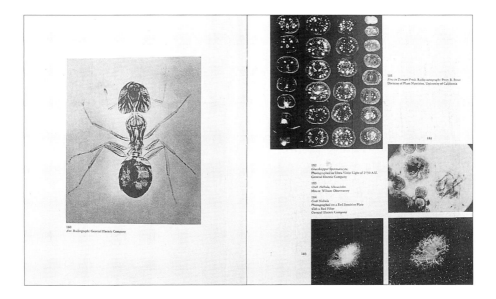

will integrate these organizational patterns into a new vision, a "pattern-seeing" that will set the guided missile of the organizational complex back on course.

Architecture itself appears in many forms in *The New Landscape in Art and Science.* One image presents one of Buckminster Fuller's geodesic domes; another compares one of his tensegrity structures with a drawing of the microorganism polystyrola. There is a photograph of a Pier Luigi Nervi roof shell. A drawing of another roof shell by Eduardo Catalano is compared with a chair by Charles and Ray Eames, and with the domed Kresge Auditorium at MIT designed by Eero Saarinen. The modular components of Eames chairs are juxtaposed with the magnetic core memory of an MIT computer. Le Corbusier's roof terrace at Marseilles and, earlier, his Modulor figure appear alongside the golden section monument designed in Milan by Banfi, Belgiojoso, Peressutti & Rogers (BBPR) and opposite Francesco di Giorgio's study of human proportion, respectively. A Paul Rudolph house is set beside a Conrad Wachsman space frame study. But these are not, like the final image of "Architecture" in Moholy-Nagy's *The New Vision,* presented as the culmination of an evolutionary process as it passes through different media. In the new landscape, architecture becomes one among many *interchangeable* media, all of which receive and transmit organizational patterns.[81]

2.16

Radiographs. Clockwise from left: ant, zinc in tomato fruit, grasshopper spermatocyte, crab nebula, crab nebula. From section on "expansion of the eye's sensitivity range" in Gyorgy Kepes, *The New Landscape in Art and Science* (1956), 168–169.

2.17

Polystyrola, drawing by Hans Haffenrichter (above); and
R. Buckminster Fuller, "Model Discontinuous Compression
Structuring." Page from Gyorgy Kepes, *The New Landscape
in Art and Science* (1956), 354.

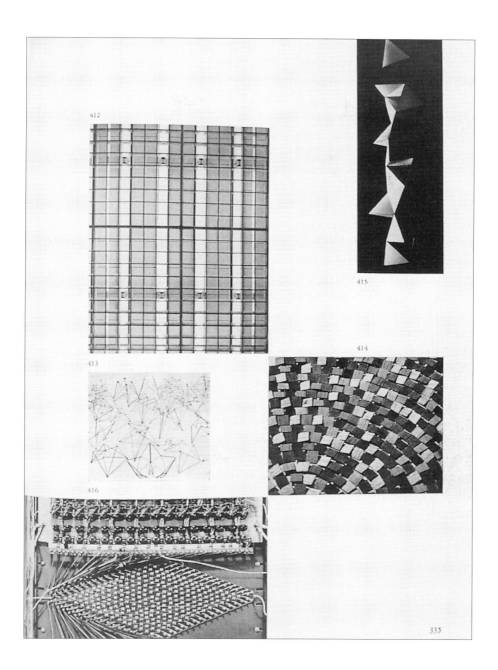

412

415

413

414

416

335

2.18
Clockwise from lower left: Digital Computer Laboratory,
MIT, magnetic core memory; Charles and Ray Eames, standard chair components; experimental ceiling lighting; student project, modular paper construction; Dorothy Pelzer,
acoustic ceiling (project). Page from Gyorgy Kepes, *The
New Landscape in Art and Science* (1956), 335.

In 1956, the same year the book was published, Kepes began convening a number of interdisciplinary seminars that became the basis for the seven-volume Vision + Value series he edited for the publisher George Braziller in the 1960s.[82] In 1960 he also acted as a guest editor for a special issue of the humanistic review *Daedalus,* titled *The Visual Arts Today.* Here again we find scientists like the theoretical biologist Paul Weiss writing about organic morphogenesis alongside Le Corbusier on architecture and the arts. But again the direct projection of these ideas onto architecture met with a certain resistance, perhaps best expressed by Kepes's friend Marcel Breuer, when he wrote privately of his reservations about ideas in *Daedalus* that he found at times "moody, confused and confusing."[83] These comments should not be mistaken for an architect's disavowal of Kepes's project. Rather, they can be seen in context as expressing something akin to the sense of exhaustion brought on by *The New Landscape.* What Breuer most likely recognized was that the *Visual Arts Today* issue was less a survey of the contemporary aesthetic landscape than a melancholic repetition, a lament.

As he repeatedly decried the disorganized phantasmagoria of postwar experience during these years, Kepes's own rhetoric became increasingly taut. He spoke to an audience at the Cooper Union in 1958 about the "lonely crowd in the wasteland" and about the subjects addressed by abstract expressionism, who occupied a postapocalyptic metropolis, which Kepes described as a "bleak, cruel, faithless environment" that was alternately "centerless, bodiless, limitless," "structureless," and "shapeless, contourless."[84] Yet, visible in the overwhelming cascade of images flowing through *The New Landscape* is the same emptied-out environment in whose physiognomy Kepes could see only what he took to be the cruelty of formlessness, of the bleakly entropic disintegration of the radiant organisms projected by his modernist predecessors. Among the latter can be counted Ludwig Mies van der Rohe's Seagram Building (completed in 1957), to which Kepes was quite likely referring in his introduction to the *Daedalus* issue:

A beautiful crystalline structure in America's greatest city (itself a symbol of the finest thinking in contemporary architecture and at the same time, like the *torre* of medieval Tuscany, a boastful symbol of wealth and power) displays, in surroundings that state an absolute control of contemporary materials and techniques and a perfect mastery of the new beauty of architectural space, images of the torn and broken man. In its offices and corridors are paintings and sculptures shaped with idioms in tune with the twilight spirit that created them: surfaces that are moldy, broken, corroded, ragged, dripping; brush strokes executed with the sloppy brutality of cornered men.[85]

While these lines clearly register Kepes's opposition to what he took to be abstract expressionism's retreat into interiority (the target of his *Daedalus* project), they also demonstrate the blindness of the new vision he promoted to the structural emptiness of its own methods for exerting "absolute control." For if the much-remarked "silence" of Mies's building resembles anything in Kepes's project, it resembles the silent awe with which the "message" of the newly organized landscape is communicated.[86] In other words, for the cybernetically oriented Kepes, silence was organization itself: the absence of noise. Like the images in his book, many of which share the "crystalline" beauty he sees in Mies (including the image of crystal growth he described as "a space-time boundary of energies in organization"), Seagram's grids and those of its less distinguished neighbors operate as organized patterns—that is, as organisms. But their empty surfaces reflect a photographically enchanted vision back outward, revealing only a desperate desire for plenitude, an overdetermined longing for the organicity of silent communication. In *The New Landscape,* Kepes insists that "it is important to organisms and social complexes that they should be able to live—and not only to live but to flourish, to realize their potentialities, to retain cohesiveness at each successive stage and, at the same time, to grow and move without frustration. For this, the inner and outer forces must be commensurate, resulting in a harmonious unity rather than in a wild oscillation about a never attained point of equilibrium."[87]

In strict compliance with the imperatives of the organizational complex, Kepes extended this desire for the "harmonious unity" of inside and outside into a feedback-driven project of self-correction whose guiding principle was the suppression of noise. His "pattern-seeing" was commensurate with the logic of the new machines and the corporations that managed them. As Marshall McLuhan would put it several years later, "Now, in the electronic age, data classification yields to pattern recognition, the key phrase at IBM."[88] But Kepes's project was always already exhausted by its own circularity, since to learn to see these patterns was to enter into an aesthetics in which everything is connected to everything else. Behind each pattern was only another pattern, and behind each network another network—all collapsed together into an infinitely extensive loop spiraling up and down in scale, like the arc of a guided missile turning in on itself, and out again.

3

The Physiognomy of the Office

In his working notes that led up to the publication of *The New Landscape in Art and Science,* Gyorgy Kepes declares that "[e]very feature of the man created environment has [an] inherent physiognomy [and] thus is an object of communication."[1] The contributions to that book by Norbert Wiener on mathematical patterns and by the physiologist Ralph Gerard on the functionality of organized systems are followed by a text by the psychologist Heinz Werner, "On Physiognomic Perception." Werner notes recent psychological interest in the contingency of vision as he declares his interest in accounting psychologically for "aesthetic behavior" by distinguishing between two modes of perception: the "geometric-technical" vision of science, and the affective, empathic, "physiognomic" vision of art.[2] This distinction, and the attendant project of restoring to rationalized postwar experience the dimension of affective physiognomics, belongs entirely within the larger project of mediating science with art through images as articulated by Kepes. But it also opens a window onto parallel efforts unfolding within the ruthlessly "scientific" realm of corporate architecture.

In the June 1957 issue of *Progressive Architecture,* an issue devoted entirely to high-rise office buildings, there appeared a reprint of "The Tall Office Building Artistically Considered" by Louis Sullivan. Sullivan's article, first published in 1896, adumbrates an aesthetic logic for the office building based on a direct reflection of the pragmatic prerequisites of its spaces. In reprinting the article, the editors of *Progressive Architecture* were attempting to provide a context for their observation that "the high-rise office building of the 1950s is the best known symbol of U.S. architecture today."[3] And like many similar presentations of the commercial architecture of the period in professional journals, the *Progressive Architecture* survey resembles nothing more than a manual of technical specifications. Works such as the Socony Mobil and Alcoa buildings by Harrison & Abramowitz; the Inland Steel Building in Chicago by Skidmore, Owings & Merrill; speculative office buildings designed by large commercial firms such as Kahn & Jacobs and Emery Roth & Sons on New York's Park Avenue; and Ludwig Mies van der Rohe's Seagram Building approaching completion nearby are shown side by side in a standardized format accompanied by vital statistics, inviting a comparison of objects in terms of their pragmatic responses to a set of technical problems. Coupled with articles on the economics of high-rise real estate, techniques of curtain wall construction, and the foreseeable effects of automation on the workplace, this comparative anatomy affords a partial glimpse of what had become, by the mid-1950s, the science of the office.

Such comparisons also tend to suppress qualitative distinctions between buildings, in favor of a general equivalence against which quantitative distinctions can be measured. In that sense, the status as a singular artwork generally attributed to Mies's Seagram Building, for example (as distinct from its many "copies"), is rendered obsolete by the very idea of the curtain wall as a generalized technological system. More than simply offering mechanical reproductions of interchangeable, reified commodities against which Seagram stands in refined "silence," such documents as the *Progressive Architecture* survey offer the very image of systematicity, inclusiveness, and flexibility within which Seagram appears as merely one module among many.

In such a context, Sullivan's effort to consider the tall office building from an "artistic" point of view seems, at first glance, out of place. Except, that is, to the extent that the aesthetics of "form follows function" advocated there by Sullivan had its own roots in a scientific discourse from an earlier period. It is well known that Sullivan borrowed the slogan—which he uses twice in the article—from the "Yankee stonecutter," the neoclassical sculptor Horatio Greenough.[4] Greenough, in turn, was a reader of the biological treatises of Georges Cuvier and his contemporaries, from whom he

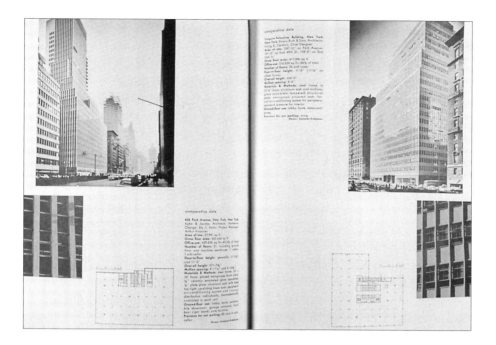

translated the notion of the organic integration of functional components into the presentation of logical—if classical—form stripped bare in art. When Greenough argued, in an 1852 essay called "Structure and Organization" (reprinted in the collection *Form and Function* [1947]), that in utilitarian structures such as ships, bridges, and fortifications "we have been emancipated from authority by the stern organic requirements of the works," he was making above all a claim for the transparency of aesthetic form to scientific principles to which the artist or architect had no choice but to surrender. Foremost among these principles was the "unflinching adaptation [in nature] of forms to function."[5]

In other words, for the artist Greenough and for Sullivan after him, "form follows function" was above all an aesthetic principle, not a technical one. A building's organization would, in effect, emerge spontaneously out of the new "nature" of the marketplace as represented by the client and his requirements, and the architect's job was to see that the results were faithfully expressed in material form—physiognomically, that is. In describing his hypothetical ideal office building, Sullivan constructs what is primarily an image of organic cellularity: "we take our cue from the individual cell,

3.1

Kahn & Jacobs, 425 Park Avenue, New York; and Emery Roth & Sons, Colgate Palmolive Building, New York. From "High Rise Office Buildings," *Progressive Architecture* 38, no. 6 (June 1957).

The Physiognomy of the Office

which requires a window with its separating pier, its sill and lintel, and we, without more ado, make them look all alike because they are all alike."[6]

But as Colin Rowe reminded his readers the same year (1956) that Kepes published *The New Landscape in Art and Science,* according to one of Sullivan's European contemporaries, the attitude expressed here pointedly confirmed that Sullivan and his fellow Chicago architects had "frankly accepted the conditions imposed by the speculator."[7] Rowe argued that the dynamic spatial potential of the "Chicago frame" was overlooked in Chicago precisely because "space" was already given, in the form of the real estate developed speculatively in the works of William Le Baron Jenney, Daniel Burnham, Sullivan, and others. It was thus left to the likes of Mies, Le Corbusier, and Sullivan's pupil Frank Lloyd Wright to liberate space as an expressive medium, but at the expense of the workaday pragmatism characteristic of fin de siècle Chicago. Comparing Victor Horta's critical project in the Maison du Peuple (1897) with the commercialism of Holabird and Root's McLurg Building (1900), Rowe declares: "In Belgium, it is evident, the *art nouveau* was one of those revolutionary movements essentially developed on a highly developed program; but in Chicago, it should be clear that the structural revolution was largely without any such theoretical support."[8] In fact, the project of aesthetic transparency to organizational imperatives driven by market forces was theorized from the start, albeit not in a form accessible to Rowe. Passing as it did from scientific thought into aesthetic discourse, the notion of the organic integration of functional components was reconverted into the theoretical basis of an "organic" architecture, the architecture of the "tall office building artistically considered."

For Rowe, whose point of departure was the preeminence achieved by the structural frame as an organizational matrix for modern architecture, comparisons between the skyscrapers of Mies van der Rohe and those of Emery Roth & Sons would no doubt have obscured his closely argued distinction between those architects who had "frankly accepted the conditions imposed by the speculator" and those of the avant-garde who had supposedly arisen in protest—Mies's work in the 1940s for the Chicago developer Herbert S. Greenwald notwithstanding. The question of Mies's, and Wright's, descent (and distance) from the likes of Sullivan is central for Rowe, who is at pains to distinguish between "architecture" and "equipment," or between discursive and nondiscursive production. *Progressive Architecture,* on the other hand, implied that the commercial skyscrapers of the postwar period were subject to the same rules as were the "tall office buildings" of Chicago, whether they were designed by architects like Mies or by architects like Emery Roth & Sons. For Rowe, and for many who have followed him, it was a matter of distinguishing sharply between the architects of the avant-garde and their commercial colleagues, whether in the 1890s or the 1950s. This distinction was also implicit in Rowe's interpretation (also in 1956–1957), of recent works by Mies and his contemporaries (including Eero Saarinen) as evidence of a neo-Palladian, classicist rejection of vanguardist ideology, including modern architecture's claims to historical necessity.[9] But a refusal to accept such distinctions leads us to a modified genealogy of the postwar office, and in particular to the curtain wall.

3.1

To take up this genealogy, we must return briefly to Chicago—but now to the Chicago of 1922, the date of the international design competition sponsored by the *Chicago Tribune* for its new headquarters, to be located on Michigan Avenue north of the city's commercial center. Sullivan's assessment of the results of the competition, which was won by the team of John Mead Howells and Raymond Hood, celebrated the second-place entry by the Finnish architect Eliel Saarinen:

> Qualifying as it does in every technical regard, and conforming to the mandatory items of the official program of instructions, it goes freely in advance, and, with the steel frame as a thesis, displays a high science of design such as the world up to this day had neither known nor surmised. In its single solidarity of concentrated intention, there is revealed a logic of a new order, the logic of living things, and this inexorable logic of life is most graciously accepted and set forth in fluency of form.[10]

Sullivan may have recognized certain affinities between Saarinen's project and the modeled, emphatically vertical facades of his own Guaranty Building (1892) and Wainwright Building (1895). Moreover, as Manfredo Tafuri has suggested, he may also have seen in Saarinen's "metamorphosis of forms" an "enchanted mountain" promising an organic relation of skyscraper to city not fully realized in his own work. According to Tafuri, though fulfilment of this promise also eluded Saarinen, it led him beyond the Chicago School's laissez-faire affirmations of competition among isolated urban artifacts, to an attempted reconstitution of the tall office building as "an element capable of exercising a formal control over the urban complex as a whole."[11] In other words, for Tafuri the urbanistic success of the skyscraper depended on extending, to the scale of the *city,* the organicist "science of design" integrating the office into the *building.*

But the "science of design" that Sullivan recognized in Saarinen's entry was to undergo numerous rearticulations in subsequent decades. One trajectory of decisive importance was its passage into the hands of Saarinen's son and successor, Eero Saarinen,

The Physiognomy of the Office

whose work for major American corporations after the war we will consider in detail in the following chapters. But the younger Saarinen's production must also be seen in the context of a parallel trajectory followed by this "science," as it passed through the many office buildings whose anatomy was laid bare on the pages of every major professional journal during the late 1950s. In the 1930s, the office complex that would set the standard for all others was the multiarchitect effort at New York's Rockefeller Center. Begun as an initiative to house the Metropolitan Opera on another site in 1927, over the course of the Great Depression the project for the development of four blocks in mid-Manhattan was transformed into a speculative real estate venture financed by

3.2
Eliel Saarinen, *Chicago Tribune* tower competition entry,
1922.

3.3
Associated Architects, Rockefeller Center, New York, 1928–
1940.

the holdings of John D. Rockefeller Jr., who was able to use his formidable liquidity to take advantage of the depressed market.

When the design team for Rockefeller Center—known as the Associated Architects, and composed of the smaller partnerships of Reinhard & Hofmeister; Corbett, Harrison & MacMurray; and Hood & Fouilhoux—studied the centerpiece of the complex (the future RCA Building) in the early 1930s, they found themselves at something of a crossroads in the history of office planning techniques. In the *Chicago Tribune* competition, entrants were required to provide two floor plans, one of the ground floor and the other of a typical office floor, but were not required to show interior layouts. Hence, no planning distinction was made between the lower floors of the building, which were to be occupied by the *Tribune* offices, and the upper floors, which were to be leased to commercial tenants. This reflected the common practice of fitting out speculative office floors to the specific needs of tenants upon occupancy, which left the architect, even the functionalist/organicist architect attentive to Sullivan's doctrine, with the question of what interior "function" to express on the exterior of an empty building. As Tafuri points out, in the *Tribune* competition the absence of "functional requirements" in the competition brief encouraged scenographic solutions.[12] But what he does not acknowledge is that the most functional architect-designed floor plan for this type of building by this time was already approaching the horizon of the empty shell.

During the office building boom of the 1920s it became increasingly evident that from the standpoint of rentability the open plan was preferable, since experience showed that prebuilt spaces would often be substantially modified upon occupancy in any case. This was an issue already confronted by Peter Behrens as early as 1910, in his Mannesmann office building in Düsseldorf (completed in 1912), as he attempted to reconcile a cellular organicism with unpredictable changes in use.[13] In other words, the only office spaces that could reasonably sustain internal layouts determined by the sort of functional requirements sought by Tafuri are those built for a single client whose needs were known in advance. Speculative office space was, by definition, functionally exempt from such a logic. Sullivan's efforts to express aesthetically an internal cellularity on the building's exterior, while emphasizing the vertical accumulation of such cells, merely reflected market conditions more sympathetic to prebuilt interiors. So it was never a question of projecting what Tafuri calls an "organic logic" onto the city,[14] since an "organic logic" such as Sullivan's had always already accommodated itself to the market. The only difference was that both market and "organism" had changed. By 1930 the professional journals could designate the open plan as the preferred alternative in office planning with a pragmatic matter-of-factness.[15] Thus, as Rockefeller Center was being designed, the volatility and unpredictability of the real estate market had already begun to be internalized in office buildings.

In Rockefeller Center itself, prospective tenants were encouraged to identify the complex as a new commercial locus whose urbanism and architecture sought to unify its disparate elements into a single, recognizable post-Depression monument to economic stability, a connotation also carried by the Rockefeller name. Its soaring verticals (reminiscent of Cass Gilbert's 1913 "cathedral of commerce," the Woolworth Building), were dedicated to the consecration of commerce as a source of urban unity and social stability, securely anchored in a base dedicated to culture and the arts—the catalyst for the center in the first place. Likewise its "five spot" site plan was at once dedicated to the modernist project of "light and air" and respectful of Beaux-Arts symmetries, complete with an abbreviated *promenade architecturale* culminating in the sunken restaurant/skating rink at the center's core.

Here it was, then: a singular spectacle of reconciliation between commerce and the city. That, as Tafuri argues, the center failed in its apparent project of actual unification beyond its borders is manifestly the case but should not be surprising. Rockefeller Center was reduced to the status of an isolated, lonely demonstration of the "civic art" from the very beginning, but not because of some internal contradiction between the drive toward organic unity and the chaos of commerce. Quite the opposite. It is precisely because Rockefeller Center succeeded—despite dire predictions to the contrary[16]—in projecting organic unity onto the disaggregated field of commerce that it "failed" as an instrument of a more general urban unification.

In that sense, Sigfried Giedion's formalistic reading of the center was accurate. He argues that its massing prevents the full apprehension of "the essential character of an organism like Rockefeller Center" if viewed from its central axis. Going so far as to describe the complex's multifaceted surfaces as "curtain walls," Giedion compared their visual effect to that of Harold Edgerton's stroboscopic photograph of a golfer's swing[17] (a photograph nearly identical to the one later reproduced in Kepes's *Language of Vision* as an illustration of dynamic visual organicity; see figure 2.11). In other words, it was the center's visual dynamism, descended from the "metamorphosis of forms" in Eliel Saarinen's *Chicago Tribune* tower project, that succeeded in harnessing the flux of capital—and ensured that it would be experienced as a source of economic and social integration, precisely because it distinguished itself from the surrounding city. What we see emerging here is the operative power of the corporate image, in which specifically modern aesthetic techniques are mobilized to project an image of dynamic, organic unity comparable to that sought by Kepes in the imagery of science. Rockefeller Center projects such an image not in some residually futile effort to unify the civic realm but as a marketing tool.

The RCA Building was also notable for its slender proportions and represents a widely recognized prototype for the so-called slab office buildings that were to follow in the 1940s and 1950s.[18] According to Raymond Hood, one of its primary architects, the process of arriving at the RCA's slim, stepped-back form was one of pure ratio—a strictly numeric relationship between the dimensions of the floor plate and the size of the elevator core.[19] Since the 1920s, and before air conditioning and fluorescent lighting came into widespread use in commercial structures during the 1950s, office planners had been engaged in debates about the marketability of windowless "deep space."[20] During the planning stages for Rockefeller Center, it was therefore decided that the ideal rentable depth of office space was 27 feet from the exterior wall. A structure the height of the RCA Building (sixty-six stories) was also necessarily divided into a series of zones stacked vertically, with each zone serviced by a designated elevator bank. As the building ascended, the number of elevators required in the core dropped off with each zone, until only those serving the uppermost floors remained. If the RCA Building had been designed as a simple, rectangular floor plate extruded sixty-six stories, substantial quantities of deep space would therefore have been produced as each elevator bank dropped off. Thus, the volume was stepped back each time an elevator bank terminated, in order to remain consistent with the 27-foot depth requirement established by market considerations.

But the principle of optimized rentability was even more visibly reflected in the exterior elevations that unified the complex. As William Jordy has pointed out, the skins, or shells, of the Rockefeller Center buildings responded to the unpredictable needs of future tenants by offering a range of possible locations for the partitions that abutted the exterior walls, since the dimension of the intervening solid piers (3' 6" and 6' 3") allowed partitions to be placed anywhere along their width. As Jordy also observes, this fenestration pattern, which repeated that of Hood's Daily News Building (1930), favored a flattened-out neo-Gothic over the less flexible but more "modern" option of continuous, horizontal fenestration allowing partitions only at the window mullions, available to the Associated Architects through the model of Hood's McGraw-Hill Building (also completed in 1930).[21] Still, the flatness of its facades already hinted at a new dynamism that was to respond to such forces as they exceeded ever-higher

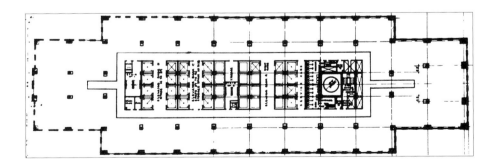

3.4

Associated Architects, RCA Building, Rockefeller Center, 1933. Typical floor plan.

thresholds of tolerance. It was as if the financial events of October 1929 were to be subsequently accounted for in an architecture in which stability was forsaken for a pragmatic recognition of the forces of unpredictable change, registered in the exterior wall of the building. Neo-Gothic verticality was converted, with the window-pier-window system, into a means of maintaining what Giedion recognized as a "dynamic equilibrium," plainly visible on the building's surfaces if one chose to look.[22] With the gridded office buildings of the postwar period, this gesture toward the dynamism of capital was made overt, in a further externalization (and internalization) of the capital-ist—and organicist—logic of growth and change.

3.2

In 1945 L. Andrew Rein-hard and Henry Hofmeister—office planning experts and two of the principal architects on the Rockefeller Center team from the start—assessed the "new trends" in office design: "The modern office is brightened and enlivened by dozens of new materials, both structural and decorative; by new forms and curves; by modern lighting and air conditioning and acoustic treatment and office machinery and conveniences of many kinds. By all the devices and arts of modern architecture, decoration, furnishing and display. This trend may have brought harrying problems to office building managers. But it has also improved the effectiveness and efficiency of the office."[23] Although these remarks clearly adhere to the requirement that architectural criticism recycle even office space through some "new trend," they also imply—at an early date—a more substantial shift in the performative character of office space.

What these planners mean by improved "effectiveness and efficiency" becomes clearer when they associate the increased popularity of modern design with office tenants ("something more advanced than the heavy dignity of tradition") with the advancing role of interior office design in corporate marketing that was directed inward as well as outward:

This salesmanship is not devoted entirely to the firm's clientele. For if this is a seller's market, it also belongs to employees. The workers in the office "bull pen" are having their day, and more is being done for them. They are getting not only better light, better ventilation and better working conditions, but also improved and more cheerful surroundings. This might be considered a long-term trend as well as a current necessity; in any case it is a factor that will increasingly improve the office and add to the problem of the office planner.[24]

Quietly, incrementally, the "cathedrals of commerce" inventoried in the *Chicago Tribune* tower competition and scattered in the myriad, isolated expressions of corporate identity in cities across the United States were being secularized. These advertisements for enchantment that invoked a proto-Gothic corporatism against the artificiality of the metropolis began to mutate into modern environments dedicated to the well-being of the worker. The office, hollowed out in Rockefeller Center into a flexible, rhythmic shell, was being proffered to employees as well as to clients as a form of community. Meanwhile workers, beneficiaries of the "light and air" sold at Rockefeller Center, were themselves in the process being converted from Taylorized machines into "humans," in recognition of the operative value of an empathic relation between manager and employee, clothed in the image of modernity. All of these changes were accessible through a "physiognomic perception" aided by modern architecture. In the name of the corporation as productive organism, offices were becoming social condensers.

"Human relations," the name given to the attempt to improve productivity by appealing to the employee's sense of identification with the corporation, is precariously rooted in the so-called Hawthorne experiments, the focus of a study conducted by faculty members of the Harvard School of Business at the Western Electric Hawthorne plant outside of Chicago from 1927 to 1933. The study eventually fell under the direction of the psychologist Elton Mayo, whose name has since become closely identified with human relations dogma. In the experiments themselves, a group of assembly workers were isolated in a "test room" in which environmental parameters and economic incentives were systematically varied to test their effects on worker productivity. To the surprise of the experimenters, productivity in the test room remained consistent or even increased under increasingly adverse environmental conditions. These results generated conflicting hypotheses, but what emerged from the subsequent publications analyzing the study, including Mayo's *Human Problems of an Industrial Civilization* (1933), was an interpretation—since shown to be largely arbitrary—that attributed the observed increase in productivity to a heightened sense of identification with the corporate institution on the part of the workers in the test room, simply by virtue of their participation in the experiments.[25]

On this basis, Mayo and his colleagues concluded that productivity in the factory could be enhanced through methods designed to relate to the worker as a member of a social group. These included interviewing workers to determine whether they were prone to, or had been subjected to, dysfunctional social relations in their family lives. For Mayo, who drew to some extent on Freudian psychoanalysis, the manager became in effect a therapist—charged with looking after the worker's psychic well-being and with systematically constructing worker identification with the corporation understood as a basic social unit, comparable to (and even substituting for) the worker's family.

Like the earlier techniques for optimizing mechanical productivity developed by Frederick Winslow Taylor and by Frank and Lillian Gilbreth, the degree to which the techniques of "human relations" were actually applied in the work environment varied from corporation to corporation. But by the late 1940s, a decade and a half after Mayo's *Human Problems of an Industrial Civilization* first appeared, and immediately following a series of bitter postwar labor disputes, a doctrine of management-worker cooperation had become conventional wisdom among many executives.[26] In a broad sense, this represented the long-term effect of a "managerial revolution" initiated in the late nineteenth century, which had seen the rise of a managerial class responsible for the administration of the day-to-day operations of the largest American corporations. As this class emerged, it established a new set of social and technological principles that might be grouped together under the heading of "control."[27] And indeed, human relations theory has significant discursive and historical ties with the systems and cybernetics-based control logics we have already encountered. Both, it may be said, seek to link diverse forms knowledge into an encompassing managerial loop.

The most direct of such ties dates to the influential seminar conducted from 1932 to 1934 by the physiologist-turned-sociologist Lawrence J. Henderson at Harvard on the works of the Italian sociologist Vilfredo Pareto. Henderson saw Pareto's thought as a model for social integration that could be mobilized against the inroads made by Marxism into American sociology, an agenda that by 1960 led one observer to characterize Henderson as "the greatest rationalizer of authoritarian conservatism of our time."[28] Among the small circle who regularly attended the seminars were Mayo, Fritz Roethlisberger (another major spokesman for human relations theory), and the sociologist Talcott Parsons, who acknowledged that the title of his 1951 book, *The Social System,* was indebted to Pareto's emphasis on the scientific concept of "system." Henderson compared Pareto's notion of social systems seeking equilibrium with a notion of the system as a functional whole in dynamic equilibrium based in part on the work of the physicist Willard Gibbs (also an important source for Wiener's cybernetics) on physico-chemical equilibria, as well as that of Walter B. Cannon (a reference shared by Wiener, Giedion, and Kepes) on biological self-regulation, or homeostasis. Along with Cannon, Henderson thus represented a major proponent of a systems-based revision to the functionalist organicism received by Louis Sullivan as "form follows function," converting it into a "science" of social organization.[29] Mayo's and Roethlisberger's ties to this endeavor underscore the organicist dimensions of the hu-

EXHIBIT I. DIAGRAM SHOWING THE INTEGRATION OF VARIOUS RELATED FIELDS

	A Science	B Techniques	C A clinical point of view and method	D Professional formulation and practice
1.	Psychology	Applied Psychology		Administration
2.	Sociology	Applied Sociology	Human Relations	Personnel Relations
3.	Anthropology	Applied Anthropology		Labor Relations
4.		Scientific Management		
5.		Technical specialist groups in business and industry		

man relations project, in which integration into the "social system" of the corporation was solicited through appeals to the employee's "humanity," made in the name of increased productivity but actualized as a social bond.

Although earlier notions of the corporation as family were reflected in architecture with such works as Frank Lloyd Wright's Larkin Building (1906),[30] during the postwar period the spatial logic of the corporate "family" visibly changed, in concert with technical innovations made by the architects of office buildings who were promoting spatial flexibility. This is not to say that architects and office planners self-consciously applied principles derived from human relations discourse (there is little evidence of this), or that the two practices simply operated on analogous or even homologous terms. Here again, in the new landscape of the organizational complex, distinct cultural practices cease merely to reflect one another's premises through such relays. Instead, they interact like the patterns cascading up and down in scale in Kepes's book, patterns that were given formal articulation by Charles and Ray Eames in *Powers of Ten* (1968, 1977), their classic cinematic short. That is, they mirror and map onto one another in different ways and to different degrees, through a convergence of communicative media—photography, film, architecture, and so on—bearing what Norbert Wiener lucidly called the "message" of organization, including management treatises written by human relations experts.

Thus, in their 1945 article cited above, the office planners Reinhard and Hofmeister take the readers of *Architectural Record* through a series of office interiors planned by their firm, including the Rockefeller Center prototype. In these examples, the "T" configuration, with two small private offices at the exterior wall sharing an internal

3.5

Fritz Roethlisberger, "Diagram Showing the Interaction of Various Related Fields." From *Human Relations: Rare, Medium, or Well-Done?* (1954), 135.

The Physiognomy of the Office

reception and secretarial space, is identified as the "theoretical unit" for office space—
an adaptable planning module roughly 16 feet wide by 27 feet deep, abstracted from
the Rockefeller Center layout. By the mid-1950s, however, this unit, into which was
condensed a basic manager-staff hierarchy characteristic of most administrative offices, had been replaced by a much smaller and more abstract module. Usually rang-

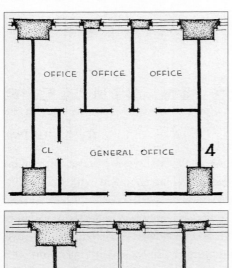

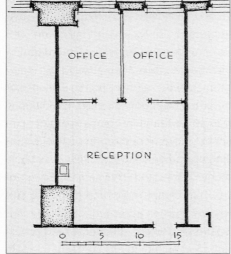

3.6
Typical office plans, RCA Building, Rockefeller Center
(1933). From L. Andrew Reinhard and Henry Hofmeister,
"New Trends in Office Design," *Architectural Record* 97, no.
3 (March 1945): 100.

3.7
Typical "T" office plan. From L. Andrew Reinhard and
Henry Hofmeister, "New Trends in Office Design," *Architec-
tural Record* 97, no. 3 (March 1945): 100.

ing from 4' 6" to 5' square, it was distributed in a virtual, organizational matrix—a grid—capable of accommodating office partitions, ceiling tiles, lighting fixtures, and furniture, in any number of combinations. Compared to the window-pier-window system of Rockefeller Center, this gridded module exhibited a lesser degree of flexibility, in exchange for a greater degree of integration.

3.3

On the outside, the new physiognomy of the office was registered in the curtain wall. And although there are numerous earlier examples of commercial buildings with large expanses of glass, the United Nations Secretariat, begun in 1948 and completed by 1950, was the first major office building of the postwar period to use a full-height curtain wall suspended off the structure for two of its main exposures.[31] The building, whose design was supervised by Wallace Harrison (one of the architects for Rockefeller Center), was clad in tinted glass on its east and west facades, with steel glazing mullions set at 4 feet on center. As a result, the prefabricated office partitions utilized in the interior of the building could be set only at 4-foot intervals—a significant reduction in interior planning flexibility, compared to that in the RCA Building. In addition, since it was the mullion centerlines (and thus only the centers of the partitions) that were 4 feet apart, the actual clear space in the minimum office possible behind this wall was slightly under 8 feet, which proved functionally inadequate.[32] Already here, a central tension that was to characterize the transformation of the office building after the Second World War also becomes evident. It was a tension between the twin imperatives of flexibility and standardization, which, though not mutually exclusive, do not necessarily imply one another, even in modular planning.

By 1957 the confusion regarding this issue was such that Richard Roth—a partner in Emery Roth & Sons, a firm responsible for thirty-seven office buildings built during the previous ten years in midtown Manhattan—authoritatively advocated continuous, modular fenestration for its superior flexibility:

> Architecturally strong and impressive as the Radio City masses may be, they do not, with their window-pier-window design, allow for this interior planning flexibility. Therefore—the new exterior design to suit interior plan spacing. It is as simple as that! Window-mullion-window (445 Park Avenue—Kahn & Jacobs); strip building with continuous windows and continuous masonry spandrels (575 Madison Avenue—Emery Roth & Sons);

metal and glass "skin" buildings (Lever House—Skidmore, Owings & Merrill); and the metal and metal with the windows losing their accent in the dominance of the metal (99 Park Avenue—Emery Roth & Sons).[33]

Unlike that found in the RCA Building, Roth's "flexibility" takes the form of a highly organized aesthetic and technological system into which units of space were to be integrated—the system of standardized components such as office partitions, lighting fixtures, furniture, and so on that American industry had generated after the war.[34] But there is more written into this discourse. For example, when *Progressive Architecture* devoted an entire issue to the question of "modular assembly" in November 1957, its editors accompanied their introduction with a series of extended

3.8
    (previous page) Harrison & Abramowitz et al., United Nations headquarters, New York, 1948–1952. Secretariat building. Photograph by Ezra Stoller.

3.9
    Harrison & Abramowitz et al., United Nations Secretariat, New York. Office interior.

3.10
    Emery Roth & Sons, various office buildings, New York, 1950s. From Richard Roth, "High Rise Down to Earth," *Progressive Architecture* 38, no. 6 (June 1957): 199.

quotations from such architects as Mies van der Rohe, Walter Gropius, Richard Neutra, and Frank Lloyd Wright on the desirability of standardized modular construction methods. They also included the following quotation from Kepes, excerpted from the section in *The New Landscape in Art and Science* on "symmetry, proportion, module" that contained various images of architecture:

Modular coordination, in its aspect of standardized products and manufacturing processes, is inherent in the condition of our time. . . . Two cans of pea soup are more alike than two peas. Units fit into the production process and combine with other units, as interest in the interconnections between modular units keeps pace with the development of the units themselves. The factors common to units become much more than repeated size and shape, and are extended to include the units' capacity for being joined together. There is an increasing tendency to produce standard modular units which interlock without the intervention of such aids as nails and glue. Implicit in this development is the search for modules with the greatest combinatory possibilities; the ideal is a standard module that can be coupled with others into the widest variety of products. Radio sets are made with standardized tubes and components; buildings are assembled from prefabricated members; machines have interchangeable parts. Even the screw lost from a doorknob is immediately replaceable at the nearest hardware store. Buildings, bridges, motorcars have endowed the modular relation with vital importance in human thought and activity.[35]

Seen in the context of Kepes's attempts to organize the visual field, the editors' inclusion of this passage is telling, since the most prominent image uniting the various studies of coordinated standardization in the special issue is the modular grid. The issue culminates in the exposition of a coordinated dimensioning system based on grids of various sizes that was never implemented. The graphic system of grids within grids would theoretically have enabled the architect to "see" standardized modules at all scales and to detail a building accordingly. This was strictly in accordance with the "pattern-seeing" advocated by Kepes in the technologized new landscape and reflected in the excerpts in *Progressive Architecture*. Although full modular coordination of the construction industry was never achieved in the United States, hundreds of office buildings constructed in the decades following the war did attain the nearly complete fusion of *aesthetic* techniques advocating modular coordination with extant technical means for implementing it, whether or not these involved actual mass production or prefabrication. With the curtain wall, the instrumentality of the corporate image went beyond the construction of the empty shell of a collective organism, as in Rockefeller Center. Through the grids shimmering across the pages of professional journals, this image began to weld itself onto the internal organization of the corporate entity itself.

Also in 1957, a special issue of the *Architectural Review* titled *Machine Made America* cited a 1955 technical report, *Curtain Walls of Stainless Steel Construction,* issued by the Princeton University School of Architecture in response to a request from industry groups.[36] This report was followed up by a conference sponsored by the American Building Research Institute (ABRI) in 1956. Both sought to classify the different types of curtain walls. But while the Princeton report noted that its classification was "based on the construction of the wall and not its finished appearance," the second study, which was cited in detail in *Machine Made America,* took the opposite position: it stated that "the first classification of curtain walls should be based on appearance."[37] Accordingly, four types of curtain walls were enumerated at Princeton and rehearsed by the *Architectural Review,* differentiated by distinct visual characteristics: "sheath" walls, in which no structural elements are indicated on the exterior skin; "grid" walls, in which horizontal and vertical structural elements are expressed with equal emphasis; "mullion" walls, where vertical structural elements are emphasized; and "spandrel" walls, in which horizontal structural elements are emphasized. Thus visual patterns became the basis for physiognomic comparisons of office buildings, whether in the Kepes-like diagrams illustrating the Princeton report or in the *Architectural Review*'s comparative physiognomy of American curtain walls, which, it noted, had become available to architects as an off-the-shelf system a year earlier (in 1956). The science and technology of the office had become an art. As the 1956 ABRI

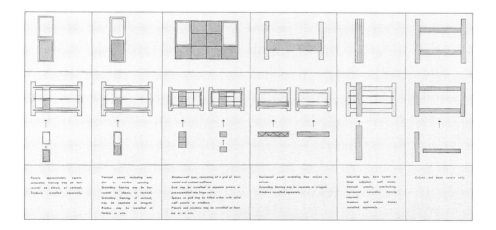

3.11

Curtain wall classifications. From School of Architecture, Princeton University, *Curtain Walls of Stainless Steel Construction* (1955), 13.

The Physiognomy of the Office

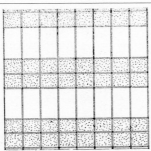

a *sheath* where no structural elements are indicated.

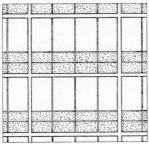

b *grid* where horizontal and vertical structural elements are expressed with equal emphasis.

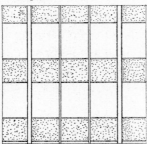

c *mullion* where vertical structural elements are emphasized.

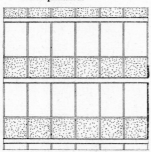

d *spandrel* where horizontal structural elements are emphasized.

3.12

Curtain wall classifications. From *Machine Made America,*

Architectural Review 121, no. 724 (May 1957): 300.

conference report put it, "Almost any system of construction can be used to achieve any one of the common curtain wall appearances."[38] What all these "appearances" had in common, however, was the direct visual presentation of an internal organizational system. In that regard, physiognomy corresponded to anatomy in a strictly organicist sense, with the difference that the expression of a structural system, celebrated since the nineteenth century as the very essence of the architectural organism, was reduced to the status of one gridded pattern among many as it conformed to the integrated rhythms of a modulated field.

In 1952, two years after the completion of the United Nations Secretariat, the "sheath"-type curtain wall found its full realization in the new headquarters of the Lever Brothers Corporation, manufacturers of soaps and household cleansers, on Park Avenue in midtown Manhattan. With its blue-tinted glazing and wired-glass spandrel panels suspended in a stainless steel-clad system of mullions and transoms, Lever House, designed by Gordon Bunshaft of Skidmore, Owings & Merrill (SOM), represented an early and relatively extreme effort to flatten out the skin. Similar efforts were visible in the many curtain walls that followed, to such an extent that during the 1956 conference Robert W. McLaughlin, director of the School of Architecture at

3.13

Skidmore, Owings & Merrill, Lever House, New York, 1952.

Photograph by Ezra Stoller.

The Physiognomy of the Office

Princeton, diagnosed a generalized "fetish for flatness" in office buildings of the period.[39] Such flatness was in marked contrast to the modeled facades of Mies van der Rohe's Lake Shore Drive Apartments of 1948, on which Bunshaft's reductive "machine-made" aesthetic was only superficially based. The editors of *Architectural Review* hypothesized that "the Lever building seems to offer a direct line of communication," as opposed to Mies's supposedly less accessible "subtleties of modeling," which they claimed accounts for the popularity of the flat wall.[40] The difference was only a matter of inches, with the applied mullions on Mies's Lake Shore Drive buildings projecting almost 6 inches from the glazing, and the face of Bunshaft's Lever House mullions projecting only 1¼ inches. But it was all that was necessary even for the editors of a professional journal to distinguish between dynamism incarnate and mere "communication."

The interior of the main volume of Lever House, a slab oriented perpendicularly to the street and rising twenty-four stories above a two-story base, was somewhat less typical of the many office towers that SOM would execute during the subsequent decade. Most distinctly, the elevator core was positioned not at the center of the slab (as in both the RCA Building and the United Nations Secretariat) but at the end farthest from Park Avenue. Except for the mullions that dictated partition locations, the interiors were decidedly devoid of grids, perhaps making it easier for the streamliner Raymond Loewy to impart to the executive suite a stylized image distinctly different from the standardized facades.

Following the completion of Lever House, SOM began in quick succession a series of high-profile office towers for corporate clients in urban contexts, many under Bunshaft's supervision. They included the Inland Steel headquarters in Chicago, completed in 1958 (and designed by Bruce Graham), and the headquarters of the Union Carbide Corporation on Park Avenue in Manhattan, completed in 1960, and those of the Chase Manhattan Bank, completed in 1961 in lower Manhattan in the vicinity of Wall Street, both designed by Bunshaft. All of these represented variations on the slab pattern, but with significant differences in the location of the elevator cores as well as in the location and expression of the building's structural frame.

One tendency that emerged with these structures—which was by no means unique to the production of SOM—was the use of materials representative of the industry to which the corporation belonged. Thus was modern architecture's obsession with hygiene converted into publicity for a soap manufacturer—a fact not lost on the editors of *Business Week,* who characterized Lever House as "spacious, efficient, and washable" in 1952.[41] As if to underscore the point, every seventh vertical mullion holding the fixed glazing of Lever House in place was equipped with a raised rail on which rode a mechanized window-washing machine.[42] Even more literal was the predominance of stainless steel in SOM's headquarters for Inland Steel and the use of a black stainless steel newly developed by Union Carbide on that company's headquarters building. More comprehensive still were the campaigns to incorporate the client's product carried out by Harrison & Abramowitz, first with their all-aluminum curtain wall, office partitions, and wiring in the headquarters of the Alcoa Corporation in Pittsburgh, completed in 1953, and subsequently with the extensive use of glass as a finish material inside and out in the New York headquarters of the Corning Glass Corporation, completed in 1959. These efforts, and others like them, were far more direct than those of Peter Behrens in his AEG turbine factory in Berlin (1909), in which the hinged base of a three-pointed arch was absorbed into a distantly classical giant order ponderously alluding to the dynamics of mechanization, a metaphoric displacement that took the detail well beyond its structural utility or any explicit reference to the company's products.[43] By contrast, in the work of SOM and their peers in the United States after the Second World War, the message was as direct as the advertisements produced for the same corporations in the national and trade weeklies.

In addition to aspiring to a communication that avoided unnecessary subtlety or allusion, these new office buildings evidenced a convergence only dreamed of in the days of the Bauhaus Corporation and its efforts to sell modern architecture to industry.[44] With companies such as Inland Steel, Union Carbide, Alcoa, US Steel, and Corning, modern fabrication and distribution methods had brought both potential standardization and a host of brand names competing for recognition in the marketplace. And as total construction volume increased fourfold in the United States between 1946 and 1956,[45] for a brief period the rhetorical "industry" of modernity, the silent antihero of Giedion's *Mechanization Takes Command,* coincided with the construction industry. Although this industry was not to remain its own client for very long, the convergence afforded architects like Bunshaft opportunities to exploit, with acute matter-of-factness, the temporary transparence of signifier to signified in the gleaming skins of the office building.[46]

While these buildings were thus corporate advertisements comparable to those exhibited by Kepes in *Language of Vision,* the mature modular systems produced by SOM during the late 1950s also attempted a further internalization of capitalist growth by inscribing "flexibility" into every surface of the office. As a newly anointed patron of modern architecture subject to unpredictable market and technological forces, the corporation was perceived as a source of unlimited organizational evolution. Consequently, it was no longer architecture's role to respond to preestablished standards like Sullivan's "cells." Instead, the architecture practiced by firms such as SOM sought to incorporate its own obsolescence into itself by dissolving its organs into three-dimensional modular matrices. In principle, everything passed through the gridded lines of the curtain wall and projected backward into every square inch of office behind it. These skins, therefore, did more than just impart an image of modernity to the many corporations they serviced. The corporation, well understood by the human relations engineers as a model for society, had opened its densely impacted layers out into the light. But the imperatives of organization as an instrument of institutional power had not dissolved along with the heavy partitions of the early-twentieth-century office. Instead, they were carried to a more advanced level.

The Inland Steel Building, completed by SOM in 1958, summarizes many of these developments. As a response to a request from Clarence Randall, the company's chairman, for a building "like a man with immaculate English tailoring," the project represented an investment in what the company's building committee called "unique institutional identification," or corporate image.[47] Located in the center of Chicago's commercial Loop, close to several of its Chicago School predecessors (including Sullivan's own Carson, Pirie, Scott department store (1904), this nineteen-story, gleaming stainless steel and glass tower designed by Bruce Graham (head designer in the firm's Chicago office) was, according to *Architectural Forum,* a "Lever-shaped tower turned inside-out."[48] The building's service core was displaced into an adjoining, smaller tower, and massive steel columns were disposed in an even spacing along the outer face of the curtain wall. The result was 10,000 square feet of open space per floor, none more than 28 feet from a window. By comparison, Lever House had 6,000 square feet per floor within 26 feet of a window, but still interrupted by a row of interior columns. According to SOM's calculations, this plan would provide office space "17% more effi-

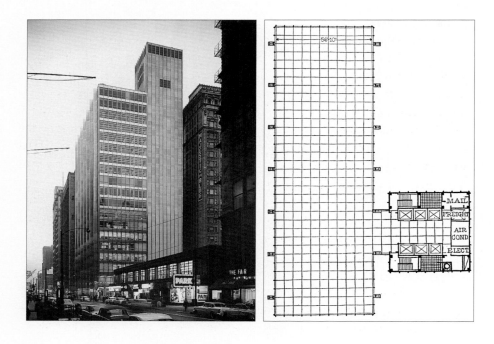

3.14
Skidmore, Owings & Merrill, Inland Steel headquarters, Chicago, 1958. Photograph by Ezra Stoller.

3.15
Skidmore, Owings & Merrill, Inland Steel headquarters, Chicago, 1958. Plan with module.

cient than average."[49] At the time the building was designed in 1955, the span of the steel frame was also the longest attempted in a tall office building, while the projecting exterior columns significantly modified the flatness of the earlier curtain walls, effectively transferring it to the building's interior. The entire building was on a 5' 2" planning grid, reflected in its curtain wall. Inland Steel occupied eight floors in the building, with the remainder rented to other businesses—including the Chicago office of SOM, which by this time had organized itself on the corporate model of many of its clients.[50]

3.4

To the degree that they employed techniques designed to maximize integrated, organized flexibility, Inland Steel and other "inside-out" office buildings designed by SOM—such as the Crown Zellerbach building then under development in San Francisco and the Chase Manhattan Bank headquarters to follow in New York—were also linked to domestic experiments carried out during the early 1940s in anticipation of a postwar housing boom.

In 1942 the editors of *Architectural Forum* asked thirty-three American architects to project "the new house of 194X," paying specific heed to the axiom of "variety within standardization." This axiom, which also applied to the office buildings that followed a decade and a half later, sought to take advantage of wartime prefabrication methods to provide housing on a large scale, while simultaneously making it possible to delineate individuated family units by means of their houses and anticipating the reorganization of the postwar nuclear family into unpredictable configurations.[51] SOM were among those architects who submitted designs for the project. Their contribution, titled "Flexible Space," was based on a diagram of an outboard structural frame and service core with an uninterrupted, flexibly divisible interior space virtually identical to that of the Inland Steel Building. Rather than design a house, SOM designed a system with, in their terms, a standardized "vocabulary" of shell, utility units, partition units, storage units, and furniture, and with a "grammar" of modular combinations that allowed a variety of "compositions" within the same basic parameters.[52] The rooms pictured, complete with modular ceilings, were uncanny prefigurations of the office spaces to come; and the accompanying text all but summarizes the approach the designers would later take when confronted with the problem of the tall office building:

How may space be divided? Rectangles, completely spanned by trusses, bents or other methods, permit freedom of interior division by storage units and screening elements for careful zoning and conditioning of space for use, and for visual space design. Areas may interlock and flow into each other. Privacy and comfort can be maintained without complete compartmentalization. In the plans shown, definite divisions have been made between activity and quiet zones.

Such rectangular space as shelter, with attached or enclosed utility units, could be fairly well standardized for construction in different regions, and left as such until a family moved in with its own dividing units which in the case of storage units may be used for packing and shipping. This does not indicate a belief in nomadism—even an established family may wish the alterations easily effected with such flexibility.[53]

This last disavowal of the "nomadism" implied by the house conceived as a standardized and easily transportable package clearly alludes to the demountable "Dymaxion dwelling machines" of Buckminster Fuller, and perhaps even more specifically to a project designed by Fuller not long before the *Architectural Forum* study. Two

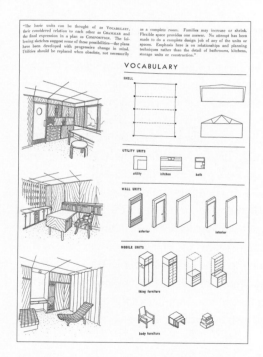

3.16

Skidmore, Owings & Merrill, "Flexible Space." From "The New House of 194X," *Architectural Forum* 77, no. 3 (September 1942): 101.

years earlier, in 1940, the same magazine published Fuller's "mechanical wing," a portable core or "compact, mobile package in which the mechanical essentials of contemporary U.S. living can be transported to the Vermont farmhouse, or incorporated in a permanent dwelling."[54] As an extension of Fuller's project for an optimized, lightweight, mass-produced house, this "wing" on a trailer was an immediate predecessor of the equally portable Dymaxion Deployment Unit, adapted from a metal grain silo and exhibited in the garden of the Museum of Modern Art in New York in November 1941.[55] But SOM's insistence in their house project on what they called the "inherent flexibility and structural stability" of rectangular form, and their rejection of the "inherent disadvantages" of the "[f]ixed geometrical forms, of the types recently suggested by a number of 'radical designers'" (again, most likely a reference to Fuller),[56] marked a significant and conscious departure from the optimal spaces designed around Taylorized dwelling activities, as seen in Fuller's 4D Dymaxion House of 1927 or the Dymaxion Bathroom of 1937. Nevertheless, traces of Fuller's treatment of the house as a logistical problem of deployment remained discernible in other experiments in domestic reorganization carried out on the pages of American professional journals during the war.

The same year—1942—that SOM submitted their contribution to the *Architectural Forum* postwar house project, *California Arts and Architecture,* the magazine that under the stewardship of its editor John Entenza would sponsor the Case Study Houses program after the war, announced an open competition titled "Designs for

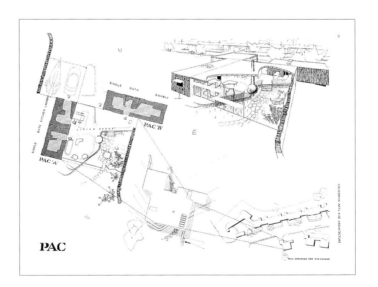

3.17

Eero Saarinen and Oliver Lundquist, proposed postwar house with "Pre-Assembled Components (PACs)." Winning entry, "Designs for Postwar Living," *California Arts and Architecture* 60 (August 1943): 28.

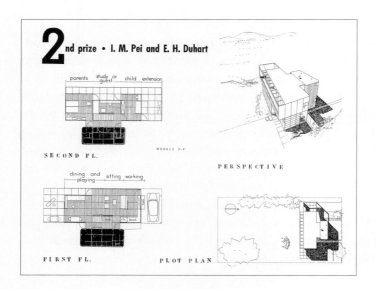

2nd prize • I. M. Pei and E. H. Duhart

Postwar Living." The winning entries, selected by a jury that included Charles Eames, were published in the magazine's August 1943 issue; first prize went to Eames's friend Eero Saarinen, in collaboration with Oliver Lundquist. Saarinen and Lundquist proposed an efficiently designed core of mass-producible, preassembled components (or "PACs"), surrounded by a more loosely laid-out modular living area. The PACs, formed out of a resin-bonded plywood hull, were reserved for what were designated as the "biological and mechanical functions—sleeping, dressing, bathing, cooking, washing, heating, and cooling"; the "living," or social, areas of the house were flexibly panelized for variety of arrangement.[57]

The two types of domestic space into which the house is divided utilized mass-produced components in correspondingly different ways. The molded "biological and mechanical functions" of the house were, like the furniture designs with which Saarinen and Eames won the Museum of Modern Art "Organic Design" competition of 1940–1941, stamped out in a plywood hull. But the modular and infinitely flexible matrix of "living" space, associated with the supposed idiosyncrasies manifest in the social context of each family, was more suited to panelization. "Biological and mechanical functions" applied to all clients, while "social" functions were variable according to local conditions internal and external to the family.

Second place in the competition went to a house for a "typical defense plant worker" by another future designer of office buildings, I. M. Pei, in collaboration with E. H. Duhart. The Pei-Duhart house was organized around a similar division: an efficiently

3.18
I. M. Pei and E. H. Duhart, second-place entry, "Designs for Postwar Living," *California Arts and Architecture* 60 (August 1943): 32.

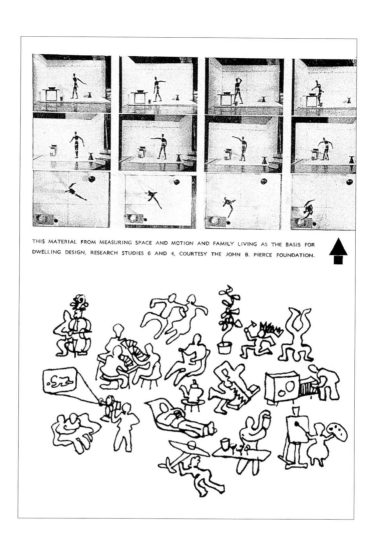

THIS MATERIAL FROM MEASURING SPACE AND MOTION AND FAMILY LIVING AS THE BASIS FOR DWELLING DESIGN, RESEARCH STUDIES 6 AND 4, COURTESY THE JOHN B. PIERCE FOUNDATION.

3.19

Models "measuring space and motion and family living as the basis for dwelling design" from the John B. Pierce Foundation (above), and diagrams of figures engaged in domestic activities (below). From Charles Eames, John Entenza, and Herbert Matter, "What Is a House?" *Arts and Architecture* 61 (July 1944): 37.

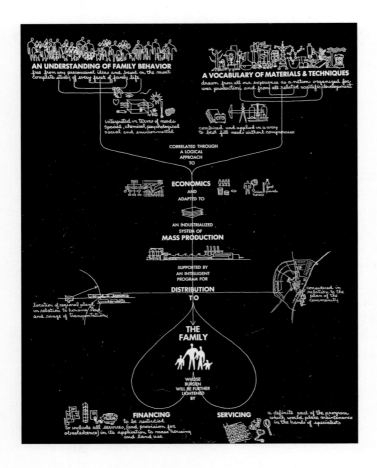

planned pressed aluminum service core was attached to a gridded and panelized "home room." Here the correlations could not be more explicit. What these architects described as an open, flexible "space for family life," the same space provided by SOM and Saarinen in their schemes for the postwar house, would be magnified (again like the photomicrographs published by Kepes and the cascading scales of the Eameses' *Powers of Ten*) into the open, modular floor plans of office buildings like the Inland Steel headquarters.[58] With this mutation, the specifically "social" as opposed to "biological" spaces of the family, as they were called, were inscribed into the social condenser of the postwar office building.

The "typical defense plant worker" of the Pei-Duhart scheme, the "housewife" and the "postwar worker" inhabiting another Pei and Duhart house project published in *Arts and Architecture* in 1944, the "Alphas" and the "Omegas" for whom Richard Neu-

3.20

Charles Eames, John Entenza, and Herbert Matter, "The Family," diagram. From "What Is a House?" *Arts and Architecture* 61 (July 1944): 32.

tra designed unrealized Case Study Houses, the "Mr. and Mrs. X" inhabiting Case Study House no. 1 by J. R. Davidson, the standardized figures in family-like clusters drawn by Ray Eames for the cover of *Arts and Architecture*'s special 1944 issue on prefabrication, and those same figures in perfectly Taylorized positions as they performed the "typical" household activities enumerated inside—all were standardized character types who formed a hypothetical clientele for the new modern house built around such a "family" reconstituted in the aftermath of war. That the corporation was figured as the institutional correlate of this very same family through subterranean links between its structures and those of houses projected by its architects a decade earlier should be no surprise. The postwar family was the ultimate "organism," the last holdout of an enchanted American *Gemeinschaft,* or organic community, now redeployed and reorganized into a flexible matrix. Contra Fuller, houses were no longer standardized "units"; and contra Sullivan, offices were no longer standardized "cells."

This condensation of modular flexibility and organic community can be seen more clearly still in one more set of examples at the domestic scale. In July 1944, *Arts and Architecture* devoted an entire issue to prefabrication. It included "What Is a House?," an article in which John Entenza, Charles Eames, and Herbert Matter, explicitly referring to Fuller, distinguish between those parts of the house that could be optimized to serve a set of standardized needs (kitchen, bathroom, bedroom, and storage rooms) and the "living" areas of the house that required a flexible organizational format in order to respond to the needs of individual families and family members.[59] This distinction was repeated at a larger scale in the distinction of service core and rentable space typical of nearly all postwar office towers. Here also, four years before the publication of Giedion's *Mechanization Takes Command,* a Taylorization of household tasks common in earlier modernisms was affiliated with an aesthetics of movement. The Herbert Matter image of a man dressing included as an illustration—a photographic record of the man's movements traced in the air with light—was later included in László Moholy-Nagy's *Vision in Motion.* And already in 1942, the Saarinen-Lundquist "Postwar House" winning competition entry had included a built-in dressing area arranged around a "dressing radius," or the space traced out by a body's movements during the act of dressing, organized around the reflective surface of a mirror.

Also in 1942, Eero Saarinen designed a hypothetical community center utilizing the products of the United States Gypsum Company. The project was published as a four-page advertisement for that company in the March issue of *Architectural Forum,* under the heading "Demountable Space."[60] It was a square pavilion lifted off the ground, again designed to accommodate the unpredictable needs of community, this time quite literally. The entire building, which bore clear traces of Fuller's 4D Dymaxion House with its central structural mast and suspension cables, was laid out on a 12-foot by 12-foot grid, into which were inserted standardized panels (to be prefabricated by United States Gypsum) interspersed with windows. Inside, it was to be entirely finished

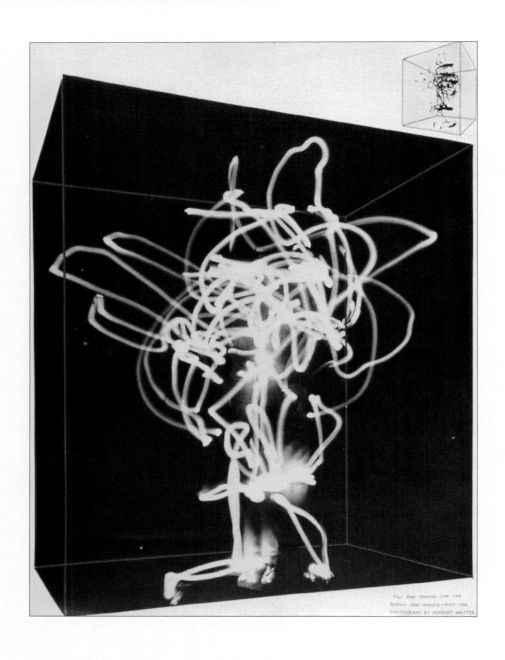

Herbert Matter, *Man Dressing,* n.d. From Charles Eames, John Entenza, and Herbert Matter, "What Is a House?" *Arts and Architecture* 61 (July 1944): 36.

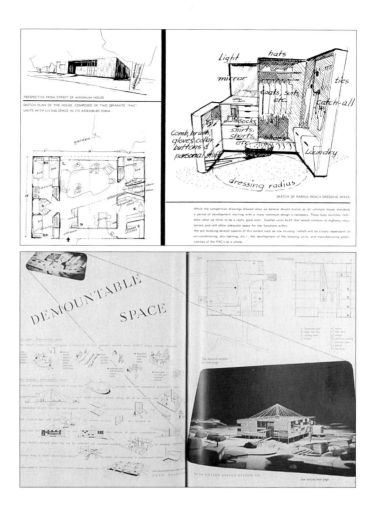

in United States Gypsum products. With its patterned, panelized, prefabricated facades, the community center anticipates the house that Saarinen's friends (and then
colleagues at the Cranbrook Academy) Charles and Ray Eames designed for themselves in Santa Monica in 1949. The connection becomes particularly clear when
the link to Fuller is passed through the 1944 "What Is a House?" article (coauthored
by Charles Eames), which effectively stated the theoretical terms under which the
Eameses would produce their own house.[61]

3.22
Eero Saarinen and Oliver Lundquist, "Dressing Radius."
From winning entry, "Designs for Postwar Living," *Califor-
nia Arts and Architecture* 60 (August 1943): 31.

3.23
Eero Saarinen, "Demountable Space." Design for a community center as an advertisement for United States Gypsum Co., *Architectural Forum* 76, no. 3 (March 1942): 50–51.

The Physiognomy of the Office

But Saarinen's project must also be seen as belonging to his own early exploration of Fuller's ideas, carried forward several years later (1945) with the hypothetical prefabricated metal "unfolding house," which was equipped with a segmented roof that could be unfolded to provide additional space. Again flexibility was associated with the unpredictable needs of a postwar American family defined by change, after having already been projected onto a multiuse social condenser (a "social center") for a postwar community made up of such families—the constituents of what its author rather mechanically referred to as a "changing civilization." Family, community, and society—three different scales of organism—are here telescoped together, in compliance with the multiply scaled images that Norbert Wiener called "pure patterns in a natural world," images laid out a decade later by Kepes as the topography of his new landscape, in which a longed-for unity of microcosm and macrocosm unfolded.

The tall office buildings of the 1950s can thus be seen as inhabiting one more scale in this self-similar cascade. Following along the lines of Inland Steel, the diagram of "flexible space" deployed by SOM in their "house of 194X"—an outboard frame spanning modular open space—was repeated in the headquarters of the Chase Manhattan Bank in lower Manhattan, designed by Bunshaft and completed in 1961, but this time with the service core absorbed back into the center of the rectangular volume. What began as a simple plan for corporate expansion was transformed into a monumental effort to revitalize New York's Wall Street business district, which had been threatened by the new concentration of corporations in the formerly residential stretch of Park Avenue in midtown, whose conversion to a new commercial center had been pioneered by Lever House. Downtown, one block of Cedar Street was closed off in order to cover the entire site with a large one-story base housing a Chase branch bank, out of which would rise the sixty-story rectangular shaft of the new headquarters.

This "little Rockefeller Center" (as it was called at the time, in reference to Chase president David Rockefeller) was part of a large-scale strategy for urban revitalization developed by SOM, including a proposal for "walk-to-work" row houses nearby.[62] The plan was promoted under the auspices of the Downtown-Lower Manhattan Association (DLMA), a group of businesses with an interest in the economic future of the area, founded by Rockefeller in 1956. By the 1970s, this initiative to expose the dark canyons of Wall Street to the planning methods of "light and air," with freestanding shafts set off by open plazas—based on research begun at Rockefeller Center—had borne fruit not only in the realization of the Chase complex and the nearby Marine Midland Bank headquarters (also by SOM, 1967) but also in the World Trade Center, designed by Minoru Yamasaki in collaboration with Emery Roth & Sons.[63] The SOM "superblock" plan for Chase Manhattan was intended to position the Chase headquarters as the focus of what Nathaniel Owings called "a new town within the city," in which, "around this twenty-first century edition of the Boston Common in downtown

Manhattan, Chase could be the visual and acknowledged leader." As Owings put it, with the appearance of the World Trade Center, "The dream of the intimately scaled downtown village was lost but an armature remained upon which the dynamics of change could grow with health and strength."[64]

Tafuri views the heirs to the legacy of Rockefeller Center, including the World Trade Center, as further symptoms of a "desperation shared by intellectuals and businessmen alike—the desperation of one who sees himself impotent to control, with his antiquated instruments, the enigmatic course of the indomitable White Whale" of the capitalist metropolis. For him, these were "antiurban paradoxes, artificial technological 'miracles.'"[65] Surely the new headquarters of the Chase Manhattan Bank, which transposed Rockefeller Center's impossible project of urban reunification onto lower Manhattan, also belongs in this category. But Owings's organicist rhetoric could not be more explicit about the concomitant shift to which Chase also bears witness; the mutation of the bounded stability of the village into an open "armature" that, like the grids of SOM's office buildings, homeostatically regulates the dynamics of growth and change in order to preserve the health of the corporate (and urban) organism. The priority of the organism and of organic community is conserved. Tafuri evaluates the failure of these complexes to overcome their "artificiality" in light of their (and his) own organicist premises, which, as Owings's remarks confirm, coincide with the interests of the corporations. But he does not acknowledge that the "organic," too—

3.24

Skidmore, Owings & Merrill, Chase Manhattan Bank headquarters, New York, 1961.

The Physiognomy of the Office

precisely because it is *tied* to capital, rather than hopelessly braced against it—has changed beyond recognition, to all but those possessed of a new vision capable of renaturalizing the artificial landscape of the city. Seen against the background of the human relations project, efforts to install organizations like Chase at the center of a newly reinvigorated downtown acquire a different patina. Their exhausted systematicity can indeed be read as symptomatic of a loss of control over the city, which was at the same moment expressed in the flight of these "antiurban" corporate machines to the outlying regions. But the prospect of their organismic success, premised on identification with the corporation as a social unit comparable to the family, cuts a significantly more ominous figure.

Still, to what extent was the project of homeostatic pattern maintenance actually achieved within these machines, even as they cut themselves off from the surrounding urban fabric? The Chase tower, designed under the imperative of maximum organizational flexibility, was supported by 3-foot by 5-foot columns positioned on its east and west faces outside the bright white curtain wall, with two more rows of interior columns running through the core. This was done to allow for future shifts within the company, such as the expansion and moving of departments, as well as to provide for one-third of the floor space to be rented.[66] Like many large corporations at that time, Chase Manhattan had also been dealing with the often unpredictable and substantial needs of the new office machines—including mainframe computers—and so sought interior flexibility to accommodate machines whose size and shape were changing so fast that their space requirements could not be anticipated.[67] The entire structure was on a 4' 6" module marked by the curtain wall, and also absorbed into those interiors that were designed by SOM. But it was in another SOM corporate tower

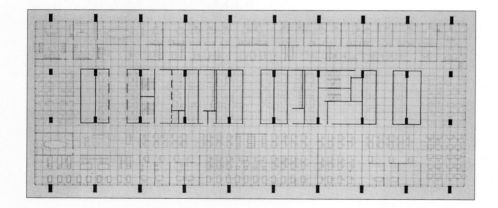

3.25

Skidmore, Owings & Merrill, Chase Manhattan Bank headquarters, New York, 1961. Typical office floor plan.

then being designed by Bunshaft that the project of controlled, flexible, modular integration was advanced most decisively.

In 1955 the Union Carbide Corporation had considered moving its headquarters from Manhattan to a suburban site in Westchester County. Instead, the company decided to commission SOM to design a new headquarters on Park Avenue.[68] The new structure, completed in 1960, rose in a fifty-two-story slab set back 33 feet from the sidewalk, backed up by a twelve-story annex facing Madison Avenue to the west. The building was, in effect, all curtain wall, inside and out. Column spacing was determined by the position of the below-grade railroad tracks between which foundations had to rest; and although the structural frame was marked on the skin by black spandrel panels and column covers, its presence was partially obscured in the optics of the

3.26
Skidmore, Owings & Merrill, Union Carbide Building, New York, 1960. Photograph by Ezra Stoller.

3.27

Skidmore, Owings & Merrill, Union Carbide Building, New York, 1960. Curtain wall. Photograph by Ezra Stoller.

(top left) Skidmore, Owings & Merrill, Union Carbide Building, New York, 1960. Office interiors. Photograph by Ezra Stoller.

(top right) Skidmore, Owings & Merrill, Union Carbide Building, New York, 1960. Lobby. Photograph by Ezra Stoller.

Skidmore, Owings & Merrill, Union Carbide Building, New York, 1960. Office interiors. Photograph by Ezra Stoller.

projecting, polished stainless steel mullions set on a module of 5' 0." In this case, a "sheath"-type curtain wall was not necessary for the planning module to declare victory over the "Chicago frame." The frame had been thoroughly absorbed into the skin's gridded pattern, to the degree that its partial expression did not threaten the integrity of a finer grain of spatial articulation, which was answerable only to the dispersal of the constitutive office cell into a flexible matrix. The interior layouts, which were to accommodate the five thousand Union Carbide employees occupying the building, were regulated by a thoroughly integrated lighting, air-conditioning, and partition system, with 65 percent of the offices within 15 feet of a window. The luminous plastic ceiling—a continuous interior skin—incorporated linear runners that also served as air-conditioning diffusers and tracks designed to accept the steel-framed modular office partitions. Executive desks, side tables, and conferences tables received polished stainless steel frames and dimensions compatible with the overall system, which also incorporated storage units, door hardware, and signage.[69]

Inside these modulated fields were occupants no longer representable as "salaried masses," whose own physiognomy had been refigured as a pattern of character types that served as receptacles for a progressive individualization announced by human relations discourse, a process that reached deep into the subjective interior of each worker-consumer in a cascade of behavioral codes.[70] At this juncture, the sociologist C. Wright Mills could still inventory the hierarchies within hierarchies embedded within the "enormous file" of the postwar office skyscraper, with a "row of clerks and a set of IBM equipment," while recording the extension of corporate power into the psychosocial realm of office "morale," which for him was still "the morale of cheerful robots."[71] Mills still saw human relations as ideology, a false consciousness that could be stripped away to reveal the alienated, machinelike soul of the white-collar worker. But, as we will see with IBM, it was precisely this worker's soul that the new business machines were digitizing, filing into memory, and reproducing as they pried it open. Thus the generic clients inhabiting the wartime and postwar house projects had grown into living symptoms of what Theodor Adorno called "pseudo-personalization," or the summons to identify with a character type as an expression of one's individuality—a summons most systematically issuing from the moralizing "messages" of television.[72] In developing his thesis, Adorno refers to David Riesman's distinction between two primary types, the "introvert" and the "extrovert," made in the landmark 1950 sociological analysis *The Lonely Crowd: A Study of the Changing American Character*. According to Riesman, the "introvert" had played an essential role in the individualistic Protestant work ethic that Max Weber found permeating early-twentieth-century America.[73] Hence, Adorno reads the obsolescence of the introvert as symptomatic of the emptying out of "inwardness," or inner experience, manifest in the emptiness of the popular stereotypes.

One such character type came under vigorous attack when William H. Whyte Jr. published his oft-cited piece of popular sociology, *The Organization Man* (1956). Referring to Weber and Riesman, and in particular to Weber's social typologies, Whyte lamented the eclipse of of the Protestant work ethic's individualism by a new conformity. The "organization man" was a product of this conformity—the ideal subject of "human relations" who identified with his corporation as though it were his family.[74] Whyte's figure had internalized the logic of organization itself. Conformist yet adaptable and resourceful, he "[does] not question the system" but rather seeks out integration at the office or at home, in the new suburbs that hold the alter ego to his corporate family in near-perfect symmetry.[75] Here is life in a dynamic equilibrium: an organized procession into the future in the custody of a social "system," its purpose coordinated with that of the larger whole.

Though *The Organization Man* remains a lucid critique of the self-regulating processes of the organizational complex, its author, like Riesman, continued to hold out for the redemptive potential of an organic social bond. Even as he urges his readers to "fight the organization" and cheat on the personality tests administered by the humans relations juggernaut, his actual target is the "dehumanized collective" he sees in what he calls the "Social Ethic" of teamwork.[76] The implication remains that the organization can redeem itself through the restoration of "humanity" to the integrated system, by tolerating a renewed, rebellious individualism as counterbalance to the body corporate. Whyte thus fails to recognize the force of his own insights, since Adorno had already found this rebellious "individual" to be one more phantom playing across the television screen, perhaps—we can add—even the ur-type: the consumer, captivated by an overdetermined belief in autonomous, internally motivated "choice" from among a variety of standardized products and behaviors, all of which refer to the same empty shell of a "humanity" left behind long ago, as mechanization took command.[77] This is what is at stake in the architecture explored above—the architecture of the lonely crowd. The organization man and the many secretaries and clerks who surround him—as well the "housewife" who stands by him[78]—constitute the units, the modules from which the postwar corporation was constructed. They are the new "humans," always already a product of the machine. Their alienation is all that interferes with their full assimilation into the organized social system. To seek a "humanity" within the infinite, modular patterns organizing the emptied-out interiors of edifices like Union Carbide is to submit to the logic of the corporate organism. Instead, the image of organization demands even more forcefully to be taken at face value, as materialized image—a depthless curtain flattening out every square inch of available space.

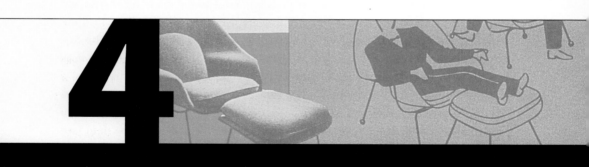

4

Organic Style

The long, low forms of Eero Saarinen's General Motors Technical Center in Warren, Michigan, appear on the screen of an automobile windshield. The photograph, published in Great Britain in 1959, says it all.[1] By 1945, when the Saarinen office began work on the project, architects had already positioned themselves as custodians of a dynamically organized social unity carried, in principle, by prefabricated modularity. But standardization also suggested homogeneity. And so modern architecture once again appealed to the machine: "We choose our automobiles within the limitations of the makes and models for the best kind of transportation adapted to our needs, but in order to put that stamp of individuality upon our automobile we do not demand that it have six wheels and two motors."[2]

This particular appeal was made in 1944 by Saarinen's friend Charles Eames, in "What is a House?," a text we have already encountered in the previous chapter. One

123   *Organic Style*

of Eames's coauthors was John Entenza, for whom Saarinen and Eames would later design a house. Their claim here was that the individual tastes of consumers can be reconciled with the standardized accommodation of typical needs. In other words, what works for the car works for the house—and also, we can add, for the office building. There a corporation's own "individuality" can be secured with the use of cladding materials specifically identifiable with its products, which are adapted to the technical, aesthetic, and organizational advantages of the curtain wall, as in the examples of Lever House, Corning, Inland Steel, and others. Consequently, prefabricated organization men and long-lost American individualism are not, despite William Whyte, mutually exclusive. There are different makes and models of organization men, identified with specific corporations, just as there are different makes and models of curtain-walled office buildings.

In 1923, comparing houses to sports cars and sports cars to temples, Le Corbusier set the standard by which all subsequent encounters between architecture and automobiles would be measured:

The motor-car is an object with a simple function (to travel) and complicated aims (comfort, resistance, appearance), which has forced on big industry the absolute necessity of standardization. All motor-cars have the same essential arrangements. But, by reason of the unceasing competition between the innumerable firms who make them, every maker has found himself obliged to get

4.1

General Motors Technical Center seen through an automobile windshield. From Lawrence Alloway, "City Notes," *Architectural Design* 29, no. 1 (January 1959): 34.

to the top of this competition and, over and above the standard of practical realization, to prosecute the search for a perfection and a harmony beyond the mere practical side, a manifestation not only of perfection and harmony, but of beauty.[3]

For architects in 1923, the perfection of the Parthenon was made possible by the standardization of the Greek temple, after which "competition"—and thus aesthetic progress—took over. But by 1955, things had changed. That was the year that Reyner Banham thought it time to reconsider the automobile's architectural status.[4] While, as Banham put it, Le Corbusier had "confronted the Parthenon with the Bignan-Sport," the New Brutalists of 1950s Great Britain delivered a "pop-eyed OK for the Cadillac convertible."[5] Far from being heralds of a classical timelessness, however, for Banham the automobiles coming annually out of Detroit with new configurations of tail fins, chrome trim, "speed-streaks," and "cineramic wind-screens" promised new "intellectual attitudes for living in a throwaway economy." Anything that claimed to be a "classic" car was merely the retrograde product of "abnormal sales conditions," since

> On the open market, where competition is real, it is the cun-
> ningly-programmed minor changes that give one manufacturer
> an edge over another, and the aesthetics of body-styling are an
> integral part of the battle for margins. Under these circumstances
> we should be neither surprised nor shocked to find that styling
> runs the same way as engineering development, and in any case
> there can be no norms of formal composition while the auto-
> mobile remains an artefact in evolution, even though particular
> models are stabilised.[6]

Le Corbusier's industrial idealism is thus confronted with the fantastical realism of the annual model change. As introduced by Banham, the automobile stylist presiding over an "aesthetics of expendability" emerges as the model architect, "continually sampling the public response to dream-car prototypes" and responsible to the desires of an entire nation.[7] Banham himself remains in awe of the sheer scale of the enterprise, citing the deference exhibited by the New York–based monthly *Industrial Design* in its review of the 1954 cars: "The most successful company in the history of the world makes automobiles; in 1953 General Motors' sales totaled $10,028,000,000, an unheard of sum. Under the circumstances, passing judgment on a new crop of cars is like passing judgment on a nation's soul."[8]

Organic Style

A tendency toward a statistical sublime was commonplace in a postwar United States emboldened by its economic and technological prowess. Indeed, in 1956 the General Motors Corporation compiled a comparable set of statistics to describe its newly completed Technical Center:[9] twenty-five buildings totaling more than 2.2 million square feet, grouped in five clusters around a 22-acre artificial lake; 11 miles of road, 85 acres of parking, more than 378 miles of wiring, 12 miles of underfloor ducts, and over 56 miles of fluorescent tubing, all on a 320-acre site, built at a cost of over one hundred million dollars. General Motors, America's largest and most powerful corporation, was proud of its achievement. At the dedication ceremony the company's president, Harlow H. Curtice, declared the new facility to be of global significance for its optimistic materialization of what he called the American "belief in the importance and inevitability of change."[10]

4.2

Eero Saarinen, General Motors Technical Center, Warren, Michigan, 1945–1956. Aerial view. Photograph by Balthazar Korab.

Curtice was frank about what he meant by change. "Some call this typical American process 'dynamic obsolescence,'" he said. Referring to the design changes made annually to each model, he noted that "The automobile industry is dedicated to the process of accelerating obsolescence." The Technical Center's purpose was to gather together the five thousand scientists, engineers, designers, technicians, and other personnel responsible for administering this process, in what Curtice described as a campuslike atmosphere "conducive to good work" and intended to "stimulate creative thinking."

For the architects, the project represented a commission of staggering proportions even for the postwar period. It also marked a transition in the Saarinen office from the leadership of the father, Eliel, to the son, Eero, as well as the beginning of a long string of major corporate commissions.[11] In the years preceding his untimely death in 1961, Saarinen's continued success with big business earned him international accolades, as well as suspicion at his willingness to produce, with singular efficiency, a series of unique embodiments of corporate identity. Writing in 1962, Banham scolded those who had earlier criticized Saarinen's eclecticism—his "style for the job" approach—but were posthumously all too eager to sing his praises:

> A section of design punditry, sensing that the whole [General Motors] scheme was in some way a personal shrine for the master-stylist Harley Earl, drew meaningful distinctions between the "true" machine aesthetic of the buildings and the "immoral" styling of the vehicles conceived in them; and a fair slice of the profession thought it saw Mies made easy, and promoted Eero to membership of a triumvirate of Junior Miesians along with Philip Johnson and Gordon Bunshaft of Skidmore, Owings and Merrill.[12]

The General Motors Technical Center earned Saarinen his status as "Junior Miesian" by eliciting frequent comparisons to the Illinois Institute of Technology campus. But Mies is not all there is to the Technical Center, as Mies himself implied: "Eero came to see me when he was doing General Motors and he asked me about the sculpture garden, 'How would you do it?' And I told him, 'I would emphasize the dignity of work. That is all General Motors is for—work. That is what you should express.'"[13]

What sort of dignified "work" did Mies believe took place at General Motors? Saarinen's former associate Kevin Roche confirms Mies's singular inability to read the signs. Roche had studied with Mies at IIT and, by his own account, was responsible for the articulation of a particularly Miesian stance within the internal discourse of the Saarinen office: "Mies came to visit, and since I was the only one he knew I drove him around. I had a Chevrolet which had a grille across [its dashboard] and the ashtray was built into the grille, so you had to know where to push to open the ashtray. So I turn around to Mies and he is smoking a cigar and pounding on that thing. It didn't express its function."[14]

As GM president Curtice pointed out, to "work" at the Technical Center was to implement the logic of "dynamic obsolescence," or what Banham called the automobile's market-driven "evolution," including the production of the stylized surface effects that prevented Mies's untrained eyes from finding the ashtray in Roche's Chevrolet. For modern architects of a Miesian or Corbusian vintage, the automobile was the carrier of an industrial logic devoted to an optimized and standardized functionality. That is, these architects did not distinguish between the marketing practices of the Ford Motor Company of the early 1920s and those of the General Motors Corporation of the 1950s. Written into his encounter with Roche's dashboard is the fact that Mies, who did not suppress the traces left on his architecture by what he called the "objective" demands of the real estate market, had no patience for the superficialities of automobile styling.[15] But in the industrialized American consumer culture of the 1950s, to produce automobiles was to produce stylized images. In that sense, Saarinen's dutiful adherence to *this* logic makes him even more Miesian than Mies, since his architecture at the General Motors Technical Center is, strictly speaking, a *mirror* of the supposedly objective technological, economic, and aesthetic conditions under which it was produced.

Until the mid-1920s, the American automobile industry was dominated by the Fordist principle of a standardized product that changed little from year to year, enabling the market-leading Ford Motor Company to optimize production and offer its automobiles to consumers at ever-lower prices. The standard was set by Ford's Model T, famously available in any color "so long as it's black."[16] But under the chairmanship of Alfred P. Sloan Jr., General Motors gradually overtook Ford as industry leader. Ford's patriarchal management model was challenged by GM's model of centralized policy making and decentralized operations, and the visually standardized Model T was pulled under by the tides of planned obsolescence.[17]

By 1926 Sloan and others in the corporation's management realized that the newly compacted automobile bodies offered unexplored opportunities to distinguish GM's cars from others, especially Ford's distinctly styleless product. So Sloan hired Hollywood custom-car designer Harley J. Earl as a consultant on the design of the 1927 Cadillac La Salle. One year later, General Motors had a new Art and Color Section devoted exclusively to automobile styling, with Earl as director. The La Salle was the first stylist-designed car to reach a mass market, commencing a process that culminated in the full implementation of orchestrated annual model changes in all of GM's lines by the mid-1930s.[18] Sloan identified this as the moment when the automobile industry became aware that its products could be submitted profitably to what he described as the "laws of the Paris dressmakers."[19]

Not coincidentally, these developments crossed paths with the techniques of so-called streamlined design.[20] In the hands of industrial designers such as Henry Dreyfuss, Raymond Loewy, Walter Dorwin Teague, and Norman Bel Geddes, streamlining reached its apotheosis in the United States in the "This Is Tomorrow" world's fair, held in New York in 1939–1940. The fair's most popular attraction was the General Motors Futurama, designed by Geddes. It was located in a sprawling curvilinear GM complex, also designed by Geddes in collaboration with Albert Kahn, with a young Eero Saarinen assuming primary responsibility for the design of the building in which Futurama was housed.[21] Futurama itself was an immense model of "the city of 1960," an exurban force field of frozen movements caught in a network of superhighways stretching across the continental United States. Here were the high-rise concentrations of Le Corbusier's Ville Radieuse, including the separation of traffic according to speed, combined with the automobile-generated dispersion of Frank Lloyd Wright's Broadacre City.

Guided by a recorded voice pointing out the pleasures and benefits of a streamlined automotive utopia, visitors embarked on a "skyride" through this landscape that touched down in a large-scale model of a representative section of the city, a mix of sleek skyscrapers and low-rise structures. From there they entered a full-scale representative street intersection. At its four corners were an auditorium, a department store, an apartment house, and an "Automobile Display Salon." This last was a piece of glass architecture on the order of Erich Mendelsohn's commercial architecture in Berlin or Mies's Adam department store project of 1928. Inside were automobiles— Buicks, Cadillacs, Chevrolets, Oldsmobiles, Pontiacs, and a "glass car" from General

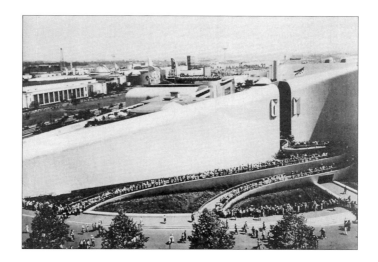

4.3

Albert Kahn and Norman Bel Geddes, General Motors
Pavilion, 1939–1940 World's Fair, New York.

Organic Style

Motors subsidiary Fisher Body—along with streamlined locomotives and streamlined refrigerators.[22]

Covering automobiles with the traces of movement was nothing less than an effort to consolidate image with function. In *Horizons,* published in 1932, Norman Bel Geddes led the way. It may or may not be the case that Geddes's definition of streamlining draws on the exposition of biological morphogenesis laid out in 1917 by D'Arcy Wentworth Thompson in *On Growth and Form,* which hypothesizes direct, mathematical correlations between the shape of organisms and the physical forces acting on them.[23] Nevertheless, with the exposed chassis and closed cab configuration of early automobiles transformed into a single, coordinated totality that combined the previously distinct functions of transport and enclosure—an "organism"—Geddes was able to compare automobiles to swordfish, seagulls, greyhounds, stallions, and bulls, claiming that "when the motor car, bus, truck and tractor have evolved into the essential forms determined by what these machines have to do, they will not need surface ornamentation to make them beautiful." Geddes observed that to transfer the "diagram of forces" (an expression associated with D'Arcy Thompson) to the machine via the automobile's skin required that the machine's "vital parts"—engine, clutch, transmission, and differential—be reorganized, arguing that "presently it will be the obligation of designers to collect this miscellany and to arrange it organically into one unit."[24]

4.4

Norman Bel Geddes, General Motors "Futurama," 1939–
1940 World's Fair, New York. Model of "The City of 1960."

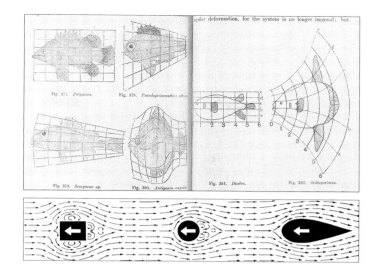

General Motors and other major manufacturers partook of this doctrine only to a certain extent, since their agenda was not necessarily to optimize performance but rather to facilitate constant change. There was therefore no contradiction in applying a streamlined aesthetic to static objects like refrigerators. While designers like Geddes claimed a scientific legitimacy for the streamlining of literally moving objects like automobiles, the General Motors stylists recognized that the automobile's modernity lay in its capacity to serve as a model for other commodities, including—as Banham rightly pointed out—architecture. The automobile as mobile organism (in Geddes's formulation) acquired a certain "look," which was in turn converted into a mutable image that nevertheless maintained the car = organism equation. *Styling: The Look of Things,* a brochure prepared by the GM styling group in 1955 (the year before the Technical Center opened) and signed by Earl, summarizes the transaction. There, the silhouettes of seals and birds (again recalling D'Arcy Thompson) accompanying images of Saarinen's Womb Chair are not just an innocent background for the declaration that the stylist "knows from his studies of morphology (the form and structure of animals), that in nature all life looks the way it does because of the forces at work on it. The rate and direction of growth of the life cells is increased at one point, inhibited at another, according to the specific need. And so it is that we can deduce the forces that are acting or have acted on a living thing simply by looking at it."[25]

4.5
D'Arcy Wentworth Thompson, diagrams illustrating morphological adaptations. From *On Growth and Form* (1917), 748–749.

4.6
Norman Bel Geddes, "Diagram Illustrating the Principle of Streamlining." From *Horizons* (1932), 45.

Organic Style

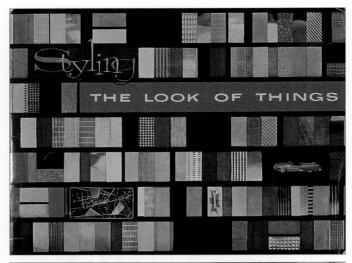

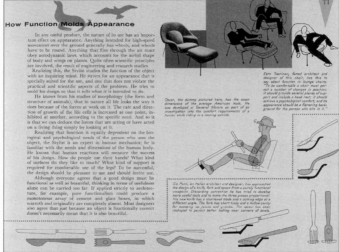

But in a section titled "Evolution of Design in the American Automobile," which repeated the logic of Raymond Loewy's 1933 "Evolution Chart for Automobiles," General Motors marks its distance from the functionalist organicism of the streamliners. The GM stylists cite the developments of the 1930s and Earl's preference for a "longer and lower" look over the egg shapes of designers like Geddes: "Many people, in describing what cars of the future would look like, predicted an evolution into a tear drop or egg form because these were known to be the most perfect streamline shapes.

4.7

General Motors Corporation, *Styling: The Look of Things* (1955), cover (above); and page 11 showing Eero Saarinen's "Womb Chair" and silhouette of swimming seal (below).

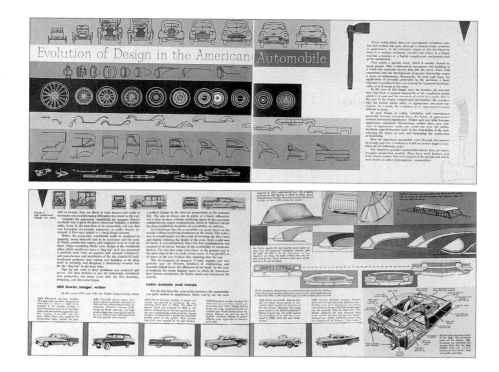

Among the automobile Stylists were supporters of this general idea. More, however, favored a different approach—that of a longer, lower silhouette which would give the impression of speed without certain drawbacks inherent in a streamline shape."[26]

As Geddes himself had noted, one of the drawbacks of a functionally stream-lined shape was that the tight integration of skin and internal organs required for optimal performance was not technically or economically compatible with the arbitrariness of the annual model change. Like many others, Geddes thus condemned styling for its violation of organic laws in favor of the laws of fashion. Undaunted, the GM stylists asserted *their* claim to organicity in the pages of their public relations brochure, presenting an evolutionary model of their own: "horseless carriage" to runabout to touring car to closed sedan to the longer and lower bodies of the thirties to the wider wheelbase of the 1940s, and finally to the "still lower, longer, wider" cars of the '50s. Thus, with the submission of *both* functional organisms (Geddes) *and* stylized images (Earl) to an evolutionary model, were the twin temporal categories of modernity—evolution and fashion—forced together onto the surface of the automobile.[27]

The General Motors brochure, a design manual aimed at automobile stylists and consumers alike, also rehearses Bauhaus fundamentals with an obvious debt to

4.8

Excerpts from "Evolution of Design in the American Automobile." From General Motors Corporation, *Styling: The
Look of Things* (1955), 26–27 (above), 44–45 (below).

Organic Style

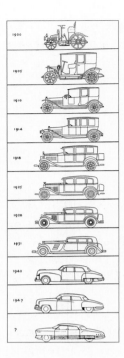

Gyorgy Kepes, who is paraphrased and acknowledged in a footnote in the section on "elements of design."[28] Thus did *Styling: The Look of Things* (1955) take its modest place in the discourse of modern design, lining up behind *The New Vision* and *Vision in Motion* (Moholy-Nagy) as well as *Language of Vision* (Kepes). Since planned obsolescence entailed a *naturalization* of market forces by representing the cyclical dynamics of fashion as evolutionary, it is no surprise to find the organizational techniques of "dynamic equilibrium," refined by the avant-garde, applied here to a branch of the culture industry through a new type of aesthetic engineering dedicated to managing the market, with its most prominent practitioner—Harley Earl—coming straight out of Hollywood itself.

The organism is what made bedfellows of Mies, Geddes, and Harley Earl. For Mies it was the "skin and bones" transparency of a building that achieved organicity by exposing the fundamentals of the building's production and its aspirations to universality.[29] For the streamliners, the organicity of machines lay in the capacity of the skin to organize the interior in response to external forces, thus reversing Mies's inside-out organicism in the name of a process of integration moving outside in. And for the GM stylists, annually evolving traces of movement were inscribed onto the skin of the automobile not by aerodynamics but by the winds of change that drove the new nature of the market. The functionalist myth of the machine as organism was

4.9

Raymond Loewy, "Evolution Chart for Automobiles," 1933.

being retooled for commodities like automobiles to advertise their annual adaptations. And the Miesian premise, even when taken to radically negative extremes, was already obsolete. Such were the ins and outs of organisms and machines, images and automobiles, by the time Saarinen completed his work for General Motors.

Beginning with his design for the Cranbrook Academy of Art (1925–1940) and continuing with the many exurban campus plans that followed—including the initial scheme for the General Motors Technical Center—Eero Saarinen's father, Eliel Saarinen, was projecting outward the internal, organic integration promised but not delivered by the new commercial concentrations like Rockefeller Center, displacing it toward the urban and suburban periphery, inside out. In so doing, he took full advantage of the capacity of such campuses, as well as the institutions to which they were dedicated, to exhibit a degree of integration and social authority unattainable in the city.[30] In the suburbs, the elder Saarinen's organicism thus became equivalent to a portentous realism no longer restricted to purely formal expression, since it coincided with the interests of the institutions that it served.[31]

Eliel Saarinen was also the author of two books: *The City: Its Growth, Its Decay, Its Future* (1943) and *The Search for Form in Art and Architecture* (1948). In the former, he offers a nostalgic and commonplace assessment of the coherence of classical and medieval town planning, lamenting its subsequent "decay" in the modern period. The book is permeated by rhetoric relentlessly promoting what Saarinen calls "organic decentralization," backed up by drawings from photomicrographs of healthy and cancerous cells resembling abstract city plans.[32] Saarinen uses this version of the city-as-organism to communicate an extreme nervousness reminiscent of the Garden City movement, bordering on panic in the face of an "urban disease" whose symptoms included "disorganized congestion, decline, dilapidation, blighted areas, and then, slums."[33] The cause, as he saw it, was lack of planning in response to a growth process that had begun to show an inexorable tendency to spread laterally outward from the dying "seeds" or cores of cities. "Organic decentralization" was his prescription.[34]

The formal principles (if not the forms themselves) by which, Saarinen argued, this was to be accomplished were notably similar to those being promoted at the same time in Chicago by figures such as Moholy-Nagy and Kepes:

Organic Style

To begin with, it must be borne in mind that man's knowledge of the construction of the universe, both macrocosmic and microcosmic, has been considerably broadened so as to offer entirely another conception of space and its organization than was man's conception heretofore. Moreover, it must be borne in mind that intercommunication between peoples and thoughts has passed through revolutionary changes. This has been true particularly during the most recent years, when all kinds of communicative means have appeared, both for fast traveling and still faster interchange of thoughts and ideas. One needs only consider the fact that in our days any thought and idea can be flashed in less than a second's time to any corner of this globe, no matter how remote—and one realizes how completely conditions have changed.[35]

The echoes of the new "space conception" announced two years earlier by Giedion in *Space, Time and Architecture* are equally apparent in Saarinen's repeated invocation of a "new form-conception" or a "new form-world." But so are the implications of his organicism, since for Eliel Saarinen "a new form-world needs a freshly new soil from which to grow," purged of the style consciousness of "World's Fairs, Local Fairs, and like spectacular things." In a kind of slum clearance plan for the urban periphery that anticipates urban purges to come, Saarinen announces "necessary cleanings" designed to remove "that dirt and disorder which frequently is spread all around; and . . . all those signs, bill-boards, and like things, such as are displayed along streets and plazas and which, for the most part, are of such a quality as is apt to foster poor taste and cultural degeneration."[36] Saarinen had in mind specifically the outer edges of cities, which represented the promised land of "organic decentralization"— spaces like that later occupied by the General Motors Technical Center, 12 miles outside the center of Detroit. These were the spaces traversed by those users of the new transportation lines (such as highways and railroads) around which the new "form-world" would be built.

According to Saarinen, who had also designed the Helsinki railroad station in 1904:

It has been said that the railroad station is the entrance-gateway of the city of today, and that its architectural forms serve the same purpose in the present-day city as was served by those of the entrance gateway of the olden town—the purpose of favorable impression. This is true when one enters the place by train and one's first impressions are derived from said depot and its perhaps orderly surroundings. But how often does this happen. Impressions are received rather from the wide outskirts, passed mile-by-mile before the station is reached—and what kind of outskirts, alas; notice them with a keen and critical eye. Littered factory grounds and dirty back-yard clutter, old junk, half-rotten fences, sheds leaning precariously, and shattered windows—these are the things displayed for one's enjoyment; and in these beauteous places one can see the unfortunate, dirty, and perhaps diseased slum-dweller. One wonders why it is necessary to advertise one's home-town by such means. Undoubtedly, such conditions are the result of shocking negligence, for at least a semblance of order is not costly. A dirty face is not a matter of money; it is lack of decency.[37]

At the time he wrote these words, Eliel Saarinen's hometown was Detroit. The same city was similarly described by Eero Saarinen ten years later to an audience at a Yale University, though without the malicious disdain for modern cities and their inhabitants exhibited by his father.

The younger Saarinen had been invited to a conference on the topic of "architectural lettering" in November 1953. Among the other participants was Gyorgy Kepes. Saarinen spoke immediately after Kepes, whom he acknowledged as having "stolen the show" by putting the issue of architectural signage in "larger terms." Saarinen continued:

> We have had this microscope put on lettering. But I think there's also another awareness that we can learn from this. We can think of it as the telescope. In other words we can become [aware] of a larger problem through lettering. That larger problem is our whole environment—the twentieth-century environment.... The real environment that our time—our industrial revolution—has created you can see best all outside of Detroit or outside of Chicago. And you see lettering and lettering and lettering; you can see hamburger stands, you can see gas stations, you can see used car lots, and it's really a terrible mess.

He even went so far as to propose a media exchange to take care of this mess: "As far as I'm concerned I would rather see all the signboards taken off our roads and one hundred percent of all the radio time used up for commercials." In fact, the elimination of messy signage turns out to be something of a personal crusade for Eero Saarinen: "I've often said that if I wouldn't be an architect and if I'd had a private income or something, I would like to devote my life to getting all the signs off the roads of America." At this point, in the casual tones of an improvised talk, the organicist diagnosis becomes explicit, as Saarinen caps his observations with an appeal to "eliminate this cancer that our period has created."[38]

Saarinen closes his remarks by proposing that Yale initiate a systematic "study of our environment" to cope with the disease. Perhaps not by chance, this is exactly what Kepes was about to do from his base at MIT. By December 1953, within a month of the conference, Kepes and his MIT colleague, urban planner Kevin Lynch, had drafted a proposal to the Rockefeller Foundation requesting support for a research project dealing with "the relation of the individual to the urban physical environment as directly perceived by the various senses."[39] At the conference Kepes had emphasized the need for street signage to address the modified sensorium of a spectator moving at variable rates, arguing that the proliferation of disarticulated signs that often overtook the buildings on which they were hung threatened architecture's efforts to "organize a continuity."[40]

The grant proposal was successful, and Lynch and Kepes worked on different aspects of the project from 1954 to 1959. One result was the publication of Lynch's book *The Image of the City* (1960), in which Kepes is acknowledged for contributing the book's "underlying concepts."[41] What is important for Lynch in his step-by-step account of the loss and potential restoration of the mobile spectator's orientation in a cityscape dominated by signs is what he calls the city's "imageability."[42] In an echo of the "pattern-seeing" that Kepes sought to bring to the "new landscape" of a technologically mediated nature, Lynch proposes that this formulation would allow architects and urbanists to "learn to see the hidden forms in the vast sprawl of our cities. We are not accustomed to organizing and imaging an artificial environment on such a large scale; yet our activities are pushing us toward that end."[43] Lynch's analysis, with its cynical efforts to restore organicity to the blighted cityscape, thus bears affinities to Eliel Saarinen's acceptance of the inevitability of urban decentralization; similarly, the two find common ground in the treatment of the city as a sequences of visual impressions by Camillo Sitte, to whose work Lynch's has often been compared.

Yet for the most part, the details of Lynch's analysis remained confined to the experience of pedestrians wandering lost in America's downtowns. Another aspect of the Kepes-Lynch research, an analysis of "the perceptual impact of the urban highway on the driver and his passenger,"[44] was more faithful to Eero Saarinen's call at Yale for the systematic study of the exurban environment. Again, this required a media convergence, as drives taken along a number of highways in the northeastern United States were documented in a combination of photographs, motion pictures, and written impressions, in order to "give a picture of the major perceptual elements and how they are organized."[45] The result was to extend Kepes's theories of a mobile spectator moving through an unfamiliar landscape into techniques for the design of America's highways. In all, the automobile had become a machine for the new vision, a vision in motion.

These studies were also made in the context of the ratification of the Interstate Highways Act of 1956—the same year the General Motors Technical Center was completed—which provided for 41,000 miles of new highway to be built with a 90 percent government subsidy. This act was the result of a lobbying effort begun with Futurama at the 1939–1940 World's Fair; the lobbying was led by General Motors, the largest contributor to the American Road Builders Association, an umbrella group formed in 1943. After a decade of intense pressure, the committee set up by President Dwight D. Eisenhower in 1954 to study the need for a federally funded highway system chaired by a member of the General Motors board of directors, Lucius D. Clay, recommended in favor of the idea. The act also drew support from the civil defense community, as Eisenhower's rhetoric made clear: modern highways were necessary, he argued, since "in case of atomic attack on our key cities, the road net must permit quick evacuation of target areas."[46] The 1956 act thus represented a victory for the automobile companies whose hegemony was expressed so thoroughly in the confident campuses being produced for them by architects like Saarinen.[47] The lobbying effort spearheaded by corporations like General Motors reinforced the grip their products already had on the American sense of manifest destiny projected onto the vast, unsettled tracts in the country's heartland.[48]

Likewise, for Kevin Lynch and Gyorgy Kepes, as for Eero Saarinen, the "city of 1960" projected by Geddes's Futurama had arrived. But it was barely a city at all, and more like an endless sprawl of disorderly signs whose capacity to carry cultural meaning was inversely proportional to the extent of its disorganization, a measure that information theorists like Norbert Wiener and students of communication like Marshall McLuhan would recognize in the term *entropy*. And so the organism was called into service as a model. The prophecies of the 1930s, built on images of streamlined organicity, had become the potent nostalgias of the 1950s. This shift was due in no small part to the formidable ability of corporations like General Motors to deploy images to sell machines that were themselves ever-evolving images figured as organisms, and to lobby for the organized construction of infrastructural networks like highways with the help of those same images. Their aim was to create an ever-increasing need for the image machines they were selling, machines through which a new vision would see organized landscapes of images in dynamic equilibrium, in a continuous feedback loop.

But the *production* of the market through the combined strategies of planned obsolescence and planned and packaged manifest destiny was not the only reason for the success of General Motors from the 1930s until its troubles in the 1960s. From the outset, Alfred Sloan was aware of the incompatibility of total redesign with the economics and organization of mass production. Partly by design and partly by default, he and his colleagues opted instead for an elaborate system of interchangeable engine, chassis, and body parts that could be combined and recombined into a variety of makes and models with minimal retooling. At the level of the automobile's mechanism, this interchangeability meant that engineering refinements made in one line could be transferred to the others. At the level of styling it meant just the opposite. Five different lines of clothing could be designed annually for these engines, based on different combinations of standard body parts. Each would impart a separate identity to the Buick, Cadillac, Chevrolet, Oldsmobile, and Pontiac lines, thus achieving the marketing ideal of product differentiation while preserving the advantages of product standardization.[49] All this required that the organization of the corporation itself be modified, since such a complex process demanded adaptability at every step along the way—a flexible attitude of mutual accommodation between styling, research, development, engineering, production, marketing, and finance.

By 1946, the year after the Technical Center project was announced, these principles were recorded by the economist Peter Drucker in *Concept of the Corporation,* a landmark paean to free-market corporatism based on his analysis of General Motors's organizational policies in a report commissioned by the company in 1943. Drucker gives the broad outlines of GM's structure of centralized management and decentralized operations, emphasizing the self-conscious nature of the company's role as a social institution in which the individual parts are subordinated to the logic of the whole. No mere assembly of machinelike workers and aloof executives indifferent to the needs of the public, no rigid abstraction, Drucker's corporation was in some sense alive: "General Motors is a functioning and moving organization of human beings and not a static blueprint."[50] In other words, General Motors is an organism.

According to Drucker, General Motors pursued decentralization to establish a more direct relation between the individual production unit and the market, thereby enabling production methods and priorities to be adjusted in communication with central management, according to market pressures. Reciprocally, "Central management not only delimits the divisions against each other, it fits them into a general pattern as part of a unified corporation."[51] In his speech at the dedication of the Technical Center, GM president Curtice also underlined the interdependence of GM's divisions, emphasizing that "[t]he result is that the whole is greater than the sum of its parts."[52] Again according to Drucker, this same principle of integration into the whole, applied to the workforce, made General Motors a model for social organization in general. As evidence he cited the Hawthorne experiments, from which the postwar practitioners of human relations drew many of their conclusions on the effects of workplace psychology and social integration on productivity. According to Drucker, Hawthorne provided firm evidence that productivity depended less on the relative monotony of the work or the environmental conditions under which it was performed than on the worker's satisfaction at feeling a part of a greater whole, achieved through recognition of the worker's contribution to the overall production process.[53]

The coordination of GM's product lines to maximize interchangeability without threatening product identity was thus made possible by the organizational structure celebrated by Drucker as a model of social integration. The evolution of each car's image was centrally controlled by the stylists in consultation with engineering and with management, while production and distribution were decentralized. At its most efficient, the entire assembly performed as a single, integrated unit, assimilating its workers into the complex process of producing surface effects as though they occurred naturally. Styling decisions in one line were coordinated with decisions made in another, in order to minimize the retooling of dies in each factory. In turn, the machinery was designed to maximize flexibility in the range of forms and parts it was able to produce without comprehensive overhaul. As Sloan explained, "engineering and production have adapted to the requirements of styling as styling adapted to mass production."[54]

This same flexibility contributed to GM's success in changing over from automobile production to military production beginning in 1940. The company continued to earn profits during the war, while by 1944 the pent-up civilian demand for automobiles (which had all but ceased production) made it clear to General Motors management that the war's conclusion would be accompanied by vast market opportunities. To capitalize on that demand the company developed a comprehensive reorganization plan, which included a new "technical center" first proposed by Sloan and Charles F. Kettering, his research-oriented vice president, in 1944. The Technical Center was to be a corporate campus devoted to the integration and coordination of scientific and technical research with styling, in line with the policy of centralized image management.

Organic Style

On 24 July 1945, General Motors thus announced its intention to build a state-of-the-art technical facility outside Detroit. A model and renderings of the proposed project by Saarinen, Swanson & Associates were unveiled at a luncheon at the Waldorf-Astoria in New York; Sloan, Kettering, Harley Earl, Eliel Saarinen, his partner Robert Swanson, and Eero Saarinen were present, along with other General Motors executives.

The Research, Advanced Engineering, Process Development, and Styling Sections of the corporation were to be housed at the center. By consolidating these, Sloan and Kettering hoped to generate a more rapid translation from scientific and technological research to practical application. The war had seen vast new technological developments on all fronts; GM was now competing with enlarged aerospace and communications industries for military contracts, and was under heavy pressure to put scientific discoveries to practical use as quickly as possible. Meanwhile, styling (known internally as the "beauty parlor") continued to play a pivotal role in General Motors' commercial operations, as a means of educating the consumer's eye to favor GM products.[55]

Earl himself was made responsible for selecting the architect for the Technical Center project. On his recommendation, in 1945 General Motors contracted with Eliel Saarinen and Robert Swanson to complete a feasibility study for the complex.[56] Hugh Ferriss's renderings of the resulting scheme show a sweeping, streamlined campus surrounding a large artificial lake. Designed by Eliel Saarinen with his son's collaboration, it consisted of four building clusters: administration, research laboratories, advanced engineering, and styling. This fragment of Futurama was dedicated to the movement of motorists circulating on the periphery and around the lake; its forms demonstrate the acceptance of streamlined design into mainstream architectural production by that time. But its formal continuities must also be understood in terms of

4.10

Eliel Saarinen, General Motors Technical Center, Warren, Michigan, 1945. Original scheme. Rendering by Hugh Ferriss.

Eliel Saarinen's efforts to integrate mechanization with an archaic organicity, where the speed of the automobile is tempered by contemplative workspaces bearing traces of a crafts-based *Gemeinschaft* along the lines of the Cranbrook Academy, or of the much earlier Saarinen family studio/house in Finland, Hvitträsk. Seen within such a context, and within the elder Saarinen's organicist discourse on the city, this project can from its inception be understood as an effort to invest the empty automobile-scape of outer Detroit—the kind of space he found littered with the "indecency" of disorderly signage and the underclass—with a form of mythic enchantment proper to what he had termed "organic decentralization."

Eliel Saarinen's streamlined materialization of speed, with automobile traffic separated off from the covered walk, collects the corporation's various constituent parts into a unified totality in a "campus-like atmosphere" for which the Saarinen firm was already well known, anticipating (GM president) Curtice's characterization of the final project in those terms more than a decade later. Moreover, this same subordination of the individual building to the legibility of a greater whole would be a worthy response to Lynch's call for visual urban unity, while bearing the distinct markings of the "metamorphosis of forms" that Manfredo Tafuri finds in Eliel Saarinen's second-prize winning entry in the 1922 *Chicago Tribune* tower competition. But here it also becomes evident why the failure of such efforts as the latter to reorganize the downtown commercial center cannot, as Tafuri suggests, be traced to the restriction of their "organic logic" to the merely formal, indifferent to the laissez-faire economics of a city of self-contained objects.

Even in this early, unrealized scheme for the Technical Center, organicist urbanism did not fail. It succeeded, precisely because its stylized formal recognition of an integrated dynamism, which was also incorporated into its planning, was coterminous with the image-based marketing and management practices of its client. Already by the mid-1940s, such corporations were being seen not as *constituents of* society, and thus active participants in the urban spectacle, but rather as *models for* society and thus for the organization of the exurban landscape. Here, at the level of the corporate organism, the myths of "human relations" and "organic decentralization" coincide. Rather than witnessing a heroic struggle of the integrated organism *against* the market, we are witnessing here their mutual implication in a fully naturalized corporate ecosystem of ever-evolving images.

Following the announcement of the Saarinen scheme, development of the Technical Center project was interrupted by the nationwide auto workers strike in 1945. By the time design was resumed the project had become the responsibility of Eero Saarinen, whose career in his father's office had been interrupted by only two outside jobs: four weeks spent in the office of Norman Bel Geddes during the 1930s and a period of consulting to the Office of Strategic Services in the U.S. War Department from 1944 to 1945, during which he became familiar with logistical techniques involving troop communication, supply, and deployment.[57] Eliel Saarinen remained involved in the project until his death in 1950; and although his son articulated the project in architectural terms different from his own, the initial organization remained intact and its efforts at spatial integration were, if anything, pursued even more vigorously.

Under the younger Saarinen, in association with the Detroit architectural and engineering firm of Smith, Hinchman & Grylls, the scheme underwent a series of significant modifications that strengthened the original commitment to organizational continuity. The lake remained but was transformed in the second iteration in 1949 into an elongated rectangle surrounded by a series of low, rectangular buildings clustered together in five groups: research, service, process development, engineering, and styling. A stand-alone cafeteria overlooked a pedestrian courtyard, and a central administration building was poised on stilts on a promontory jutting into the lake. The architecture was now one of rigorous, mechanical repetition carried on horizontal bars sliding past one another; it absorbed the influence of Mies and of the industrial archi-

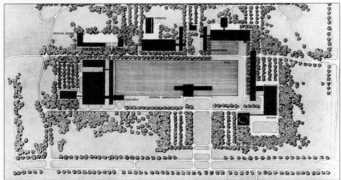

4.11

Eero Saarinen and Eliel Saarinen, General Motors Technical Center, Warren, Michigan, 1949. Intermediate scheme, rendering.

4.12

Eero Saarinen and Eliel Saarinen, General Motors Technical Center, Warren, Michigan, 1949. Intermediate scheme, site plan.

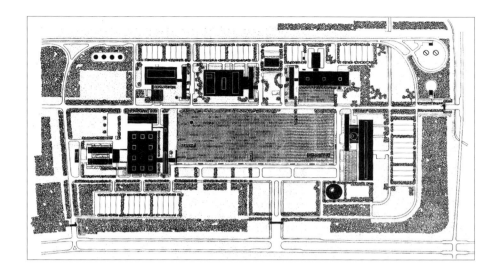

tecture of Saarinen family friend Albert Kahn,[58] but it also refined the strategy of integrating the parts into a dynamic, dispersed whole. In the final scheme, the basic dispensation of elements remained the same but the central administration building was eliminated, contributing to the dissolution of large-scale administrative hierarchies in favor of lateral integration.

The first cluster of buildings to be constructed was the engineering group, completed in 1951. Like the others, it consisted of several rectangular buildings differentiated according to function—in this case, a shop, a dynamometer building, and a three-story office building, all connected by attenuated passageways. The entire grouping was planned on a 5′ 2″ module, which allowed larger offices than were usual, while also accommodating nonstandard 5-foot fluorescent tube lighting in a specially designed modular ceiling grid with nodes at each intersection for a high-pressure air-conditioning system developed earlier by Smith, Hinchman & Grylls. The office building was framed by long-span three-dimensional trusses supported on hollow, rectangular steel columns composed of two angles tip-to-tip and clad in black; these were spaced at 5′ 2″ intervals along the external walls, with brightly glazed brick end walls. The result was a column-free space subdivided with custom-designed movable metal partitions. Its skin effectively incorporated the structure into its curtainlike thinness.

A three-story bright aluminum frame with matte black aluminum column covers and 2-inch panels with honeycomb insulation sandwiched between porcelain-glazed

4.13
Eero Saarinen, General Motors Technical Center, Warren, Michigan, 1956. Final scheme, site plan. Clockwise from left: research, service, process development, restaurant, engineering, styling.

Organic Style

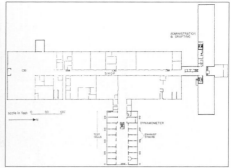

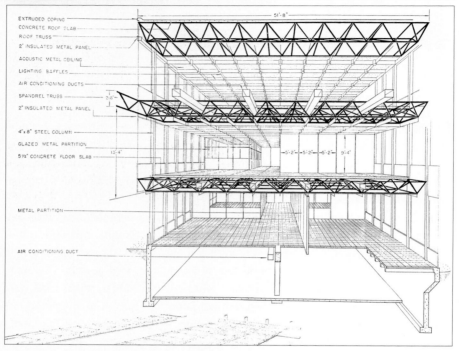

4.14
(top left) Eero Saarinen, engineering group, General Motors Technical Center, Warren, Michigan, 1951. Administration wing. Photograph by Ezra Stoller.

4.15
(top right) Eero Saarinen, engineering group, General Motors Technical Center, Warren, Michigan, 1951. Plan.

4.16
Eero Saarinen, engineering group, General Motors Technical Center, Warren, Michigan, 1951. Sectional perspective.

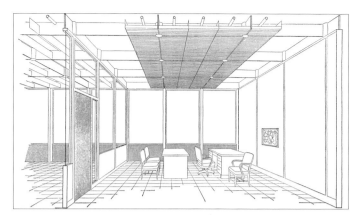

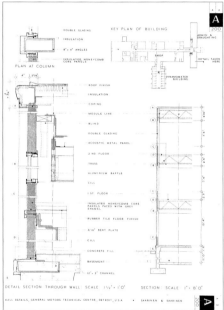

4.17
Eero Saarinen, engineering group, General Motors Technical Center, Warren, Michigan, 1951. Typical office interior.

4.18
(bottom left) Eero Saarinen, engineering group, General
Motors Technical Center, Warren, Michigan, 1951. Curtain
wall details.

4.19
(bottom right) Eero Saarinen, with Smith, Hinchman &
Grylls, General Motors Technical Center, Warren, Michigan,
1956. Luminous modular ceiling. Photograph by Ezra
Stoller.

Organic Style

steel sheets, all suspended under a rounded, bright aluminum coping set off with black trim—these were the components of this proto-curtain wall with its integral structure. In addition to reflecting the project's organizational system, it synthesized a number of technical advances, including the metal panels and the solar-resistant glass. In many instances, the Technical Center served as a laboratory in which new products later introduced into the postwar construction industry were proto-typed and tested, at times with the direct participation of General Motors technical personnel. For example, the caulking that held the metal panels in their frames began to fail as the next set of buildings, the research complex, was being designed. A new detail was developed in collaboration with General Motors engineers: a neoprene gasket like those already in use on automobile windshields, easy to install and remove with its integral neoprene "zipper" compression seal, manufactured by a General Motors subsidiary. Other technical innovations underwritten by GM included the glazed brick on the buildings' end walls (developed in collaboration with a Cranbrook ceramicist, thus underlining the debt to the crafts tradition) and the luminous ceiling. The development of the latter culminated in a ceiling of curved, translucent plastic pans and linear baffles that diffused the fluorescent light for better viewing of the automobile finishes in the styling studios and elsewhere.

In the research administration building, the most visible of the research buildings that were next in the construction sequence, the planning module that was thenceforth to organize nearly all of the center's two million square feet was adjusted to 5' 0". A long, three-story rectangular bar spanning the northern edge of the artificial lake, the building contained mostly offices with modular metal and wood partitions strung along a double-loaded corridor. The structure repeated that of its predecessor, except that the columns embedded in the exterior walls were now spaced at 10 feet on center and supported conventional steel framing, while the extruded aluminum frame had acquired thinner lines. The exterior wall therefore remained a hybrid: part suspended curtain wall and part expressed structure, all in an alternating rhythm pulsing along the sheer grayish-bluish-greenish skin. Next were constructed a series of special-purpose buildings again on the 5-foot module, with the process development and service administration buildings returning to 5-foot structural bays incorporated into their surface articulation.

The sleekness and efficiency with which Saarinen accommodated his client's complex functional requirements while providing a coherent image of technical virtuosity and stylish, forward-looking optimism would later draw these remarks from Banham: "When you see client-orientation of this kind you realize there was no irony in [Saarinen's] work for GM at all—it was the building Harley Earl wanted. Like a good advertising agency, Eero really serviced his clients, and in finding for them the 'unique solution,' he did, fairly painlessly and without short-calling anybody's cultural standards, exactly what David Ogilvy has to knock himself out to do in advertising— he bestowed status, improved the image."[59]

4.20

    Eero Saarinen, research group, General Motors Technical Center, Warren, Michigan, 1953. Photograph by Ezra Stoller.

4.21

    Eero Saarinen, process development group, General Motors Technical Center, Warren, Michigan, ca. 1954. Photograph by Ezra Stoller.

Eero Saarinen, styling group, General Motors Technical Center, Warren, Michigan, 1956. Photograph by Ezra Stoller.

The styling complex in which Harley Earl and his staff were housed was the last of the major components to be realized. It may not have been exactly what he had in mind, but it did come closer still to the stylized exteriors of GM's cars.[60] Saarinen's version was another group of low rectangular structures anchored by a linear administration wing. The styling complex contained separate design studios for each of GM's divisions, plus a color-matching studio and other design facilities. Here the structure returned to the 10-foot spacing but retreated behind the skin at the upper two levels; its largely transparent lower story revealed a lobby designed to permit the display of automobiles, repeating the configuration of Futurama's "Automobile Display Salon." By now the aluminum frame had acquired thinner lines; at the first floor the glazing was set back to the column faces, while at the top, the protruding coping found on the earlier buildings was now set back so as to be invisible from below. The result was a tightly stretched skin no longer bracketed between columns or capped off at the sky—pure "curtain" at the upper two stories, concealing the structure behind an orchestrated rhythm of reflections, color, and glare.

In his written comments on the project Saarinen paid homage to Mies, referring to the "purity" of the latter's walls and the "clarity of the structure."[61] But this was no simple repetition of the IIT campus at a grand scale. Ultimately, Saarinen's repetitive curtain walls owe more to Mies's Lake Shore Drive apartment buildings in Chicago, which present an optically variable skin to passing motorists, than they do to the pedestrian-oriented planning and details of the IIT campus. Despite Saarinen's claims, what "clarity of structure" there is derives from the subordination of the structural frame to the regime of the module, made most explicit in the styling complex.

Saarinen's own assessment of the project emphasized its qualities as a flexible but unified system that could be expanded and altered at will. In his words, "maximum flexibility" was its imperative.[62] With its modular partitions and luminous ceiling grids mapped onto the rhythms of the exterior walls, this project was an immense logistical and management exercise steered by Saarinen and General Motors together. Designed by an architect who as a consultant to the U.S. Army had been responsible for depicting graphically the logistics of military staffing, this system materialized GM's corporate image-management process in a network of interchangeable parts. What Saarinen called the "architecture of metal, of repetitious metal, in a sense in character with what General Motors stands for"[63] enabled him to impart visual *and* organizational unity to the entire complex, while also making it possible to mark crucial differences between the separate functions of this productive nerve center with distinctive lobbies—especially in the research and styling buildings, with their glistening ornamental staircases designed by Kevin Roche. The module also allowed Saarinen to experiment with surface treatment on different buildings in an overall evolution toward a skin purified of all traces of the structural frame, leaving the modular curtain wall free to declare its authority over all internal organization.

No longer confined to its original streamlined shell, this updated Futurama followed the logic of decentralization that it served: it extended itself horizontally, devoting its sprawling acreage entirely to the automobile's velocity, which nevertheless threatened to break it apart. And so, according to Saarinen, "our most important problem was to hold the whole project together, and thus the pools of water, thus the color, thus the modular that runs through all parts, thus the masses of the buildings, and the way the landscaping was designed. All was done for the purpose of [a] sort of unity of one total environment."[64] In this manner, Eliel Saarinen's earlier experiments with urban waterfronts were absorbed into a complex that produced its own waterfront in order to turn itself inward, referring itself to the controlled movements of a spectator looking through a windshield and cruising around the lake. In Saarinen's words, the Technical Center was a "group of buildings where the horizontal dimension was 10 or 20 times that of the normal relationship between horizontal and vertical in any grouping of buildings." Like the "longer and lower" automobiles designed by Earl, the GM complex had speed literally built into it. So in a gesture toward the compatibility of the modular pattern with the speed of the automobile, Saarinen named 30 miles per hour as the privileged vantage point for the ensemble, while elsewhere pointing to "the unification of the whole group into essentially one kind of architecture so that not only at the instantaneous vision but also in memory vision the group held together."[65]

What Saarinen called "memory vision" was, in principle, a transposition of the physiological phenomenon of the persistence of vision responsible for the illusion of cinematic movement onto the architecture.[66] In that regard, it is completely consistent

4.23

Eero Saarinen, research group, General Motors Technical Center, Warren, Michigan, 1953. Lobby with stair. Photograph by Ezra Stoller.

with the methods later proposed by Kepes at the Yale conference to organize the urban and exurban visual field. Saarinen's module sought to prepare the architectural
surface to integrate fleeting optical effects into an organized system reminiscent of
the "virtual volumes" produced photographically by Moholy-Nagy and reproduced in
Roche's staircase in the research lobby. But this organism was empty, its central organizing element—the artificial lake—ultimately too feeble to protect it from intrusion
from without, the intrusion of an exurban emptiness spilling over from the peripheral
parking lots. In the end, the nature at the center of the General Motors Technical Center turned out to be dead, dried up. The coiling of the complex around the lake in order to preserve the interiority of a corporate organism torn from the commercial
downtown and relocated at the periphery was itself turned inside out by the automobile. This double inversion was marked by the empty surfaces of the buildings parked
like cars along the side of a highway, and it was reflected in the surfaces of the cars
driving by.

Only two elements stood out in this landscape. One was a stainless steel-clad
water tower, and the other was the low, flat, aluminum-clad styling dome. At Earl's request, the auditorium required to present and exhibit the new styles was designed
primarily to highlight the surface effects to which the annual model change was dedicated. The reflectivity of the General Motors cars, with their chrome trim and bright
colors, required an even lighting, and Saarinen's problem was that the inevitable joints
between lighting elements suspended in a rectilinear shell would be reflected by
the car bodies. The design went through a series of permutations, including a tentlike

4.24

Eero Saarinen, General Motors Technical Center, Warren,
Michigan, 1956. Styling dome, right. Photograph by Ezra
Stoller.

4.25

Eero Saarinen, styling dome, General Motors Technical
Center, Warren, Michigan, 1956. Interior.

4.26

Skidmore, Owings & Merrill, United States Air Force Academy, Colorado Springs, 1958. Photograph by Hedrich-
Blessing.

version that ultimately became an indirectly lit dome, inspired in part by a similar dome in teardrop form at the plant of a fabricator of steel water towers.[67] The final structure was a 65-foot-high shell with a 188-foot diameter, made of welded steel plate $3/8$ inch thick. General Motors and Saarinen proclaimed in unison that this structural steel shell was "as thin in relation to [its] area as $1/30$ of an egg shell would be to its area,"[68] with Norman Bel Geddes and D'Arcy Thompson not far behind.

Like D'Arcy Thompson's gridded organisms, the dome's reflective exterior sheathing registered the movements around it. As a critic of the period observed, "Its surface is aluminum, reflecting the sky and therefore always alive with light and even with movement when there are clouds."[69] It also signaled its function: to provide a reflective surface that would distribute light evenly over the automobiles housed inside. This was accomplished by cladding the inside of the dome with a perforated stainless steel skin onto which was projected an infinitely variable range of lighting effects. It was an architectural egg evolved to structural perfection; inside, the automobile industry's reliance on styling was underscored by an elevated stage with three turntables—a runway for displaying the "dream cars" designed to whet the public appetite for next year's model.

"An automobile is essentially a colored mirror which reflects its source of light." This was how General Motors described its products in relation to the dome designed for them.[70] The design and engineering of such mirrors formed the bulk of the work performed at the Technical Center. Like the stylized skin encountered by Mies in Roche's Chevrolet, Saarinen's surfaces, too, worked together to generate the image of an integrated corporate whole. In this system of mirrors, consumers were meant to see themselves endlessly reflected and changing annually—evolving, even—in the great stream of technological progress carrying America into the future.

That techniques genealogically affiliated with those used by Saarinen at General Motors were applied in equal measure (and at approximately the same time) by Skidmore, Owings & Merrill to a corporate headquarters for the Connecticut General Life Insurance Company and to the United States Air Force Academy reminds us once again of the mutability of the organizational complex, and further confirms the growing indistinction of boundaries between the military, industry, and the university, as each sought out the services of organicist integration.[71] At General Motors, the anatomy of this open-ended organizational system is inventoried by the statistics compiled by the company to describe its scope, while its physiognomy is given by the curtain wall, an infinitely repeatable surface designed to mirror the infinitely variable desires of a corporate subject—the consumer of planned obsolescence—peering into and through the glass at 30 miles per hour. It is in this sense that Saarinen's architecture and the practices of his client coincide at the Technical Center. Together, they were devoted to the production and maintenance of an integrated organism that had incorporated into itself the logic of style.

5

Computer Architectures

In the section of his compilation of scientific photographs in *The New Landscape in Art and Science* (1956) devoted to the "modulation of signals," Gyorgy Kepes included several oscilloscope images that recorded graphically the output of different kinds of computers. A series of luminous spirals registered the continuous processes of an analog machine, while patterns of dots linked up into similar lines registered the discontinuous actions of a digital machine. Kepes commented in this section of the book:

> Instruments bring us fresh knowledge of the world and further control over nature. With instruments we are gradually finding a common denominator in all sensed experience; it is possible to convert sound to sight, space to time, light to form, and interchange phases and events, static and dynamic, sensible and

Computer Architectures

conceptual. Through modulation of signals we extend experience, letting the blind see, the deaf hear. We can introduce new
relations into any set of signals—extending, condensing, dis-
torting, magnifying, reducing. By feeding punched cards into
electronic devices linked to atomic power we might alter our environment to an extent limited only by our own imagination.[1]

He used the term *modulation* here to describe the conversion of one form of
sensory information, conceived in the terms of information theory as a "signal," into
another. For Kepes, patterns of data like those punched into what were called "IBM
cards" and fed into the powerful new computers that were just coming onto the market made visible what was invisible. Those who could read them were thereby em-
powered with supranatural capabilities on the order of "atomic power." But what is
only barely discernible here is another media translation, another modulation, in
which representations of the internal processes of computers are accorded a status
equivalent to the representations of natural phenomena collected in that section and

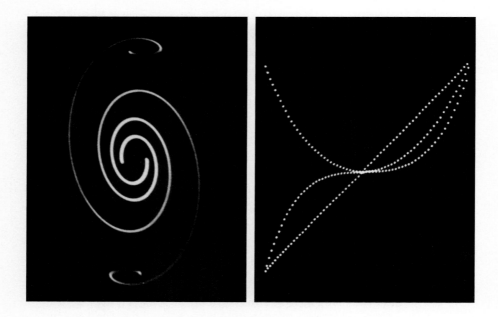

5.1
Oscilloscope pattern of an analog computer. From Gyorgy
Kepes, *The New Landscape in Art and Science* (1956), 180.

5.2
Cathode-ray oscilloscope display of a problem being solved
by a digital computer. From Gyorgy Kepes, *The New Landscape in Art and Science* (1956), 183.

throughout the book. Keeping in mind the neurological terminology that permeated the early discourse on computers, we can say that Kepes treats the "thought" processes of computers as natural equivalents to the hidden properties of minerals or of organisms made visible under the regime of "modulation." Alive or dead, machine or organism—all is pattern, transmitted as signal, measured against noise.

5.1

In a publicity booklet released in 1955, the International Business Machines Corporation reminded visitors to its plants as well as potential employees that "IBM first came into your life when your birth was recorded on a punched card. From then on many such cards have been compiled, giving a lifetime of history of your important decisions and actions. If you went to school, entered a hospital, bought a house, paid income tax, got married or purchased an automobile, the chances are that permanent punched records were made of these and other personal stories."[2] Any and all social transactions had thus become convertible into patterns of holes stored in a database. Each transaction a different pattern. All of them together: "you."

But should we be surprised by this capillary penetration of corporate data collection techniques, and the controls they imply, into the deep recesses of "personal" experience? No, since the countless modular office buildings that followed the examples set by Eero Saarinen, Skidmore, Owings & Merrill, and others throughout the 1950s had simultaneously begun to stage this process in reverse. They offered a potentially infinite mutability, in which the architectural module was a unit of variable content (partitions, glazing, lighting, etc.) through which spatial identification with— and the visual identity of—the integrated system of the corporation was engineered. Corporations like IBM linked modulated flexibility with organicist notions of open-ended yet controlled growth, correlated with pseudo-freedoms of self-realization within a flexible framework. Thus corporate identities, consolidated into integrated wholes with unpredictable needs, were made up of modular, patterned units of variable content. And the "individuals" inhabiting these units were the prototypical subjects of an organizational regime—subjects without an inside, whose own identities consisted of patterns of holes punched into an IBM card.

For example: IBM's brochure identifying the human with the punched card from birth was circulated on the occasion of an announcement, in early 1956, of the company's plans to construct a large new manufacturing plant in Rochester, Minnesota. Eero Saarinen was to be the architect of the plant, which was to be one of several new

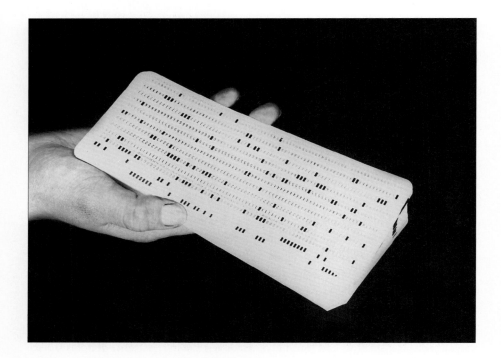

facilities that IBM planned to build as it decentralized its functions and sought to establish a corporate presence beyond the northeastern United States. Upon the plant's completion in 1958, as part of a systematic effort to solicit the approval of the local community, IBM circulated in Rochester a punched card onto which was printed data about the corporation and the plant. The device was clear. For subjects whose identity was constructed as patterns in a card, IBM presented itself as a corporation whose own identity could be recorded in a similar card, and so on. Caught somewhere in this transaction—a transaction between IBM, its employees, and its publics—was Saarinen's building.

The building itself seems simple enough: a sprawling two-story steel structure, wrapped on all sides with a 5/16″ thick two-tone blue skin composed of porcelain enamel aluminum panels laminated to both sides of a cement asbestos core, locked into place between slender aluminum vertical members with a neoprene zipper gasket also designed to accept the 5/16″ glazing arranged in horizontal bands. Indeed, in many ways this wall is all there was to the administrative, manufacturing, and educational facility designed by Eero Saarinen & Associates between 1956 and 1958. Despite the rhetoric of U-values and "overall wall performance" utilized by Saarinen's

5.3
"A person's first 'IBM' record—THE VITAL STATISTICS CARD
TO RECORD HIS BIRTH." From IBM Corporation, "IBM:
People . . . Products . . . Progress" (1955).

associate John Dinkeloo in his reply to readers of *Progressive Architecture*'s June 1957 news survey that celebrated the IBM wall's thinness,[3] its most noticeable attribute was its colorful pattern. Set against the 4-foot planning module registered in the spacing of the vertical supports, each panel was composed of a one-third/two-thirds rhythm of alternating fields of light and dark blue, offset above and below the continuous bands of tinted glazing. As we have seen, the neoprene gasket was originally adapted from automobile windshields, in a 1953 collaboration with General Motors engineers, for Saarinen's General Motors Technical Center.[4] This time, however, Saarinen carried the logic of the GM curtain wall to a provisional conclusion, reducing its thickness dramatically and allowing the wall's colors to drift in and out of each panel's frame, in frank acknowledgment of the variability of surface effect achieved by a technically refined enclosure system into which was condensed a simple imperative: make the thinnest wall possible.[5]

When read through the archives of the architectural profession—including such items as the *Progressive Architecture* news report and the extant documentation of Saarinen's activities and intentions—the bravado of the wafer-thin IBM wall set against the harsh Minnesota winter would seem to represent only the latest step in an irresistible march toward optimizing construction technologies in which the Saarinen office played a significant role, in particular through the expertise of figures like Dinkeloo. Maximize performance and minimize material cost and erection time, all to maximum aesthetic effect. The wall's thinness might also be seen as belonging to a project of dematerialization associated with the reflectivity and transparency of many

5.4

Eero Saarinen, IBM manufacturing and training facility, Rochester, Minnesota, 1958. Photograph by Balthazar Korab.

Computer Architectures

5.5
Eero Saarinen, IBM manufacturing and training facility,
Rochester, Minnesota, 1958. Curtain wall. Photograph by
Balthazar Korab.

curtain walls and—through a common commitment to image-based communication—with postindustrial capital and media technologies, both realms in which Saarinen's client was prominent.

Saarinen's own unpublished remarks on the project are consistent with his facility for converting architectural problems like enclosure systems into representations of corporate identity. Indeed, they suggest that we may very well be witnessing
the devolution of architectonic research into an efficient sound bite: "The vibrancy
of the two blues, which helps avoid monotony at close view, changes when seen from
the distance. Then the total effect is a dark blue band making a transition from the
tawny-green, rolling landscape to the sky. In winter, the blue vibrates with greater in-
tensity against the snowscape. The result is a building made up logically and appropriately for IBM of precise, machine-manufactured parts[.]"[6] In this light, Saarinen's

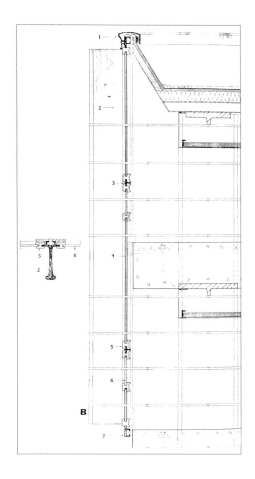

5.6

Eero Saarinen, IBM manufacturing and training facility,

Rochester, Minnesota, 1958. Curtain wall details.

vibrating blue band appears as nothing short of a skillful consolidation of nature and culture: from the mystique of the ineffable, deep horizon to the mystique of Big Blue.

To be sure, by 1958 IBM had not yet acquired the nickname uncannily encoded in Saarinen's wall, although the process of remaking the company's image had begun. Indeed, rather than merely dematerializing the industrial object into the ethereal, dissimulating haze of corporate spectacle, the thinness of Saarinen's wall and the primacy of its patterns substituted for the reassuring solidity of structure a *modulation,* in which organizational logics are programmed into the very substance of the building itself. In order to recognize this substitution, we must seek out evidence of a complex series of exchanges among *different* technological processes, including the cladding of a building, the organization and public image of a corporation, and the design of that corporation's products.

The choice of Saarinen as the architect for the Minnesota facility was itself part of an overall reorganization of IBM's corporate image, initiated in 1954 by the company's president and later chief executive officer, Thomas J. Watson Jr., and coordinated by the architect and industrial designer Eliot Noyes. In an effort to distinguish himself from his famous father, and to demonstrate his own sense of direction for the company, Watson hired Noyes—a former Air Force acquaintance—as a general consultant with the title "director of design." Noyes was responsible for overseeing the design of everything with the IBM name on it, from business machines to letterhead to buildings; he instituted companywide policies intended to heighten awareness of modern design precepts and to unify the company image. Toward those ends, he brought in Paul Rand to redesign IBM's logotype and graphics, and he proposed architects for IBM's new buildings. Saarinen, whose work with Charles Eames had already

5.7
Eero Saarinen, IBM manufacturing and training facility, Rochester, Minnesota, 1958. Photograph by Balthazar Korab.

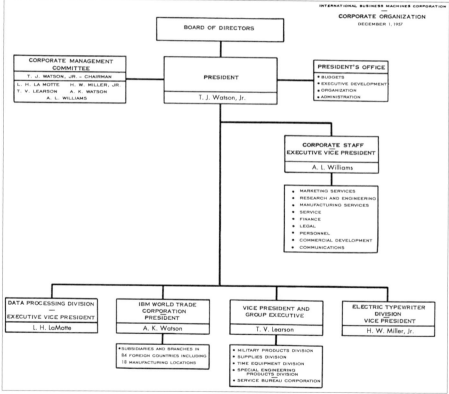

5.8

IBM official photograph of Thomas J. Watson Sr., late 1940s. Photograph by Yousuf Karsh.

5.9

IBM Corporation, organization chart, December 1957.

been awarded a prize in the Museum of Modern Art "Organic Design" furniture competition run by Noyes in 1941, and who had just completed the much-acclaimed General Motors project, was later to be joined by Marcel Breuer, Gordon Bunshaft, Ludwig Mies van der Rohe, and other architects to design major new IBM buildings.

By 1955, riding the wave of war-related advances in information-processing technologies, IBM sales were growing at close to 20 percent per year. This growth translated into a major building campaign to accommodate expansion from the original headquarters in Endicott, New York, westward, southward, and eventually overseas, as well as into a comprehensive overhaul of its internal organizational structure. Until 1956, IBM basically followed a centralized chain of command under the leadership of Thomas J. Watson Sr.; according to his son and successor, "our way of getting things done consisted mostly of wisdom carried in a few people's heads." Thus the younger Watson declared defiantly that "I remember the first thing we did [upon his ascension] was to break Dad's taboo against organization charts."[7] Not long after Noyes was appointed (consultant) director of design, a new "director of organization" was appointed, and the process of decentralization was begun.[8]

Watson observed, "Dad must have felt as if IBM wasn't entirely his anymore—but I didn't feel as if it were mine, either."[9] Indeed, more than just another Oedipal conflict, this family drama substantially reconfigured the channels and relations of power within the company. Although Watson replaced his father atop the corporate leadership, that position was no longer properly patriarchal. No less than all the other so-called IBMers under him, Thomas J. Watson Jr. became a component (albeit a key one) in a complex system designed to regulate its own functioning and growth.[10]

Listing the old practices in IBM branch offices dedicated to the maintenance of corporate unity, practices that his new program replaced—company songs, banners, slogans—Watson also recalls "a photograph of Dad in every room."[11] Written above this image was the company command, which was eventually to apply equally to its machines and its employees: "Think." Watson Sr.'s photograph-as-corporate logo was thus already identified with the primary productive activity of the company, thought itself. Watson Jr. simply replaced his father and his photograph with new managerial techniques, including nonfigurative, decentralized, modernist forms of image management.[12] In his words, "I decided I could put my stamp on IBM through modern design."[13] The initiative was modeled on that of the Olivetti Corporation, whose recently opened New York showroom, designed in 1954 by the Milan-based BBPR Studio, had so impressed Watson that he had traveled to Italy to meet with Adriano Olivetti to discuss the program.[14]

In 1955, after further consideration of Olivetti design provoked by an IBM executive in Holland, Watson organized an executive retreat to compare IBM's design program with that of other companies. The retreat coincided with the production of the

IBM IBM

700 series of business machines, referred to by Watson as "our first family of computers," which according to him "seemed from the inside design to be the very epitome
of modern technology." Consequently, "we thought it was time for the outside to
match the inside."[15] The mandate given to Eliot Noyes, then, was to oversee the redesign of the corporation's products and buildings in order to convert a technologically unified "family" into a visually unified one. Significantly, this visual unity was fully
operative, in the sense that it was expected to *produce* organized integration even as it
represented it.

In addition to hiring Charles Eames and the critic Edgar Kaufmann Jr. as general
design consultants to the director, one of Noyes's earliest moves in his new role was to
bring in Paul Rand to coordinate IBM's typographic output. Rand's first contribution
was an IBM logo in a bolder typeface that permitted more variation in spacing and col-
oring, thus making it more adaptable to use in a wider range of situations. In this manner, the organicist mandate of "flexibility" at work in modular planning attended the
redesign of IBM even at the scale of its letterhead.[16] This, coupled with Rand's own definition of the logo's function—"a logo does not sell (directly), it *identifies*"[17]—further
confirmed the functionality of the corporate image as a technological effect designed
to produce in turn a coherent identity. Rand had acquired a predilection for modular
thinking from the writings of Le Corbusier, whom he had met while traveling in Europe;[18] and if his modular logo had anything to do with the architectural reproportion-
ing of the human body visible in the logo Le Corbusier invented for "Le Modulor," it
was through a common commitment to identifying a constituency for modern design. For Le Corbusier this constituency was condensed into a heroic male profile submitted to the proportions of the Golden Section. For Rand the IBM logo, like the IBM
punched card, encoded the abstract, modulated identity of a lonely crowd working for
the company and mapped by its machines into patterns of holes. It was the password
into the soul of the IBMer.[19]

5.10

Paul Rand, IBM logotype (two versions), 1956.

Computer Architectures

In *The Organization Man*, William H. Whyte Jr. cites Sloan Wilson's 1955 novel *The Man in the Gray Flannel Suit* (at the time being turned into a film starring Gregory Peck) when he characterizes the "well-rounded man." That is the man who doesn't sacrifice wife and family for the sake of the firm—not because they are more important, but because their well-being and participation in the logic of organization are necessary for the well-being of the corporate organism itself.[20]

More modest, more conformist—and both more and less "human"—than Le Corbusier's upward-reaching silhouette, the modular figure lurking in the IBM logo was in fact this "man in the gray flannel suit," a dress code made famous under the leadership of Thomas J. Watson Sr. and carried forward, with minor modifications, under the auspices of his son. One of Watson Sr.'s most widely quoted slogans was that "to build a business you must first build men."[21] And so after the corporate reorganization and the redesign under Noyes, Watson Jr. was able to say: "I did manage to break away from the stiff collar. We now wear more comfortable collars. People still smile at our dark suits and white shirts. But we in IBM smile along with them. The stockholding public also smile happily at our growth and success."[22] This figure dressed in dark gray with a stiff white collar had been known in the company and to its public for some time as the prototypical IBMer. Thus, the identity constructed in the corporate dress code had for some time been expressed in the three letters that named the company. All Rand did when he redesigned those three letters in 1956 was ensure their uniformity companywide, in a logotype officially described as "one of several connecting links in the design program that unify the visual impression of IBM"[23]—the flexible, modular graphic equivalent of a "more comfortable collar."

A similar intersection between modern design and the design of the subject of corporate capitalism was also visible in IBM's commitment to the doctrine of human relations. For IBM, as for many corporations, this project served two simultaneous purposes: to equilibrate its relations with its workforce and to project an image of dynamic but stable growth to the general public. In the case of Rochester, Minnesota, these coincided, since the town was chosen in part for its demographics, which the company believed would support its personnel needs.[24] For IBM the general public of

Rochester represented a reservoir of potential IBMers, 2,000 of whom would work in Saarinen's plant.

As part of a public relations and recruiting campaign that began when construction plans were announced in February 1956 and continued through the plant's opening in September 1958, IBM's human relations policy was detailed in the local press at the start and again (in almost identical terms) after the opening. The Rochester Chamber of Commerce reported:

> Under the guidance of Thomas J. Watson, chairman of the board of IBM, good human relations have prevailed in the kind of environment where they thrive naturally.
>
> What is this environment? It is the realization that everything starts with the individual.[25]

Thus proceeded the production of future IBMers as "individuals," with the bulk of the report referring to standard human relations touchstones such as employment policies, benefits, and job security. The corporation as family is also made literal, as the chamber notes that "IBM encourages members of the same family to work within the organization. The steady growth in membership in the IBM Two Generations club and Three Generations club points up the fact that parents think IBM is a good place for their children to work."[26]

And as it sang the praises of IBM's human relations program, the local press also dutifully paraphrased Saarinen's comments on the design of the building (such as the reference to the Minnesota landscape cited above):

> The central core, from which the unit pavilions extend laterally, contains the dining and recreation areas and, on its north side, a small entrance pavilion for visitors. The importance of the front entrance, so often emphasized in monumental terms in manufacturing plants, has been de-emphasized. The emphasis in this building has been placed on those who work within the plants. The visitors' entrance has no superiority over those to each of the employees' pavilions and since administrative and manufacturing activities are treated equally there is no special distinction between manufacturing and administrative employees.[27]

Saarinen's own way of putting it was that the plan made "no special distinction between white-collar or overall-clad employees."[28] In other words, the architecture of modular blue patterns—nonhierarchical and flexible in order to accommodate an "individualized" constituency ready to follow IBM into an unpredictable future—was mobilized in Minnesota to displace (or dissimulate) the social hierarchies written into white collars and gray flannel, in the name of "human relations" among mass-produced IBMers. As Saarinen had done in his unpublished description of the building, the article announced that the IBM plant had been designed for two objectives: "one, to provide an orderly scheme for maximum flexibility and growth, and two, to create harmonious and efficient working conditions."[29]

Saarinen's Rochester plant was in fact one of several built under the expansion program; among the first was what was called an "industrial campus" designed by John Bolles in San Jose, California (in the future Silicon Valley). It was planned very much in the manner of Saarinen's recently completed General Motors Technical Center and described in *Architectural Forum*, in terms that echo Saarinen's characterization of his own design, as a "white collar factory," based on open, "multi-use space" that could be converted or expanded to accommodate the production of any as-yet-unknown future IBM product.[30] Already in San Jose we see pixellated patterns adorning the surface of an IBM plant, perhaps even distant ancestors of those "punched card" facades that Noyes himself was to design for IBM in the 1960s.[31] But not yet, since at the moment Noyes was preoccupied with several major design commissions of his own for IBM. One was the design of an engineering and development laboratory and an educational facility in Poughkeepsie; another (in collaboration with the design firm Sundberg-Ferar) was the styling of the new IBM 305 Random Access Memory Accounting Machine (or RAMAC), which was released in 1956 and manufactured at the San Jose plant.

Both Poughkeepsie projects followed more or less directly from Saarinen's lead at General Motors. Noyes's engineering laboratory echoed Saarinen's earlier distribution of building components into functionally differentiated wings, with a curtain wall

5.11

John Bolles, IBM manufacturing and research facility, San Jose, 1958.

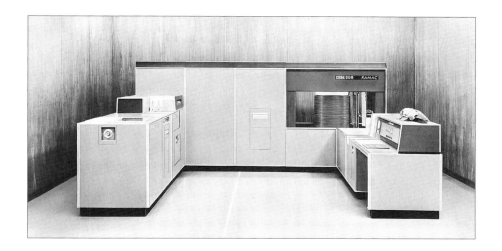

patterned in two tones of gray. His educational facility, built later, followed the GM curtain wall even more closely. It too was clad with a two-tone gray skin on porcelain-coated steel panels alternating with glazing, all on a regular (though larger) module marked by bright stainless steel mullions.

Noyes's approach to the RAMAC was absolutely identical. Presented with a hap-hazard collection of disparate components, he first moved to articulate their functional differences through simplified massing. At the same time, he unified them by wrapping everything in two-tone gray metal panels and chrome trim, effectively initiating a translation of the curtain wall into a cladding for IBM's machines—a practice of architecturalization in which, according to Noyes, the machines were submitted to the imperatives of "a Mies house."[32] Moreover, what distinguished the RAMAC was a singular innovation in hardware design that Noyes's wrapper did not fail to recognize: the RAMAC was the first computing machine to incorporate a random access memory (RAM) assembly, which consisted of fifty magnetized disks each 2 feet in diameter, scanned by read-write heads providing random access to regularly updated data such as inventory records. In the words of one design critic, "This gave the machine its memory, and in conjunction with the processing unit, its brain."[33] In the RAMAC, this aspect of its brain function was made visible through a large window, another feature that would appear repeatedly in the design of IBM's machines under Noyes.

Noyes had used a similar strategy in designing the IBM 705 computer, which went onto the market in 1954. He described the exposure of the inside of this machine as follows:

> Take the central processing unit of the 705 machine. This is an in-
> teresting case in point. The IBM designers in Endicott and myself

5.12

Eliot Noyes with Sundberg-Ferar, IBM Random Access Memory Accounting Machine (RAMAC), 1956.

Computer Architectures

were working over an early version of its design. It was completely covered in gray panels. We started stripping off the panels, and the more panels we stripped, the more beautiful it became. We found blues and oranges and wonderful reds, and wound up exposing the entire unit behind glass. And besides the coat of many colors, this revealed the machine's true character.[34]

But what, besides this "coat of many colors," was the machine's "true character"? The profundity of this last statement apparently escaped even Noyes himself, although comments made later by Watson Jr. about the redesign of IBM's machines under Noyes illustrated the degree to which the machines were being treated as aesthetic objects comparable to the spaces in which they were made and sold: "The actual mechanisms themselves make lovely pictures, so we finally put in safety glass and let the customer or observer look into the machine mechanism itself, rather than try to hide it under a cover. At the same time we began to work on good office and good showroom interiors."[35]

The first of these interiors was the overhaul of IBM's New York showroom, done by Noyes in 1955. There the electric typewriters redesigned earlier by Noyes and now available, like General Motors cars, in a range of colors, were displayed in an array reminiscent of Olivetti.[36] Beyond the typewriters was a functioning gray IBM 702 computer, "tended by well-dressed technicians in its brightly lit room."[37] The machine, on which customers could rent processing time, was set off against a bright red wall—a decisive move away from the room-size installations of earlier computers, in which the machine effectively *was* the wall. This slow process of granting the machine a spatial autonomy reached its apotheosis in the so-called white room, a futuristic interior of all-white walls, floors, and ceilings constructed by IBM at its Poughkeepsie facility in the 1960s. In it, design reviews with Noyes were held, and the company's new, colored machines were photographed.[38] Here, the styling dome designed by Saarinen to simulate daylight for the viewing of General Motors automobiles had more than met its match. Information machines had, in all senses, a space of their own.

The nature of the machines themselves, however, including their potentially functional autonomy, remained a question. Posed in the form "Can machines think?" it was a rigorous extension of the motto suspended over the head of the iconic photo of Thomas Watson Sr. that became synonymous with the identity of the IBMer: "Think." But when Alan Turing revised the question into something like "Can machines *imitate* thought?" it became evident that what was inside machines—and, by extension, humans—had nothing to do with their identity as intelligent beings.

In the so-called Turing test, devised in 1950, the mathematician whose name was synonymous with universal computing proposed an "imitation game" played by three players: two humans and a digital computer. One of the humans is isolated in a separate room as the "interrogator," posing questions through the medium of a teleprinter to the other two players. The questions are designed to reveal which of the two is the machine and which the human. If the frequency with which the computer leads its interrogator to identify it as human matches that with which the same interrogator mistakes a man for a woman or vice versa in a version of the game played by three humans, the computer can be said to have passed the "Turing test."[39] Thus, the question of machine intelligence is converted into a question of identity (comparable to that of gender) enacted through mimetic representation ungrounded in a primary referent: distinctions between humans and machines are either maintained or dissolved on the basis of their mutual participation in a communications network. Here it is not the "actual" resemblance of machines to humans that counts but the likelihood that a human "receiver" will see a resemblance in the representations that humans and machines produce. The ontological question of whether machines possess the capacity for thought is replaced with a probabilistic measure of their capacity to *imitate* the thought processes of humans. In that sense what is at stake in the question of the "true character" of these machines is ultimately the humanity of the "interrogator." Just as the machine whose representations approach those of humans is no mere "machine," so the observer who can no longer distinguish between teleprinted patterns produced by humans and those produced by machines, and whose actions since birth have been recorded in similar patterns generated by similar machines, can no longer be identified unproblematically as "human." Machines and humans thus cross paths on the slippery slope of representation.

5.13

Eliot Noyes, redesigned IBM New York showroom, 1955.

Photograph by Ezra Stoller.

Computer Architectures

Likewise, for subjectivity circa 1950—the subjectivity of the Turing test—to "think" was to transmit and receive signals. There remains no thought without media, if indeed there ever was. It should not be surprising, then, that as architecture began to organize the space of the computer, the primary concern was with what machines *looked like,* in the sense not of a first order of figurative resemblance (it was never a question of machines looking like humans) but of a second order of resemblance, based on a machine's capacity to integrate itself into a communications network also populated by humans—to disguise itself, as it were, in representations resembling those produced by humans. Such representations were generated by modern architecture: panelized curtain walls and glass skins. But these media effects, these public constructions of a corporate image—an image of humanity itself—on the surfaces of its enigmatic offspring, also amplified an instability that had long characterized modern architecture's identification with machines. Like the patterns of signals issuing from Turing's teleprinter, those thought patterns also defined the mimetic horizon, the mirror, in which humans were no longer able to distinguish their own reflection.

Along these lines, Watson Jr. noted of Eliot Noyes that "[b]asically he believed that machines should look like what they are, not be dressed up in phony streamlining or frills"[40]—a comment that reveals an underlying nervousness permeating the attempts to manage IBM's public image. For if designers like Noyes were supposedly dedicating themselves to ensuring that IBM's machines (like the RAMAC) "look like what they are," nobody, it seems, was quite sure exactly what they were to begin with.

Well into the 1950s Thomas J. Watson Sr. was refusing to allow his company's products to be called "computers," because that term had been in use for some time to describe humans who performed calculations with the help of machines. Since the 1920s IBM had built its business on a wide assortment of special-purpose tabulators and calculators conceived around its patented punched card, input-output system. The company did not enter the computer market competitively until the mid-1950s, when its 702 gained a market share approaching that of the innovative UNIVAC (Universal Automatic Computer) manufactured by Remington Rand. But even then, IBM executives preferred the term "calculators" to describe even the company's most advanced machines, fearing that "computer" would imply the replacement of humans altogether.[41] Such nervousness often surfaced at the most telltale moments, including dedication speeches for buildings, as evidenced by the following excerpts from Watson Jr.'s comments at the ceremony dedicating Saarinen's Rochester facility in September 1958: "[P]eople think we build electronic brains. . . . Nobody, of course, can build a brain. We build tools to lighten the burden on men's brains and enable them to do greater things with their brains, and we would like to disavow any connection to the brain maker."[42]

Whatever these machines were, then, from IBM's point of view they were certainly not "brains," despite the provision (and celebration, by Noyes) of even a "memory" as part of their hardware. But this disavowal was nothing if not disingenuous, given the company's earlier celebration of the top secret "brains" it had been constructing for some years for U.S. Air Force bombers, revealed in an article in the 1 July 1954 issue of *IBM Business Machines* (an internal publication) titled "We Build Brains for Defense." That article also described the development of "a powerful defensive weapon: a huge electronic calculator" larger and faster that the IBM 701,[43] which would eventually be called the 702 Defense Calculator. And again the presence of an electronic "brain" was represented less as a matter of the machine's physiology than of the reactions of its human "operators." As the article reports: "To the pilots of the Air Force [the B-47 jet bombers] are known as 'birds with brains.' IBM manufactures the 'brains'—the uncanny bombing navigational computers that make these planes 'live' for that split second when the bombs are dropped."[44]

An important source for the dissemination of neurological terminology within the early discourse on computer design was the mathematician John von Neumann, who collaborated on the pioneering ENIAC (Electronic Numerical Integrator and Computer) and EDVAC (Electronic Discrete Variable Automatic Computer) at the University of Pennsylvania in the mid-1940s. Von Neumann was preoccupied with the analogy of the computer to the human nervous system, frequently referring to the machine's storage component as a "memory organ" and contemplating the possibility of constructing artificial brains right up until his death in 1957.[45] He was also largely responsible for outlining the operational principles of the "stored program" computer—the basis for most modern computers—a concept that later became known as "von Neumann architecture."[46]

The term *architecture* was itself applied as early as 1959 in an IBM report to the logical organization of computers independent of their actual physical configuration and hardware constraints, and it entered common parlance not long thereafter.[47] Several years later, in a text precipitously titled "Architectural Philosophy," describing the logical organization of the IBM 7030 computer, Frederick P. Brooks Jr. asserted: "Computer architecture, like other architecture, is the art of determining the needs of the user of a structure and then designing to meet those needs as effectively as possible with-in technological and economic constraints."[48] Thus, a nascent computer science internalized the notion of an architecture of abstract components performing specific operations, analogized to the organs of the human nervous system and addressing themselves to the needs of the humans making contact with the machine. Brooks further distinguished between computer architecture and engineering, declaring that "the emphasis in architecture is upon the needs of the user, whereas in engineering the emphasis is upon the needs of the fabricator."[49] This "philosophy" formed the basis for the IBM System/360, also designed under Brooks.

The System/360 was a colorful, modular, fully compatible *system* of recombinable components released in April 1964 that ushered in a new era in computer design and completed the reinvention of IBM.[50] Like Saarinen's architecture, its integrated flexibility was addressed to the ever-changing "needs" of a market that in turn was constructed through the identification of the user/consumer with an image of individual choice between various models or configurations that could themselves be reconfigured within the system over time, again like Saarinen's architecture. Not only did the design and production of this system require the flexible coordination of all branches in the worldwide IBM organization, but both its "architecture" (or logical organization) and its image, made up of combinable, modular, color-coordinated units,

5.14

IBM System/360, ca. 1964. Designed under the supervision of Eliot Noyes.

internalized the notion of a universally computable familial "compatibility." At that point, the architecture of computers could legitimately be said to have approached that of the buildings designed by modern architects like Saarinen for the companies that produced and used them. This is a question not of the "influence" of architectural design on the design and engineering of computers, but rather of their common adherence to a shift in organizational imperatives, from the functionalist notion of an internal logic of "organs" (e.g., "brains") made visible by Noyes through the architectonic windows of the RAMAC to the systemic, open-ended logic of the module and the surfaces in which it was registered—no different, in principle, from the patterned "coat of many colors" that Noyes found inside the IBM 705.

But Noyes himself (to whom Watson Jr. referred, with respect to the redesign of IBM's image, as "the brains behind this project")[51] was unable to recognize the implications of the process in which he was a major participant. He did not disavow humanistic denials such as Watson's insistence that "[o]ur machines should be nothing more than tools for extending the powers of the human beings who use them. As a consequence, our design, our colors, our building interiors are intended to complement human activity, rather than dominate it."[52] Speaking about IBM's "corporate character" in the same terms in which he had described the "true character" of the company's machines, Noyes declares: "I don't believe in corporate images. This image game is very superficial, using design as a sort of slipcover, and I think that the practitioners do the world of design great damage with such a shallow game. But I do believe in corporate character, and that design programs can both identify and express that character." He adds, "In my experience, the designer has to identify this character for himself. It is terribly easy to look at a company in too small terms, and this generally is what goes on inside. For example, it's easy to say that IBM is simply a maker of business machines. But if you get to the very heart of the matter, what IBM really does is to help man extend his control over his environment."[53]

"Control" is certainly the issue here, but by exactly what means was it effected? IBM's first major experiment with mainframe computing, the Harvard Mark I or Automatic Sequence Controlled Calculator (ASCC), was built in 1944 by IBM engineers at Harvard University in collaboration with the mathematician Howard Aiken. A Harvard press release referred to the machine as an "algebraic super-brain," while IBM engineer Leslie J. Comrie described the Mark I as follows: "The brains of the machine lie in the control tape, which is code-punched in three sections. The first instructs the machine where to find its data; the second gives the destination of the data or answer; the third dictates the process."[54] The ASCC's "control tape" was basically an elongated version of the patterned punched cards that IBM had been using for decades to input data into its business machines, with an additional purpose: it now regulated the machine's functions. Four years later, this strict physical separation of hardware (machine) and software (control tape) was superseded in the architecture of the stored program computer. These machines could store and transmit both data and instructions in and through a number of interchangeable media, including magnetic tape and electronic circuitry.[55] This meant that the machine could be programmed to adjust its operations midstream in response to the data being generated,[56] initiating an implosion of hardware and software into a single technological nexus: the ability to record, store, read, and respond to two-dimensional regulating patterns had been internalized. The stored program computer was a machine that effectively stored its "brain," or logical control (to use von Neumann's terms), in memory.[57]

If we interpret Noyes's mandate in these terms, we must conclude that as the control systems built into the new machines seemed increasingly to usurp brain function, IBM felt it could not, in fact, afford to show them for what they were. As had been traditional with both IBMers and IBM machines before his arrival, Noyes chose to clad the RAMAC in a neutralizing pattern of grays—a gray flannel suit—that made it look like a not-too-distant relative of the curtain-walled materializations of corporate identity in the postwar office building. What is more, this "IBMer" also came complete with a memory that suggested that it, too, could respond to the corporate command "Think."[58] But that move left the architecture of computers vulnerable to the organizational advances made in the architecture of buildings. Despite the idealist rhetoric of "computer architecture," the absolute separation between what a computer looked like and its logical organization was untenable, in terms both of market conditions and of the construction of a corporate subjectivity. With the System/360, available in a range of coordinated colors, patterned surfaces *did* in fact describe something like the "true character" of the machine. As IBM's mainframes took on the property of flexible expandability implemented earlier at the level of corporate organization with the help of so-called modern design, color-coded modular components made it possible to recognize this line of computers *as an integrated system*. Modular compatibility thus became the basis of the 360's logical and visual organization alike.

The System/360, whose name alludes to a full circumference of functional mutability, was itself designed, controlled, and maintained by a corporation that had reorganized itself—and its image—into a comparable system beginning in 1956. Indeed, it was reportedly the ubiquity of blue System/360 components in corporate offices across the country that earned IBM the nickname "Big Blue,"[59] for which Saarinen's Minnesota plant can thus be seen as something of a prototype. The gray flannel suit had been exchanged for a colorful print and sent spinning into a new landscape in which it was increasingly difficult to tell whether the identity that it encoded (in both the denotative and performative sense of the term) was that of a human or a machine.

In response to IBM's program of controlled, decentralized expansion, Saarinen's plant was itself programmed to grow according to the modular checkerboard of its

IBM System/360 Model 85 configuration, ca. 1968.

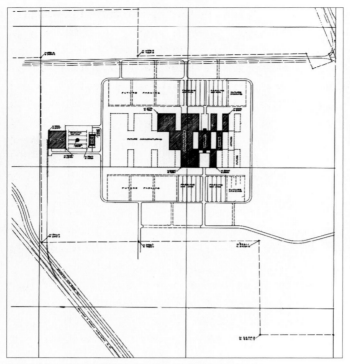

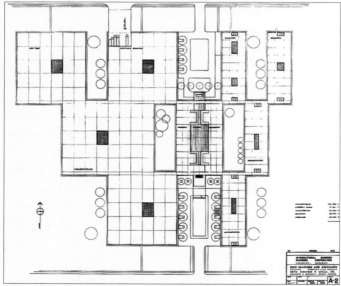

5.16
Eero Saarinen, IBM manufacturing and training facility, Rochester, Minnesota, 1958. Site plan.

5.17
Eero Saarinen, IBM manufacturing and training facility, Rochester, Minnesota, 1958. Plan.

site plan, regulated by the 4-foot module of the skin projected into the building's interior. That module was emphatically marked on the facades and reinforced by the offset checkerboard pattern of blues. In plan, the ratio of the footprint of the administrative pavilions to that of the manufacturing pavilions was 1:3, with dimensions determined by the maximum interior distance from a window allowed by the doctrine of "outdoor awareness" that Watson Sr. had long projected onto his employees;[60] the two blues on the skin covered $1/3$ and $2/3$, respectively, of the 4-foot module. These patterns within patterns imparted a regulating logic to the overall building, while simultaneously gathering its parts into a unified, open-ended system. In principle, such an organizational pattern did not have to make a distinction between what Saarinen called "white collar" and "overall-clad employees" to maintain dynamic equilibrium. But what presented itself as emancipatory was in fact merely a displacement, since as the company "flattened" itself out (in the lingo of management consultants), top-down, pyramidal power dissolved into pattern-based control—with operational parameters stored in corporate organization charts and modular skins alike.

The modular patterns of Saarinen's plan, like the thin curtain wall, were to give way to more pragmatic strategies as the plant grew. Yet right there on the surface of a piece of IBM's corporate image, in plain sight of all those attending the dedication ceremony and listening to Watson's disavowals, was a technology that implied a displacement of the human into the abyss of machine logics that—as Turing had predicted—were based on patterns of signals transmitted and received through media, including architecture. While IBM represented itself as a mere maker of business machines and "calculators," even its buildings were experimenting with "logical controls" encoded into a paper-thin skin. Even more than the RAMAC, this building's "brain" was on its surface. In that regard, its image was integral to the organizational strategies that kept the company growing and enabled it to expand its research into artificial intelligence, pattern recognition, and related arenas. Such work eventually made possible the construction of another colored brain whose architecture took shape during the 1990s in the laboratories of Saarinen's next IBM commission—the Thomas J. Watson Research Center in Yorktown Heights, New York, completed in 1961. I note this here, since for Norbert Wiener (in a note appended to the concluding chapter of *Cybernetics*), "There is one question which properly belongs to this chapter, though it in no sense represents a culmination of its argument. It is the question [of] whether it is possible to construct a chess-playing machine, and whether this sort of ability represents an essential difference between the potentialities of the machine and the mind."[61] In 1997 IBM's chess-playing machine was able to beat humanity at its own game. Perhaps not coincidentally, its name—and color—was "Deep Blue."[62]

6

The Topologies of Knowledge

During the Second World War and thereafter, facilities housing sophisticated information-processing equipment manufactured by companies like IBM were crucial agents in extending the scope of the work performed by large, technology-oriented corporations into a domain previously reserved for educational institutions. Undistinguished as many postwar laboratories were, together they occupied a specific region of the organizational complex, in which the interests of the corporations and of the military were combined increasingly with those of major research universities.[1] It thus should not be surprising that when we examine two laboratory buildings designed by Eero Saarinen in the late 1950s, the fact that the patterns Gyorgy Kepes collected for the benefit of architects and artists in *The New Landscape* had theretofore lain "buried in research laboratories" is converted from a comment on the opacity of science into a characterization of the new topologies of knowledge.[2]

The tendencies of the military-industrial complex are twofold. The first is precisely toward the type of public relations-oriented visibility that led former General Motors president and Eisenhower secretary of defense Charles E. Wilson to declare that what was good for General Motors was good for the country, a position reflected in the affinities between Skidmore, Owings & Merrill's U.S. Air Force Academy and Eero Saarinen's earlier General Motors Technical Center. The second, perhaps paradoxical tendency of the military-industrial complex is toward disappearance, stealth. In that regard, what General Motors and the Air Force (as well as numerous other Saarinen and SOM clients) had in common more than anything else was their commitment to an organizational project that dissolved institutional identity into a diffuse, integrated network through which circulated affective power relations irreducible to the agency of any one individual or group.

Brought on by the increasing need to access and encourage the highest levels of scientific and technological research, the postwar proliferation of research laboratories effectively reterritorialized the corporation, disengaging the centers of industrial research from the manufacturing plants out of which they had sprung during the 1920s and 1930s and granting them a separate identity within the corporate hierarchy.[3] The work done at these earlier centers was typically determined by an overall commercial strategy and was coordinated functionally with the production, marketing, and sales divisions of a vertically integrated, centrally managed entity. Research was directly linked to the supply lines of industry, which served as a source not only of raw materials or finished products but also of manufacturing techniques and processes. Initially this research involved relatively little "basic science," but by the mid-1920s what was already called a "fever of commercialized science" had begun to spread from the new laboratories of American industry into the halls of the university.[4]

During that same period, the stratum of American universities that had been the primary locus of advanced scientific research since the end of the nineteenth century began to benefit substantially from the resources of private, industry-based foundations. Supported by efforts at coordinating a national scientific research agenda that were a response to the First World War, philanthropic groups and commercial corporations joined with the universities, in an alliance aimed at maintaining a balance between research perceived as disinterested and as interested. While the foundations remained focused on the overall advancement of science as an index of social and cultural advancement, the corporations, whose technological products benefited from the research carried out in universities and who hired their graduates, had a material interest in supporting the type of research they considered most likely to yield advantageous results. During the 1920s these two institutions were the primary extramural funding sources for university-based scientific research; but the subsequent economic depression eventually restricted their outlay, and the federal relief policies of the New Deal tended to favor more direct economic stimulants.[5] Yet despite a shortage of resources, both industrial and university research continued to grow during the 1930s.

What changed during the Second World War was the organization of the political, economic, and discursive networks though which scientific knowledge was produced and transmitted. During that time, the federal government became a major source of funding for research taking place in the universities. In addition, work on technologies intended to have military application, such as radar, atomic weaponry, and information-processing and communications systems, required the increasingly close collaboration of industry and the military, usually coordinated through governmental agencies. Most prominent among these was the Office of Scientific Research and Development (OSRD), whose director, Vannevar Bush, authored a key report in 1945 titled *Science, the Endless Frontier*. This report was instrumental in setting the agenda for the research that would emerge from this intertwining of universities, corporations, and the military.[6]

Bush, a former colleague of Norbert Wiener's at MIT and the inventor of the computing device known as the differential calculator, came to the conclusion that "war is increasingly total war, in which the armed services must be supplemented by active participation of every element of the civilian population."[7] It was this observation, together with his recognition of the importance of the role played by technologically advanced weaponry in resolving the first ever "total war," that underlay Bush's argument for supporting basic scientific research by maintaining close ties between the military and civilian institutions. The OSRD was disbanded immediately after the war, but Bush's proposal to establish what would become the National Science Foundation (NSF) was quickly acted on. The first bill was vetoed by President Harry S. Truman, but the War Department responded by establishing the Office of Naval Research (ONR), an agency that effectively acted in the stead of the NSF until the latter's charter was authorized in 1950. The mandate of the ONR was to fund what its founding legislation referred to as *"free* rather than directed research," in anticipation of the possible uses that unforeseen scientific advances could have for "national security."[8]

This identification with "free" research carried out on an "endless frontier" was characteristic of scientific institutions during the postwar period in the United States. The prototype for its requisite blurring of boundaries between the military, the corporations, and the university was the Manhattan Project, a vast network of university, military, and private laboratories coordinated by what was nevertheless a single and fairly restricted mission.[9] After the war the mission of much government-funded scientific research was extended from the short-term project of weapons development to the more ambiguous project of national security. That extension was clearest in the Korean conflict, when military appropriations for research and development doubled, and university outposts such as MIT's Lincoln Laboratory and Berkeley's Lawrence Liv-ermore Laboratory were established on the strength of increased military contracts.[10] These developments should not be mistaken as evidence of a "corruption" of aca-demic ideals by the vulgar instrumentality of the military, however. The coordination of these processes depended on complex organizational systems to manage and dis-tribute information; they absorbed the production of scientific knowledge in both the social and natural sciences into what was essentially an organicist project of military-corporate control and communication. This was made possible by the same scientists whose interdisciplinary efforts grew out of the dream of an organic unity of science based on communication and teamwork between specialists. Just as the colonization of modern architecture after the war by the corporations represented not simply a corruption of a socially conscious modernist utopianism but rather the logical conclu-sion of an organicist project written into the very curriculum of modernism, so "big science," as it has come to be called, was always already written into the organicist dreams of the scientists themselves.[11]

By 1970 the collusion of the universities in perpetuating the cold war was so pronounced that Senator J. William Fulbright could extend Eisenhower's earlier figuration—the "military-industrial complex"—to the "military-industrial-academic complex."[12] And, as was also true of the apparently emancipatory project of open-ended flexibility around which modern architects gathered during and after the war, the unpredictability of open-ended scientific research was, in both a theoretical and a practical sense, fundamental to the organizational complex as it linked the university with corporate and military research agendas. The Manhattan Project itself had been subjected to the shock of unexpected experimental results that had reorganized its research agenda mid-stream, an event that demonstrated the instrumental value of being able to respond flexibly to new scientific developments.[13]

Correspondingly, from an architectural point of view, in the new postwar labora-tories the cultivation of "free" research went hand in hand with the requirement that the spaces provided by architects be as flexible as possible—in anticipation, as it were, of that which cannot be anticipated. This temporality was inscribed into the lab-oratories designed by architects like Saarinen. Indeed, in the suburbs "flexibility" and "communication" were the watchwords that signaled the distillation of new communities of knowledge from the corridors of the university—academic communities dedicated to the most dangerous research there was.

At the same time, corporations were redistributing their own resources to accommodate their new research needs. At IBM, running parallel with the reorganization begun in 1956 under Thomas J. Watson Jr. was a comparable reorganization of the company's research and development practices. Before the war, in addition to its ongoing but relatively slow development of business machines and related technologies, IBM had helped establish an "astronomical computing bureau" under Wallace Eckert at Columbia University in 1937. Thomas J. Watson Sr. had become a Columbia trustee in 1933, and in 1939 his company entered into an agreement with Harvard University to construct the the Harvard Mark I computer. During and after the war, this early support of the academy was converted into an internalization of academic research models within the company itself.[14]

In 1944 Watson Sr. invited Eckert to join IBM and form a "department of pure science," which would emulate the research groups found in academic institutions. The following year Eckert helped establish the Watson Scientific Computing Laboratory at Columbia; and in 1946 an engineering group was set up in IBM's Poughkeepsie facility that would eventually become a second research arm of the company. By 1951 the definition of and relation between research and development had become a management issue within the company, and the Management Committee on Pure Research was formed. By the mid-1950s, steps were taken to separate research from development in IBM as a whole; as a result a new and independent organization, devoted primarily to basic and applied research, was established at the Poughkeepsie facility in 1956. In September 1956, the physicist and former chief scientist at the Office for Naval Research Emmanuel R. Piore was named director of research, and a "purified" science was institutionalized at IBM. Two years later, the company announced that Piore was also to serve as a member of President Dwight D. Eisenhower's Science Advisory Committee under MIT president James R. Killian. Thus Eero Saarinen's 1956 commission for the IBM Thomas J. Watson Research Center at Yorktown Heights, New York, planned to accommodate an expanded research organization then located at Poughkeepsie, placed him—and his architecture—in the very midst of the military-industrial-academic complex.

This was also the moment that saw the realization of the civil defense initiative SAGE (Semi-Automatic Ground Environment). SAGE, too, had its own architecture. Indeed, prominently positioned in the foreground of a photograph taken on the occasion of the press conference announcing the SAGE system in 1956 is a "radome" designed by Buckminster Fuller to house the search radar positioned at the Defense Early Warning (DEW) line, which ran along the Arctic Circle at the outermost perimeter of this enormous servomechanical network. Fuller was contracted to design these

lightweight, deployable fiberglass geodesic domes by the Lincoln Laboratories at MIT, where the first tests of his design were conducted. The first production model of the radome was subsequently installed at the Whippany, New Jersey, facility of Bell Telephone Laboratories, whose sister manufacturing company in the Bell System, Western Electric, was the prime contractor for the DEW line.[15]

In the numerous black box-like SAGE command centers located inland, the data collected by the radar equipment housed in the radomes was combined with other

6.1

Press conference announcing the Semi-Automatic Ground Environment (SAGE) air-defense system, with Buckminster Fuller's radome in the foreground, January 1956.

6.2

R. Buckminster Fuller, geodesic radome installed at the Defense Early Warning (DEW) line by Western Electric Co.

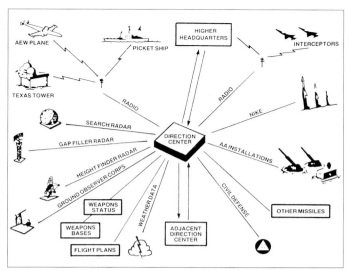

6.3

Diagram of data flows in the Semi-Automatic Ground Environment (SAGE), with direction center.

6.4

Semi-Automatic Ground Environment (SAGE) human-machine interface, with "operators," ca. 1960.

relevant information by IBM computers and mapped onto the cathode-ray displays and consoles of a "man-machine component" designed with ergonomic precision. The luminous images on these screens were processed through the eyes and brains of "operators" entrusted with recognizing aberrant patterns. The operators and their consoles were housed in windowless "blue rooms"—so named because of the blue light emanating from the screens, which illuminated the rooms.[16] Every 2.5 seconds the SAGE computers would regenerate two hundred types of displays that recorded specific types of information pertaining to the air space being surveyed. The orderly flow and interpretation of these data were maintained by a human and a machine in an interactive dynamic equilibrium, where the judgment of the operator could be superseded at any time by that of the computer.[17] Thus, the SAGE interface was intended to distribute an excess of information into an organized array of organized patterns. The geography mapped in these patterns, scanned by the operators via the remote sensing system housed in Fuller's architecture, was the *very same* "new landscape" mapped by Kepes, deployed here in the networks of the organizational complex through which art and science had no choice but to interact.

The brain of the SAGE system was the FSQ-7 computer manufactured by IBM. Central to the development of this machine were a series of experiments in real-time control by a digital computer that were carried out at MIT's Digital Computer Laboratory as part of what was known as "Project Whirlwind,"[18] an ONR-sponsored project supervised by the engineer Jay W. Forrester. Real-time control, or the virtually instantaneous regulation of informatic processes with negligible computational delays, required a general-purpose digital machine far faster and more accurate than the special-purpose analog devices with which Forrester and his colleagues had been experimenting at MIT's Servomechanisms Laboratory since the 1940s.[19] Among the resulting technical innovations was the development of a high-speed ferrite-core memory that replaced the slower and bulkier vacuum tubes, thereby making possible the further development of the stored program computers of the sort necessary to operate SAGE.[20] In 1952 Forrester toured IBM's Columbia and Poughkeepsie research laboratories in order to evaluate the company's ability to develop and manufacture these machines. Subsequently IBM, which had been developing a version of the ferrite-core memory similar to Forrester's, was awarded the FSQ-7 contract.

Thus SAGE exemplified in both its architecture and in the logistics of its design and production the dispersed, computerized spatiality of the organizational complex as it passed through the research laboratories of universities and corporations.[21] But the details of SAGE are also worth recounting since the spaces in which it was produced were themselves being modified by architects like Saarinen. As we have already noted, in the case of IBM the Poughkeepsie laboratories toured by Forrester in 1956 were about to be transplanted into the Thomas J. Watson Research Center in Yorktown

Heights, begun by Saarinen that same year and completed in 1961. Likewise, Bell Telephone Laboratories, which had hosted Fuller's radome and designed the SAGE interface, was about to add a major new facility in Holmdel, New Jersey, also designed by Saarinen. The first phase of the project, which began in 1957, was completed in 1962; the second phase was completed in 1966. The reorganization of research thus represented both a site and a programmatic brief for these projects, which internalized the topological nestings figured in the string "military-industrial-academic." This internalization, followed through the space of the campus that underlay Saarinen's schemes, in turn precipitated changes in the organization and production of the knowledge to which the laboratories were dedicated. Feedback.

Saarinen had already been working on the design of the IBM laboratory by the time he began the Bell Telephone commission, but it appears that the latter stimulated a rethinking of the laboratory planning strategies that would eventually be utilized in both buildings. The early sketches of the IBM scheme, located atop a hill on a semirural site, show a campuslike series of small buildings clustered around courtyards and cascading gently down the slope. In the scheme that was published in *Architectural Forum* in February 1957, the clusters are linked in a large, semicontinuous network. These clusters are likely descendants of those courtyards around which

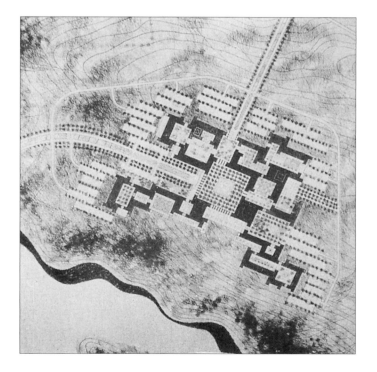

6.5

Eero Saarinen, IBM Thomas J. Watson Research Laboratory,

Yorktown Heights, New York. Early site plan, 1957.

Saarinen's father had planned the Cranbrook campus and of similarly episodic sequences of spaces developed in the campus-planning work done by the Saarinen firm in the 1940s, as well as that done for the IBM Rochester facility then under construction. The building units from which these initial studies for IBM were composed had been inventoried as a series of types, which included laboratory, education, shop, and special-purpose facilities. Variations were studied for each, but the basic diagram of rectangular wings organized around double-loaded corridors was consistent throughout.[22] This topology was residual in that it combined the individualized functional units of the General Motors Technical Center with the kinds of pedestrian-oriented spaces which that project had previously evacuated to make room for the automobile.

Writing in *Architectural Record* about campus planning in 1960, the year before his IBM laboratory was completed, Saarinen gave an indication of what he took to be the essence of the academic environment. He enjoined the profession to be more receptive to traditionalist efforts to maintain a "total unity of form" on neo-Gothic campuses like Yale University. Likewise, he praised the uniformity of William Welles Bosworth's planning at MIT and at the University of Chicago, citing Bosworth's Chicago Medical Center and identifying his work with a modernist "universal space." For Saarinen, "The esthetic purpose of the building must be to enhance the total organism."[23]

Saarinen concludes his remarks about campus planning by passing on a favorite piece of advice from his father: "Always look at the next larger thing."[24] This meant that in designing a university building one should consider its integration into the campus; and when designing the campus, its integration into the city, and so on, up and down in scale. The problem at Yorktown Heights, however, was that there was no "next larger thing" into which the project could be integrated. There was only the green, rolling landscape of suburban Westchester County, north of New York City. For organicists like Saarinen, this problem was repeatedly encountered in the exurban sites in which they frequently worked. The corporate laboratory, disengaging itself from the manufacturing plant, was adrift in this landscape. Efforts to treat it as a quasi-urban fragment akin to a university campus, as pursued by Saarinen and his associates in the early IBM schemes, were quickly abandoned to the encompassing vastness of parking lots, lawns, and highways. The Thomas J. Watson Research Laboratory thus saw a collapse into the interior derived directly from a critique of the laboratory as campuslike sprawl, in which the contact with nature was through windows—the scientific instruments—opening onto a pastoral new landscape. From the laboratories of the Bell Telephone Company, transplanted onto IBM's hillside, came a figure that turned itself inward toward the landscape made visible by the machines it housed, and then back out again.

Saarinen received the Bell Telephone commission in April 1957, and by July a preliminary scheme had been drawn up to be presented to company executives.[25] An initial site plan, which described a checkerboard system of contiguous pavilions and courtyards, was shown and compared to the plan of the principal Bell Laboratories facility in Murray Hill, New Jersey, which had been designed by the New York firm of Voorhees, Walker, Foley & Smith and completed in 1941. This juxtaposition is the key to understanding both the Bell and IBM laboratory projects that emerged in the subsequent months.[26]

In 1925 the Engineering Department of the Western Electric Company had been incorporated as Bell Telephone Laboratories in New York City. In the following years the company began acquiring property nearby in New Jersey, where it set up a series of field stations for conducting experiments using communications equipment that required large open environments.[27] In 1934 the Development and Research Department of AT&T (which owned Western Electric) was consolidated with Bell Laboratories, and by the late 1930s the company had outgrown its original accommodations in New York City. In 1941 Bell Laboratories groups began moving to the Murray Hill facility, which later became the company's corporate headquarters and the center of its most advanced scientific research. By 1960 Bell Laboratories scientists working at Holmdel in another facility developed an antenna capable of receiving signals bounced off the Echo high-altitude balloon, inaugurating the age of satellite-based telecommunications.[28] In the new Holmdel building, research and development were to be undertaken on switching, transmission and customer services, network planning, and quality testing. And in 1966, in a return of its repressed origins in the university campus, a second phase of the Holmdel facility was carried out to house the company's education center.[29]

The Bell Laboratories facility at Murray Hill consisted of a series of pavilions organized around double-loaded corridors, branching off a central spine that ran the length of the plan. This system was designed for expansion, in anticipation of future growth in the company's research needs.[30] Flexibility in interior planning was declared a top priority, and so the entire structure was planned on a 6-foot module, with laboratory spaces aligned along the perimeter on one side and offices on the other. Despite the relative matter-of-factness of the architecture, this flexibility was articulated in

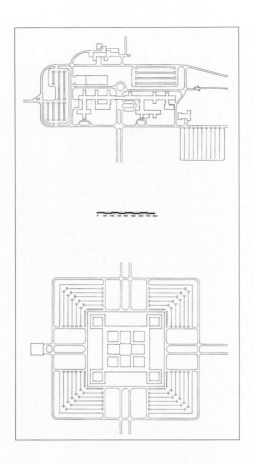

organicist terms through a logic of cellular aggregation in the 1944 planning guide produced by the architects of the facility. Like much technical literature, it must be read as a theoretical document, announcing the architects' devotion to the cellular organicism that was about to dissolve into modulated patterns on the skins of the office buildings of the 1950s. Thus the laboratory's functional organs were miniaturized as 6-foot-square planning modules, or "cells"; and it was exactly these units that Saarinen would collapse still further in his own proposals. Murray Hill already contained traces of what was to come, in the form of the modular metal partition system that enclosed the entire interior. Indeed, the spatial requirements for producing scientific knowledge during and after the war were already such that Bell Telephone calculated in 1975 that each partition in the facility was moved on average every seven years.[31]

6.6

Eero Saarinen & Associates, comparison of the site plan of an early scheme for the Bell Telephone Laboratories at Holmdel, New Jersey (bottom), with the site plan of the Bell Laboratories campus at Murray Hill, New Jersey (top), July 1957.

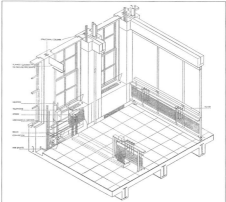

First at IBM and then at Bell Laboratories in Holmdel, Saarinen transformed the topology underlying the earlier Bell Laboratories at Murray Hill by turning it inside out. He replaced the workers sitting at tables looking out windows with an organized community of introverts inhabiting the "deep space" of air-conditioned office buildings. The scientist to whom his laboratories were dedicated was a figure inoculated against the alienation of the lonely crowd by an inwardness that Theodor Adorno during these same years had observed being emptied out into the cold, overexposed surfaces of the mass media. He (since the scientist was assumed to be male, despite significant numbers of women working in these fields) was an organization man whose

6.7
Voorhees, Walker, Foley & Smith, Bell Telephone Laboratories, Murray Hill, New Jersey, 1941.

6.8
Voorhees, Walker, Foley & Smith, Bell Telephone Laboratories, Murray Hill, New Jersey, 1941. Laboratory module.

The Topologies of Knowledge

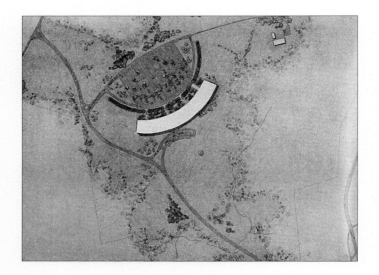

individuality nevertheless needed to be protected from the onslaught of group life in the corporation, and who played a role in the corporate organism comparable to that of the cybernetic brains being grown by IBM. This scientist, the processor of information, was also seen by many as a primary source of organic equilibrium for a society irradiated by the fallout of its own technological success. And so Saarinen tracked the movements of this figure in the spaces of the modern laboratory with care and precision.

Driving Saarinen's conclusions was the fact that air conditioning and fluorescent lighting had largely replaced windows as a source of light and ventilation in many newer laboratories and offices.[32] The result was what he called a "bold new plan": all laboratories and offices were on the windowless interior, surrounded by continuous corridors lining the curtain-walled periphery.[33] This was a full inversion of the modernist project of "light and air" as it had been absorbed into early slab office buildings like those at Rockefeller Center. The spaces of work were now entirely artificially conditioned. And in Saarinen's imagination, a new introvert-scientist would step out periodically from the deep space of his communication with other introverts and with machines, and enjoy the view: "The individual, emerging from concentration in laboratory or office, will come upon magnificent, uninterrupted views of the surrounding countryside and the winter-garden interior courts as he walks, in moments of relaxation, down these periphery main corridors."[34]

Written into Saarinen's plan and recorded in his words is thus an entire economy of intellectual labor. Inward-directed concentration and outward-directed relaxation are two poles of a continuous, naturalized oscillation akin to what Adorno and Max

6.9

Eero Saarinen, IBM Thomas J. Watson Research Laboratory,

Yorktown Heights, New York, 1961. Site plan.

Horkheimer had already characterized as the instrumentalization of aesthetic purposelessness: "At last, in the demand for entertainment and relaxation, purpose has absorbed the realm of purposelessness."[35] But this moment at which the scientist-introvert emerges alive from his skirmish with machines is also evidence of a realignment affecting the conjunction of power and knowledge, a realignment that takes the form of a singularity unassimilable into the "dialectic of enlightenment" on which the critique of the Frankfurt theorists was hung. It is exactly at this moment that we can observe the bourgeois inwardness in which enlightenment was anchored through the autonomy of the subject not merely evacuated by the dialectic's incessant process but reproduced—even celebrated. There is no longer, at this moment, anything against which a presumed "dialectic" could play. There is no outside to the utter exteriority of the organizational complex; inwardness itself is merely an effect generated by vanishingly thin surfaces folded back into the deep, dark spaces of the scientific laboratory.

The strategy of fully internalized laboratories and offices appears to have arisen after the initial comparisons to the Murray Hill facility presented to Bell executives in mid-1957. Among the extant documentation of the project's development is a series of undated sketches, some of which may have been drawn by Saarinen, exploring a variety of planning options for the Bell facility, one of which was used in the Murray Hill comparison. In four of these studies, different patterns of repetitive pavilions and courtyards test systematically two degrees of exposure: both offices and laboratories receiving natural light, or offices at the perimeter and laboratories on the interior. These symmetries are even more pronounced in two other, highly formalistic figures in which the fully internalized system is studied. In one, an equilateral triangle distributes the entire program around a central, triangular open space. A final sketch inverts this configuration, by shrinking the central court considerably and running secondary corridors supporting program space laterally, thus collapsing the triangle into a three-pointed star.[36]

The rigid geometries of these figures may suggest a classical tendency that periodically surfaced in Saarinen's work, exhibiting affinities not only with the contemporaneous work of Philip Johnson but also with that of Louis Kahn—in particular, the latter's laboratory complex for the Salk Institute in La Jolla, California (1959–1965), then under way.[37] Seen in series, however (and regardless of the chronological sequence in which they were actually produced), these drawings must first and foremost be

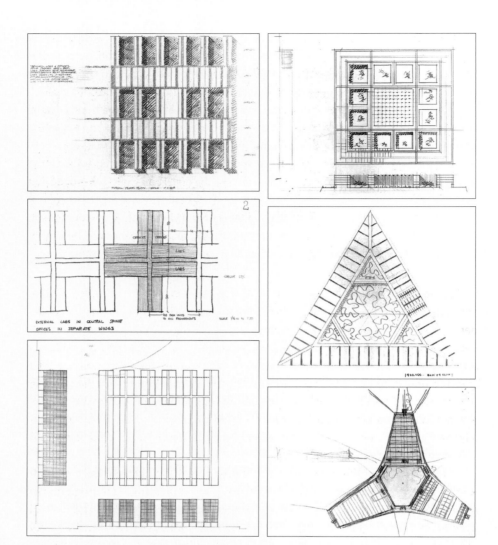

6.10

Eero Saarinen & Associates, study sketches for the Bell
Telephone Laboratories, Holmdel, New Jersey, ca. 1957.

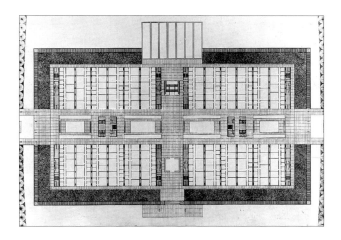

understood as *topological* studies. That is, their primary function is to study relations of inside and outside—contiguity and separation; solid, void, and perimeter—as they pertain to the distribution of the laboratory and office spaces, independent of a definitive formal resolution. In that sense the final scheme, a "superblock" of four quadrants arranged around a cruciform atrium, is almost entirely present in the three-pointed star. The only difference is in the addition of a fourth component and the collapse of two pairs of adjacent arms toward one another until their external corridors merged into the lateral atrium. To the extent that the future atrium was conceptually equivalent to the outside in the earlier courtyard schemes, the basic relation was already in place.

Moreover, even the uselessness of the atrium had already been instrumentalized by Saarinen: it was designed as an inside-out exterior landscape for programmed relaxation. The hollowness of the nature for which the atrium stood was underlined even more clearly in the early design stages, when the landscape architect Dan Kiley proposed suspending within it an open grid supporting tropical plants interwoven with a piping system that would distribute a misty "rain" simulating what he called a "tropical rainforest type of climate."[38] But the technologically mediated landscape to whose conquest the building was dedicated was all on the inside, in the deep space of the laboratories. Furthermore, what Anthony Vidler called (in his review of the building) the "communal basement," housing "all that could give [the system] life," contained not only the auditorium, cafeteria, and lounges but also the mainframe computers in which the information generated by this architectural machine was to be processed.[39] At one level, the position occupied by machines within the topology of Bell Laboratories was purely practical, since their weight and service requirements made placement at ground level or below desirable. Nevertheless, it was the logic of

6.11

Eero Saarinen, Bell Telephone Laboratories, Holmdel, New Jersey, 1962 (phase 1), 1966 (phase 2). Plan.

The Topologies of Knowledge

these machines that also "gave life" to the system at Holmdel, a function anticipated by Saarinen in his nearly parallel studies for the IBM laboratory at Yorktown Heights.

According to Kevin Roche, during the initial design phase of the IBM project Saarinen toyed with the idea of an electronic display in the lobby that would light up each time the building's mainframe performed a calculation.[40] Indeed, in an intermediate scheme dated several months after the initial "campus" studies, two courtyards within a monolithic volume are separated by a double-height interior "computer room." Visitors entering from the front at the terrace level would be confronted with the machines in this room directly upon arrival, while workers entering from the rear parking lot level at the second floor would view the machines from above. Most of the laboratories have access to natural light at the courtyards, while all of the offices line the outer perimeter. The only exceptions are the groups of rooms at either end of the plan ("Physical Research" and "Cryogenics Research") at the second floor, in which laboratory spaces flank a narrow service core and are separated from the courtyards by a corridor running along the inner face. In that respect, this scheme anticipates the planning of the final design, which was largely in place by early 1958.[41] But the entry sequence also indicates that for a time the entire facility was organized around a functional computer "showroom" very much like that designed by Eliot Noyes in New York in his new role as IBM director of design in 1955.

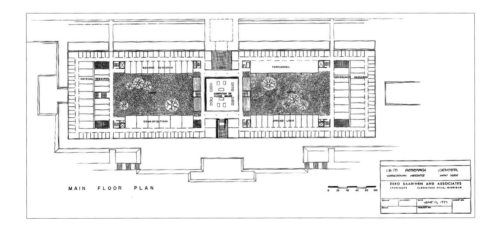

MAIN FLOOR PLAN

6.12
(previous page) Eero Saarinen, Bell Telephone Laboratories, Holmdel, New Jersey, 1962 (phase 1), 1966 (phase 2). Atrium. Photograph by Cervin Robinson.

6.13
Eero Saarinen & Associates, study of an early scheme for IBM Thomas J. Watson Research Laboratory, Yorktown Heights, New York, 12 June 1957.

The Topologies of Knowledge

What happened to the machines? By November 1957 they had been shunted to the side in the new curved scheme that ran along the contours of the hill. They would still have been visible from the visitors' entry but were only to be passed by rather than confronted directly. As built, the computer facility was assimilated into the modular planning arrangement that duplicated the one designed several months earlier for Bell Laboratories. Again, the relaxation of the scientists, fresh from the campus, was treated as part of their work. In Saarinen's words: "It has always seemed to me that many scientists in the research field are like university professors—tweedy, pipe-smoking men. In contrast to the efficient laboratories, we wanted to provide them with a more relaxed, 'tweedy,' out-doors sort of environment."[42] The organization man—the man in the gray flannel suit walking down Park Avenue or performing an administrative function for IBM—had here become a "tweedy" university professor roaming about the suburban landscape, his functional extroversion replaced by an equally functional introversion.

The spaces that Saarinen designed for occupation by this character type were also organized around a systematic eversion, or turning inside out, of the corporate office building. Planned on a 4-foot by 6-foot grid oriented horizontally, the interior of the curved bar at IBM was composed of a repetitive series of modular bays distributed around secondary corridors. Along each corridor was a row of 12-foot-deep offices, and opposite a row of 24-foot-deep laboratories, all divided by movable steel and glass partitions. The laboratories in adjacent bays were arranged back-to-back, sandwiching a narrow service core. The accompanying bay of back-to-back offices had along its spine a continuous storage wall. Stone end walls terminated each bay inside the curved perimeter corridors on either side. This rhythm was periodically interrupted by wedge-shaped utility spaces and entry points. There were no columns visible

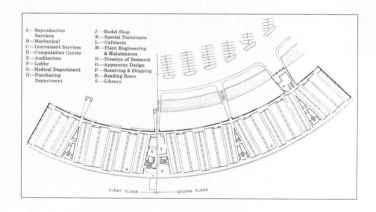

6.14

Eero Saarinen, IBM Thomas J. Watson Research Laboratory, Yorktown Heights, New York, 1961. First- and second-floor plans.

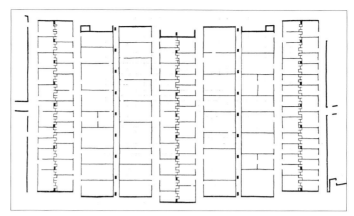

6.15
Eero Saarinen, IBM Thomas J. Watson Research Laboratory,
Yorktown Heights, New York, 1961. Planning modules.

6.16
Eero Saarinen, IBM Thomas J. Watson Research Laboratory,
Yorktown Heights, New York, 1961. Front.

The Topologies of Knowledge

anywhere. The rear, concave face of the building was clad in alternating bays of stone and bronze-tinted glass curtain wall. The front, convex face was clad entirely in the three-story curtain wall. This wall, front and back, was set on a 4-foot horizontal module; consequently, it did not register the corresponding 6-foot horizontal dimension of the module organizing the interior.

Instead, the interior module was marked on the surfaces located *deepest within* the building—the surfaces of the two spines, the service core and the storage wall, which ran down each bay of laboratories and offices. The linear core servicing the laboratories was clad in standardized panels whose modularity was echoed by that of the machines occupying the spaces they enclosed. Each storage wall running between rows of offices was also made up of panelized surfaces finished in different shades of the same color. Within each 4-foot module were a wide panel and a narrow panel, both running floor to ceiling in alternating light and dark colors, a design that accommodated storage units of different widths—an offset, patterned "curtain wall" (like that at IBM Rochester) turned completely inside out.[43] Instead of colorful modular patterns organizing the exterior of the building, here at Yorktown Heights—in a building designed for stereotypically introverted researchers—there were colorful modular patterns projected outward from the deepest cores of deep space, thus declaring their organizational authority *from within*.

Consistent with Eliel Saarinen's exhortation to "look at the next largest thing," this eversion was also carried out at the scale of the bays themselves, since the actual colors running in gradations down the backs of the offices along each corridor varied from corridor to corridor. Colors ran from cool to warm along the length of the curved bar—reportedly in recognition of the gradation of seasonal hues visible in the landscape outdoors, thereby acting as an orientation system within an otherwise highly repetitive plan. As one observer put it, "If the partitions were taken down, a visitor could see a gigantic spectroscope."[44] This mapping of the exterior landscape onto the interior surfaces of the building was carried out even more literally in the walls made of fieldstone quarried from the site that terminated each bay at the perimeter corridors. Selected stones in the walls were identified with numbered white dots, which indexed them to a map showing the location on the site from which they had been gathered.[45]

At IBM we thus find another piece of the new landscape, visible only to those who—like Kepes—peered inward through scientific instruments. Saarinen, the architect who perhaps best understood the logic of the curtain wall, used it both to obscure the inner workings of this space with a tinted mask and to map it from the inside out. The computers to which the entire operation was dedicated turned out to be not

6.18
Eero Saarinen, IBM Thomas J. Watson Research Laboratory, Yorktown Heights, New York, 1961. Fieldstone walls in corridor.

a unique and privileged figure to be exhibited to the visitor in a centralized show-room, but merely part of the pattern, integrated into the modular system through their own imminent systematicity. What mattered most was the pattern itself, a pattern that unfolded gradually as one penetrated deeper into the inner sanctum. But ultimately, deep space was found to be empty, shallow, as thin as a curtain wall. Its enchantments, including the mythical inwardness of the scientist, were only the residue of a longing for an organicity integrating the depths of scientific knowledge into a unified whole. For Saarinen this organicity had been provided earlier by the recognizable totality called the university, with its neo-Gothic surfaces and inter-linked quadrangles. But as that institution dissolved into the matrices of the military-industrial-academic complex, it had to be submitted to a visual and organizational regime capable of integrating Vannevar Bush's "endless frontier" of science—the new landscape—into another species of unified totality. This was the mission, indeed the obsession, of the organizational complex to which Saarinen was beholden, not be-cause he subordinated himself to the will of the corporations but because it was archi-tecture, the architecture of the computer and of the curtain wall, that was called on to give life to—to organize—a nature dead and dying in the radioactive winds.

That was the nature visible to the "tweedy" scientist taking a break from the ma-chines and staring out the window. It was the formerly sublime nature of the Hudson River School, soon to be populated by corporate campuses at every exit along the highway. Its pastoralism was rapidly being evacuated by the automobile, which was the silent constituent of all corporate campuses. Despite the undeniable attractions of the view, carefully managed to this day, there was little out there but machines, highways, and communications networks, the offspring of the corporations for which Saarinen worked.

Inside, at IBM, the research activities of the corporation were initially organized into six scientific divisions, distributed in loose concentrations throughout the cen-ter. These were disciplinary formations dedicated to basic research into the tech-niques of the organizational complex—business theory, operations research, pattern recognition, machine organization, communications networks, and other systems. The company's president, Thomas J. Watson Jr., described the facility in his address to stockholders on the its opening day as "an international center for unifying the mas-sive amount of information already existent in the computor [sic] field and that which will be added in the years ahead."[46]

In other words, the company slogan and principal command—"Think"—em-blazoned above the head of Watson Sr. in the old company photographs had pro-duced a new thinking machine, a corporate equivalent of the "think tanks" of military research designed to cope with the threat of a scientifically induced information over-load, by unifying knowledge unattainable at universities that were organized according to the old disciplines. As an IBM brochure on the building put it, "Although most of the classical scientific disciplines are represented in the Research program, they appear to form the parts of a newly emerging discipline—computer science."[47] In that sense, for IBM "computer science" was science itself, as it advanced into the unknown spaces of the "endless frontier." Along that frontier, the organization of knowledge into disciplines, each with its own building on a university campus, was abandoned for the integration of disciplines into a single system. As the brochure put it, "so many of the projects in computer research turn out to be interdisciplinary that we must almost of necessity talk of computer science as a new, unifying discipline."[48] Thus did the topologies of Saarinen's architecture, its inside-out, flexible, patterned matrix, assist in the reorganization of scientific knowledge itself.

At Bell Telephone Laboratories in Holmdel, completed several years after Saarinen's death on 1 September 1961, the same holds true. One characteristic that distinguished the Holmdel facility from its IBM counterpart in Yorktown Heights was its emphasis on "development," or the search for practical applications of the discoveries and innovations by scientists conducting "basic research," which remained centered at Murray Hill. But as at IBM, Bell Laboratories also saw the need to reorganize research that had traditionally been classified according to the academic model as belonging to either the physical or the chemical sciences. By 1962 the company had organized its research into more finely divided fields.[49] Participation in university activities was encouraged, and indeed many Bell Laboratories scientists divided their time between corporate research and university teaching, while university-based scientists frequently gave presentations to Bell Laboratories researchers. In the booklet welcoming visitors to Holmdel, the building is described as the company's center for "studies and development in military communications systems, data systems, data communications systems, telephone traffic, customer telephone systems, and much of Bell Laboratories' engineering information."[50] So the work performed at Holmdel in support of what its director had described elsewhere as "the world's largest computer"—the nationwide communications network then presided over by the Bell System—belonged, in an enlarged sense, to the "computer science" that had remapped academic disciplinarity into colored modules inside IBM.[51]

There were few bright colors inside Bell Telephone Laboratories at Holmdel—mostly grays, off-whites, and whites, with the occasional brown or green carpet or upholstery—but the panelized storage walls and service cores still ran down the spines of offices and laboratories, and a modular steel and glass partition system was inserted into inverted channels in the 6-foot ceiling grid.[52] Side and aisle partitions terminated in a glass panel, thus visually underlining the continuity of the ceiling's gridded field. In this case, the grid was carried into the curtain wall that enclosed the perimeter corridors, pointing to a slightly different inside-outside relation than at IBM. Saarinen's site plan positioned the building within a vast ellipse of parking, but its he-

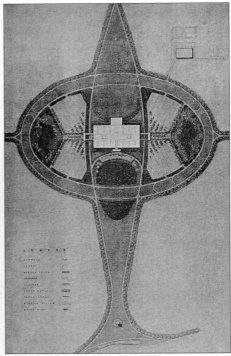

roic geometries were helpless against the even vaster emptiness of the setting. The inside-out topology of the Holmdel building echoed that at Yorktown Heights, but the emptiness of the suburban landscape was registered even more incisively on its surfaces, inside and out. The dullness of the interiors reflected the institutional grayness of the nondescript laboratories being built by the military-industrial complex in suburbs across the country, tinted only—as in the "blue rooms" of SAGE—by the colored light of the computer screens mapping new informatic landscapes. The same aesthetics of dead neutrality was materialized in the Bell Laboratories mirrored curtain wall.

The curtain walls at both IBM and Bell Laboratories contained refinements on the mobile optics with which Saarinen experimented at General Motors and IBM Rochester. In Yorktown Heights, the light aluminum sections of Rochester's vertical mullions were also inverted, to form an extruded "T"; their faces were all finished in matte-black

6.19
Eero Saarinen, Bell Telephone Laboratories, Holmdel, New Jersey, 1962 (phase 1), 1966 (phase 2). Interiors with modular partition system.

6.20
Eero Saarinen, Bell Telephone Laboratories, Holmdel, New Jersey, 1962 (phase 1), 1966 (phase 2). Site plan.

Eero Saarinen, Bell Telephone Laboratories, Holmdel, New
Jersey, 1962 (phase 1), 1966 (phase 2). Curtain wall. Photograph by Yukio Futagawa.

The Topologies of Knowledge

THE BIGGEST MIRROR EVER

porcelain enamel, except for the two narrow arms protruding laterally, which were given a bright aluminum finish. The result was a wall composed of a series of vertical lines, black and white, whose density varied with the angle from which they were viewed, an effect accentuated by the curve of the facade. The verticality of the wall was further emphasized by holding the thickness of the intermediate floor slabs back from the skin, thus eliminating intermittent opaque spandrel panels. The wall's bronze color connected it abstractly with the wooded spaces beyond, and with the fieldstone walls with which the curved bar was terminated. As was also true of the interior, color was used as a signifier for "nature," onto which were consequently projected all of the characteristics of the empty sign, flattened out into the organizational messages of the curtain wall.

The evacuation of mimesis was taken still further at Holmdel. There, the thin protruding vertical mullions of IBM were basically retained, but with a slightly different profile now rendered all in black. Their spacing was narrowed to accept the planning grid on a 3-foot half module. Spanning these verticals, and running up all five stories of the facade and entirely around the rectangular building—the long side of which

6.22

Title page from feature article on Eero Saarinen's Bell Telephone Laboratories, Holmdel, New Jersey. From *Architectural Forum* 126, no. 3 (April 1967): 33. Photograph by Cervin Robinson.

was nearly a quarter-mile long—were mirrored glass panes designed, according to Saarinen's directive, "for image reflection on one side, yet visual transparency through the other."[53] This technological innovation, which consisted of an aluminum film sandwiched between two sheets of glass, represented the first major construction application of two-way vacuum-coated mirrored glass, which had previously been used only on precision lenses. The wall was designed to reflect nearly 70 percent of the building's exterior heat load, resulting in a dramatic reduction of the high peripheral air-conditioning load typical in glass-walled buildings. This reduction was accompanied by the lower priority assigned to cooling the perimeter corridors that were not inhabited full-time, and the higher priority accorded to controlling the temperature of the interior offices and laboratories with their heat-generating equipment and precise temperature requirements. Thus did Saarinen and his associates design, with uncanny precision, what *Architectural Forum* called an "inside-out" air-conditioning system, whose primary channels followed the service cores running through the deep spaces of this inside-out laboratory.[54]

But there was nothing in the mirror. The "image reflection" sought by Saarinen was not the reproduction of the landscape of huge parking quadrants surrounding the building. Saarinen, an architect of the corporate image, had produced the image of the organizational complex itself—the vast, empty network of networks into which Bell Telephone Laboratories was embedded. This complex was utterly faceless, its physiognomy reduced to nonfigural patterns in an alien landscape of staggering new knowledge and new threats. Like the patterned punched cards fed into IBM's machines, Saarinen's mirror at Bell Laboratories did not reproduce nature; it encrypted it in innumerable tiny reflections flickering across its screens. Just as IBM was using the techniques of pattern recognition to teach American machines to read Russian at its Yorktown Heights laboratory,[55] so too could its code be read only by trained "operators," organization men turned inside out, who wore their empty introversion—their "reflective" personalities—on the *outside* of their gray flannel suits.

Thus Saarinen had no choice but to clothe the *interiors* of Bell Laboratories in grays. Gray was the color of both organization and its entropic dissipation, the reflexive key that made visible the irreversible degeneration of a new nature. It was the colorless color of organizational overload. To all who may once have been human, looking across the parking lot at an outside that had formerly been inside, the domestic mirror—in front of which Saarinen had, twenty years earlier, positioned a prototypical office worker dressing himself in his "postwar" house, and had subsequently converted into an interior sky to illuminate new automobiles—was now clouded over with atmospheric interference modulated only by the thin lines of a blank screen.

Epilogue: Hallucinations

Organization and entropy. The relation between these two terms was understood by information theorists during the late 1940s and 1950s as an opposition that concealed an affinity. For Norbert Wiener, on whose work we have concentrated, entropic de-differentiation was mathematically opposed to informatic organization. But also for Wiener, as for his contemporaries Claude Shannon and Warren Weaver, an increase in overall entropy within a system brought with it an *increase* in the measurable information contained by any given message within that system, since its emergence from a cacophony of possible messages would be less probable. As we have seen, cybernetics treats organization as a message in itself, independent of semantic content. And as Wiener writes in *The Human Use of Human Beings,* "the more probable the message, the less information it gives."[1]

Thus, as certain forms of organization (such as modular planning) become more prevalent, they exhibit a tendency toward entropy, as in the gridded interiors of Gordon Bunshaft's Union Carbide Building, or in the mirrored emptiness of Eero Saarinen's highly organized Bell Laboratories. And increased entropy can mean stasis, rigidity. But—counterintuitively, perhaps—it can also mean something like what Weaver calls, with technocratic detachment, "freedom," or an *increase* in the field of possible outcomes.[2] Far from legitimizing the control tactics of the organizational complex, this implies the potential for critical, destabilizing maneuvers—undertaken from within the very infrastructures of organization itself—that amplify this tendency, through what information theorists call "positive feedback."

Still, for the network of networks that we have been mapping, art rose to the level of science precisely to the degree that it exhibited a measure of patterned organization comparable to that made visible in the new nature revealed by advanced imaging technologies, and vice versa. For figures such as Sigfried Giedion and especially Gyorgy Kepes, this same nature served as a source of organizational patterns capable of regulating the entropic effects of the military-industrial complex, precisely to the extent that the patterns generated by information machines were comparable to those images of the new, already naturalized micro- and macroscopic landscape that were coming out of the laboratories.

The same was true for humans and machines: the two categories were inextricably linked through communicational flows that were themselves subject to organizational logics in a "defense-by-communications" not against the machine per se, but against the destabilizing dissipation of the "human" into commingled sociotechnological networks. In that sense, enterprises like "human relations," dedicated to preserving the organicity of the corporate whole, were extended not in the service of an already-constituted subject but as disciplinary measures that both constructed and controlled the new human-machine assemblages that constituted the corporations. Such enterprises reterritorialized the corporations' inherent instabilities (including the psychic instabilities tended to by the human relations counselors), an effect reenacted by the modular surfaces of the office landscape. Ultimately and paradoxically, the crisis of the "human" to which this conformist production of "organization men" (and women) belonged was the same crisis that cyberneticists saw threatening the integrity of the liberal humanist subject, to whose well-being many of them remained dedicated.

In all cases and on all sides *organization,* as the agent of a new, horizontally equilibrated organicity, effected a conjunction where there might otherwise have been opposition: art opposed to science, technology opposed to nature, human opposed to machine. All became linkages that were themselves linked in the network of networks of the organizational complex. Architecture was integrated into this complex precisely to the extent that it fulfilled the organizational imperative. Again, we are confronted here with a situation of control through feedback. Organization, as a means of control, is necessarily a function of the various nodes through which its forces flow. And architecture, as one constitutive node among many in the network, acts as both receiver and transmitter of patterned organizational codes, thereby gaining its status as one among many technologies of organization.

But technology also fails, in two ways. First, it fails to the extent that it does not succeed in living up to the external performance criteria established by technocrats who, again reflexively, are themselves functions of the machines they manage. When these criteria are not met, performance is less than optimal. In certain cases, that dropoff may also evidence a contradiction embedded within the criteria themselves. I have argued that something like this was happening with modular office planning, as the actual optimization of functional flexibility was systematically limited by the overriding imperative of organizational integration. Ultimately, the two criteria were incompatible—thus the difference between the planning of the RCA Building at Rockefeller Center, which addressed itself to the unpredictabilities of an external market, and the planning of the curtain wall office buildings that followed, which incorporated this unpredictability into their modular systems and projected it back out as image, sacrificing actual flexibility for heightened corporate identification.

Second, technology fails internally. That is, the new machines can only do what they are programmed to do (or perhaps, what they program themselves to do). Which is also to say that their performance can never be fully predicted. According to Horkheimer and Adorno, "chance itself is planned."[3] But notwithstanding all efforts to establish performance criteria capable of anticipating even that which cannot be anticipated (again, the building in of unpredictability through modular flexibility), the resolutely dissipative logic of the organizational complex prevents the consolidation of a sufficiently stable ground, an "inside," from which such criteria can be determined and measured. This blockage is the primary effect of the various topological inversions we have observed. There is no outside to the control society or to the organizational complex, but neither is there a self-consistent, continuous inside. Networks are, by definition, full of holes: not the empty spaces between lines and points, the interstices that get smaller as the network gets denser, but the holes constituted by the media themselves. Like the television sets populating living rooms across the country or the inscrutable black boxes populating the laboratories of the military-industrial-academic complex, these holes are infinitely deep and infinitely shallow at one and the same time. The unfathomable depths of a new nature—the nature of mass culture and the nature of the laboratories—are projected onto impenetrable surfaces, initiating a crisis of inside and outside that can be resolved only in gestures of overcompensation that collapse back onto themselves, emptied out into the depthless interiors of their own networks. The crisis accounts for the tendency toward entropy that we have observed in Saarinen's corporate architecture. It implodes, leaving only the pixellated particulate of its media—the modular units of the organizational complex—reflected in its mirrored screens.

With these observations, I will close by invoking a series of extended excerpts from the aesthetic culture of the mid-1950s and thereafter that refer, both explicitly and obliquely, to the architecture and urbanism of the organizational complex. These examples can be thought of as images projected backward onto the preceding analysis—images taken from outside architecture and fed back into it, in keeping with the topologies of our subject. In this manner, with all due respect for disciplinary and discursive boundaries but also despite them, the stakes in the conjunction of architecture and the organizational complex may acquire further definition, in place of the formal conclusions to which the incomplete map we have drawn will remain permanently inadequate.

7.1

The first excerpt is taken from a transcript of a seminar discussion on urban form, between Gyorgy Kepes, Kevin Lynch, and the composer John Cage, held at MIT on 10 December 1954, early on in the research project on "perceptual form in the city" on which Kepes and Lynch worked through the mid-1950s.[4] Cage begins the discussion by explaining his interest in utilizing sound to "introduce people to their environment" by setting up a "field situation," in which six categories of sound—"1- city sounds; 2- country sounds; 3- synthetic sounds; 4- manually produced sounds; 5- vocal or wind sounds; 6- sounds so quiet they have to be magnified to be in concert with others"—are played in continuous variation with respect to all of their characteristics. Kepes immediately translates this to the visual register, in keeping with the modulation of effects in a cybernetic regime from one medium (for Cage, magnetic tape) to another (for Kepes, the photograph). After Cage explains further, Kepes takes a cue from the scheme's implicit urbanism ("city" vs. "country" in Cage's classification), again making it clear that this discussion is not restricted to music but rather is premised precisely on the translatability of media effects. He asks: "If you could articulate the existing city sound patterns, what would you do, what would be your needs to be satisfied?" Kepes then answers his own question: "With purposeful organization of city sounds, we could enrich the experience of the city."

Cage: My feeling is that this is already the case.

Kepes: Ordered pattern, not a fixed, fully controlled or rigid one, but one partially defined, such as the 12 o'clock bell, in contrast to the chaotic flow of the random sounds, could help to structure our response.

Cage: Regularized events, such as the 12 o'clock bell, form a rhythmic situation, for the bells never completely coincide. If they were really controlled, they would not do what they actually do, that is to produce an overlapping situation. With magnetic tape, many have considered the possibility of controlling sounds completely. The results have proved the contrary. In Cologne they have created synthetic sounds to produce harmonious controlled sound, but the material resists control. Now they are using the card method, on the plan of a Cybernetics machine. I think it would be better to give up the idea of control and merely enjoy the absence of control.

At this point the divisions in the discussion become clear, as Lynch chimes in with the predictability of the twelve o'clock bell, suspiciously: "You believe, then, that the person should be trained to enjoy what is there, rather than attempt to control the environment." Again Cage replies: "What would be the intention of imposed order?" Kepes responds, "Because the average sound environment is a random situation, small islands of ordered pattern within the randomness could help to catalyse an overall ordered pattern, e.g. a theme, such as Christmas, would provide a symbolic focus by means of which random patterns would be related. It is possible to conceive of such sound focuses of cityscapes to enrich the whole environment."

Later it becomes clearer still that both Kepes and Lynch find the entropic degeneration of cultural meaning intolerable. Kepes persistently attempts to mobilize organizational principles dating from the Bauhaus and passed through perceptual psychology to regulate the new landscape. As he says to Cage, "The perception of a city is primarily a rhythmical experience. For example, the variety of tempos—walking fast in the early morning and walking more slowly later in the day. Perhaps soundwise each street has a characteristic experience: would it be possible to scaffold this experience to a rhythmic unity?"

Cage replies, "But rhythm is a changing concept now, too. With magnetic tape we see that the situation is logarithmic rather than arithmetic. It is a field here too rather than a series of discrete steps. This is true even of tempo, each event going on at its own pace. Thus from the most empty one moves to the greatest density in time, and from this to fragmentation; i.e., things grouping in time, until finally you merely get a dust." Here Cage is restating the cybernetic principle of increasing entropy, except that his "field" is different from the digitized noise of information theory that was expressible, like everything else in a universal Turing machine, in what Cage calls "a series of discrete steps."

In appealing to the analog medium of magnetic tape, which records and plays back a continuous field of sound, Cage is displacing his own nervousness with regard to what he calls the "Cybernetics machine" by associating the entropic degeneration to "dust" with what he calls "continuity in the infinite sense" that enacts the unlimited "potentiality" of an urban environment. For Cage, speaking urbanistically about sounds, this analog continuity is what holds things together in the absence of an organizing pattern. Cage's own nostalgia for media specificities predating the digital translatability that broke sound into bits is thus brought out when he confronts the logics of control that he recognized in the IBM "card method" of patterned ones and zeroes. His distribution of urban sounds into the categories of "city" and "country" is likewise symptomatic in omitting the vast, empty spaces in between, in which architects like Saarinen had begun to work. For Cage, urban decentralization threatened to break up the continuities of the sonic field itself, thereby nullifying a condition crucial for the liberation of environmental "potentiality." As he said to Kepes, "If sound is decentralized, you are taking sounds apart."

7.2

Our second example is drawn from the discourse on minimal art that emerged in the United States in the wake of the abstract expressionism to which Kepes was so strongly opposed in the early 1960s. The writer is the artist Robert Smithson, who would later engage Kepes directly.[5] But here I focus on Smithson's early essay titled "Entropy and the New Monuments," first published in *Artforum* in June 1966. Smithson begins: "Many architectural concepts found in science-fiction have nothing to do with science or fiction, instead they suggest a new kind of monumentality which has much in common with the aims of some of today's artists."[6] His "new monumentality," illustrated with minimalist sculpture, inverts that announced by Sigfried Giedion in two texts devoted to that theme written in the 1940s (both are also included in Giedion's *Architecture, You and Me,* the 1958 translation of *Architektur und Gemeinschaft*).[7] Where Giedion sought symbolic plenitude in the postwar civic center inspired by the model of Rockefeller Center, Smithson, two decades later, found—and celebrated—entropic emptiness. Here is Smithson, at length:

> The much denigrated architecture of Park Avenue known as "cold glass boxes," along with the Manneristic modernity of Philip Johnson, have helped foster the entropic mood. The Union Carbide building best typifies such architectural entropy. In its vast lobby one may see an exhibition called "The Future." It offers the purposeless "educational" displays of Will Burtin, "internationally acclaimed for his three-dimensional designs," which portray "Atomic Energy in Action." If ever there was an example of action in entropy, this is it. The action is frozen into an array of plastic and neon, and enhanced by the sound of Muzak faintly playing in the background. At a certain time of day, you may also see a movie called "The Petrified River." A nine-foot vacuum-formed blue plexiglass globe is a model of a uranium atom— "ten million trillion trillion times the size of the actual atom." Lights on the ends of flexible steel rods are whipped about in the globe. Parts of the "underground" movie, "The Queen of Sheba Meets the Atom Man," were filmed in this exhibition hall. Taylor Mead creeps around in the film like a loony sleepwalker, and licks the plastic models depicting "chain-reaction." The sleek walls and high ceilings give the place an uncanny tomb-like atmosphere. There is something irresistible about such a place, something grand and empty.
>
> This kind of architecture without "value of qualities," is, if anything, a fact. From this "undistinguished" run of architecture, as Flavin calls it, we gain a clear perception of physical reality free from the general claims of "purity and idealism." Only commodities can afford such illusionistic values; for instance, soap is 99 44/100% pure, beer has more spirit in it, and dog food is ideal; all and all this means such values are worthless. As the cloying effect of such "values" wears off, one perceives the "facts" of the outer edge, the flat surface, the banal, the empty, the cool, blank after blank; in other words, that infinitesimal condition known as entropy. [8]

Although, as the preceding analysis of the Union Carbide Building and its contemporaries has shown, such works of architecture are anything but uncommodified "facts," Smithson's own reversal of the sign of entropy is striking: from index of negative degeneration to index of positive release from the selling of the scientifically mediated future. Smithson's future—a science fiction future that, as he says, has nothing to do with science or fiction—is exposed in the art of his minimalist colleagues like Sol LeWitt:

LeWitt's first one-man show at the now defunct Daniel's Gallery presented a rather uncompromising group of monumental "obstructions." Many people were "left cold" by them, or found their finish "too dreary." These obstructions stood as visible clues of the future. A future of humdrum practicality in the shape of standardized office buildings modeled after Emery Roth; in other words, a jerry-built future, a feigned future, an ersatz future very much like the one depicted in the movie "The Tenth Victim." LeWitt's show has helped to neutralize the myth of progress. It has also corroborated Wylie Sypher's insight that "Entropy is evolution in reverse." [9]

This entropic future, a future that reverses the evolutionary myth of progress, is also fundamentally counterorganicist (and not merely inorganic, as were the crys-

7.1

Ronald Bladen, untitled, 1965. Illustration from Robert Smithson, "Entropy and the New Monuments," *Artforum* 4, no. 10 (June 1966): 26.

talline obsessions of Smithson's work). It is a counterfuture that incorporates architecture, digitized and shrunk down into the modular units of minimal art. For architecture this meant, strictly speaking, an "evolution in reverse." It was a film run backward, in which the sequence of visual media issuing from the Bauhaus was now reflected back onto itself in the mirror of the curtain wall: from painting to photography to film to sculpture to architecture to sculpture . . . But the first principle of entropic degeneration is its irreversibility, illustrated elsewhere by Smithson with the help of the sandbox that constitutes the last in his series of "monuments of Passaic": Divide a sandbox into two halves, one filled with white sand and the other with black. Put a child in the sandbox, and ask him or her to run hundreds of times clockwise in the box "until the sand gets mixed and begins to turn grey." Then ask the child to reverse direction. "The result will not be a restoration of the original division but a greater degree of greyness and increase of entropy."[10]

Here, to run evolution backward—counterorganically—toward an ersatz counterfuture does not mean regression. There is no room for nostalgia in entropic time. Instead, for architecture, looking back on itself through the mirror of history means coming to terms with the faceless "facts" of its own unrecognizability in the dull grayness of the organizational complex. There the myth of progress was evacuated into the cool exteriority of a media effect, even as it was absorbed into the silence of an encompassing modulation whose sole purpose was to remove the noise in the channels that prevented humans from communicating with one another and with the machines into which their humanity had been drained. Smithson himself was aware of the entropics of communication, though not (apparently) of communication theory's indifference to the cultural "value" or meaning of a message. He was therefore suspicious of the moralism implicit in measuring information content in organizational terms, declaring that "[o]ften the false has greater 'reality' than the true. Therefore, it seems that all information, and that includes anything that is visible, has its entropic side. Falseness, as an ultimate, is inextricably a part of entropy, and this falseness is devoid of moral implications."[11]

The true/false binarism structured all of Smithson's discourse, to the extent that the only option with which he left himself was endless oscillation between organic order and entropic decay. But in its moral neutrality this begins to approach the morally neutral—though ethically charged—binarism of ones and zeroes that underlay the architecture of the organizational complex itself. To raise falseness to the level of truth in the form of "standardized office buildings modeled after Emery Roth" is to refuse, as did Cage, the moralizing values of organization, but for more ambiguous reasons.

The third example, which is in fact a series of linked examples, returns us first to Saarinen, and specifically to two other major office buildings he designed that we have not examined. These were the headquarters of John Deere and Company in Moline, Illinois, and the Columbia Broadcasting System headquarters in Manhattan, both completed in 1964. In 1975 the Deere corporate campus, consisting of two linked buildings on a modular plan with an inside-out structural system rendered as a Cor-Ten steel sunscreen on all sides, was the subject of a study by the anthropologists Mildred Hall and Edward Hall, *The Fourth Dimension in Architecture: The Impact of Building on Man's Behavior.* Edward Hall, who had collaborated elsewhere with Marshall McLuhan, was the author of a number of widely read books on communication and culture, including *The Silent Language* (1959)—containing chapters with such titles as "Culture Is Communication," "The Organizing Pattern," and "Space Speaks"—which McLuhan quoted repeatedly in *Understanding Media* (1964). In 1966 Hall published *The Hidden Dimension,* an extension of his earlier work whose chapters include "Culture as Communication," "The Perception of Space," "Visual Space," and "The Anthropology of Space: An Organizing Model" and that quotes Kepes on the contingency of vision.

In other words, the Halls' study of the Deere headquarters itself belonged to the organizational complex. Their account, based on a series of interviews conducted with Deere employees between 1964 and 1969, posits the Deere headquarters as a behavior-inducing environment. They introduce their study with a quotation from Roger G. Barber's *Ecological Psychology* (1968) that defines "environment" as an "improbable arrangement of objects and events which *coerce behavior in accordance with their own dynamic patterns*[.]" This definition of the physical environment as a dynamic, coercive apparatus leads Hall and Hall to hypothesize (and to conclude): "In a word, Barber finds that the environment provides a setting which elicits standard behavior according to binding but as yet unverbalized rules which are more compelling and more uniform than such individual variables as personality."[12]

This form of environmental behaviorism was, in turn, very close to the logic of the black box as explained in 1956 by the cyberneticist W. Ross Ashby: "The child who tries to open a door has to manipulate the handle (the input) so as to produce the desired movement at the latch (the output); and he has to learn how to control the one by the other without seeing the internal mechanism that links them. In our daily lives we are confronted at every turn with systems whose internal mechanisms are not fully open to inspection, and which must be treated by the methods appropriate to the Black Box."[13] For Hall and Hall, environmental stimuli, "dynamic patterns," are input; behavior is output. Subjective interiority, including "such individual variables as personality," is seen as subordinate to the externality called "environment." The anthropologist, like the human relations engineer, further assumes a position comparable to that of the "interrogator" in the Turing test, interviewing the human black boxes to determine the degree to which their humanity has been constructed or compromised by the architectural pattern machine they inhabit.

The interviewees have one complaint: not enough color. It is a complaint that registers, according to Hall and Hall, the organization's gender gap, since the few colored accents dotting what one architectural commentator called the "pervasive plaid" of Saarinen's interiors[14] were to be found only in the attire of the female employees— gray being the color of choice for organization men. But from our perspective, such a study, with its earnest deployment of control logics in the name of human subjects, can only be read as a kind of architectural Turing test, its interrogators posing questions to a human-machine assemblage that only deepen the crisis of the anthropological a priori—the human—that they seek to defend.

A striking attribute of the Deere headquarters is that this space, analyzed fundamentally as a space of communication by Hall and Hall, systematically hides its communications equipment. Telephones and consoles are tucked into desks that are wired to the floor and thus locked into position by the hardware of communication.[15] Modular flexibility is again compromised, this time by the physical positioning of input-output ports, all in the name of smoothing out the surfaces. The somewhat paradoxical effect, ultimately, is to detach the communicative and supposedly behavior-inducing organizational software—the modular patterns—from the actual communications hardware that underpins the entire operation.

That effect is even stronger in the headquarters Saarinen designed for the Columbia Broadcasting System (CBS) in Manhattan. This "tall office building" (Sullivan), nicknamed "Black Rock" within the communications industry, is an architectural black box that extends the inscrutability of media into the urban scale. That for Saarinen there was no opposition between the "organic" forms with which he experimented in other works (such as his iconic TWA terminal) and the organicism of the office is evidenced by the early sketches for the project, which show him experimenting with a naturalistic structural morphology that gradually metamorphosed into a solid block. Literally a node in a communications network—the network called CBS— this monolith, consisting of 5-foot dark gray granite-clad piers alternating with 5-foot vertical stripes of black glazing, was conceived as a single impermeable surface, inside and out. As Saarinen put it to CBS president Frank Stanton in 1961, "the design is the simplest conceivable rectangular free-standing sheer tower."[16] In announcing that

design, the corporation described it as "[giving] expression to the worlds of communication and to the arts of which CBS is so vitally a part."[17] That the building in fact "expressed" nothing but its own impenetrability, however, was reinforced by Florence Knoll's treatment of the interiors. Reception areas were color-coded from floor to floor, but all the communications hardware, as well as other infrastructural termini (such as light switches), was again hidden. Executive offices contained pieces of furniture in which were concealed three television sets (one for each network), secret communications panels were built into receptionists' desks, and telephones were suspended below the tops of tables.[18]

This object, cut off from its surroundings on the outside and suppressing its ties to invisible communications networks on the inside, thus stood as a silent observer of

7.2

(previous page, top) Eero Saarinen, John Deere and Company headquarters, Moline, Illinois, 1964. Office interiors. Photograph by Ezra Stoller.

7.3

(previous page, bottom) Eero Saarinen, John Deere and Company headquarters, Moline, Illinois, 1964. Desks with built-in communications equipment. Photograph by Ezra Stoller.

7.4

Eero Saarinen, CBS headquarters, New York, 1964.

Hallucinations

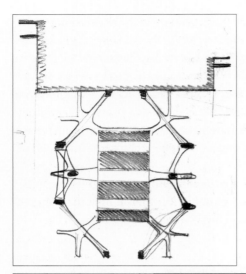

7.5
Eero Saarinen, study sketch for CBS headquarters, New York, showing biomorphic structural system, 31 October 1960.

7.6
Florence Knoll and Eero Saarinen & Associates, CBS headquarters, New York, 1964. Interior with concealed television sets.

what Peter Blake called in 1965 the "slaughter on Sixth Avenue." Blake lamented that the "complete organism" of nearby Rockefeller Center, linked underground, had been eviscerated by the autonomous, isolated towers built along its western flank during the 1950s and early 1960s; in the process, the entire zone had been converted into "a giant sample-case for the curtain wall salesman." For Blake, indifferent as he was to the enigmas of Knoll's internal dissimulations, Saarinen's building was redeemed only by its calm otherworldliness, "a mute but unmistakable commentary on the chaos all around it."[19]

In 1968 an uncannily similar—but no longer mute—monolith appeared in the media networks, projecting the chaos of the sixties forward into the eerie, empty calm of outer space. This was the monolith at the core of Stanley Kubrick's *2001: A Space Odyssey,* a mysterious black slab that appeared first among prehistoric humanity with the code to the secret of tools; again at the beginning of the twenty-first century as a communications beacon emitting piercing, inscrutable signals on the moon that secured for it the status of black box—a node in a network—and finally in orbit around Jupiter, in communication with the computer HAL at the threshold of a "stargate" leading humanity to a new order of being. It was a minimalist "new monument" worthy of Robert Morris or Donald Judd and an aesthetic precursor of the chess-playing IBM supercomputer, Deep Blue, that merged color-coded corporate identity with the topologies of the black box. And like Saarinen's "Black Rock," Kubrick's monolith was utterly detached from its surroundings but invisibly linked to a communications network.

In keeping with the externalization of thought that we have found on the surfaces of other information boxes, Gilles Deleuze has analyzed *2001* as a mise-en-scène of the brain:

7.7

Stanley Kubrick, dir., *2001: A Space Odyssey,* 1968. Monolith.

©Turner Entertainment Co. An AOL Time Warner Company.

The black stone of *2001* presides over both cosmic states and cerebral stages; it is the soul of the three bodies, earth, sun, and moon, but also the seed of the three brains, animal, human, machine.... But if the calculation fails, if the computer breaks down, it is because the brain is no more reasonable a system than the world is a rational one. The identity of world and brain, the automaton, does not form a whole, but rather a limit, a membrane which puts an outside and an inside in contact, makes them present to each other, confronts them or makes them clash. The inside is psychology, the past, involution, a whole psychology of depths which excavate the brain. The outside is the cosmology of galaxies, the future, evolution, a whole supernatural which makes the world explode.[20]

This space is, for Deleuze, among the spaces of a postwar cinema caught up in a transition from the sensory-motor extension of the body in the prewar "movement-image" to its reversal in the "beyond of movement" that he calls the "time-image," in which past and future are confronted with one another in the memory machine of the cinematic membrane.[21]

That is to say, "the membrane which makes the outside and the inside present to each other is called memory," a complex spatio-temporality that "makes relative insides and outsides [pasts and futures] communicate like interiors and exteriors."[22] Deleuze further divides the "cerebral space" he finds in the cinema of Kubrick and others into three subspaces: "a topological cerebral space, which pass[es] through relative mediums [*milieux*] to achieve the co-presence of an inside deeper than any internal medium, and an outside more distant than any external medium[;] ... a probabilistic or semi-fortuitous cerebral space, 'an uncertain system'"; and the space of the "irrational cut," of the unlinking and relinking of images not reducible to the sequences of montage and summarized in the insertion into cinema of a black or white screen, "which stands for the outside of all the images." For Deleuze, in the history of cinema these spaces unfold into a "new image of thought." By this he does not mean a representation of some externality. Rather, he means a new way of thinking. "A flickering brain, which relinks or creates loops—this is cinema."[23]

These observations are relevant here not only for their decoding of Kubrick's film, at which we have arrived after a space odyssey of our own through the organizational complex. We found at the beginning of our tour, after a survey of the cybernetic terrain, a cinematic tendency toward architecture already present in the visual thinking of the Bauhaus as expressed by László Moholy-Nagy. The curtain wall subsequently fulfilled cinema's projection forward, through photography, as an architectural membrane for the manipulation of light. Its organizational codes were linked to

insides and outsides forced into contact—and turned inside out—by topological inversions. Projected backward onto architecture, then, Deleuze's cinematic philosophy of time and space functions not merely as an interpretive mechanism but also as another reversal of the terms, comparable to Smithson's spatiotemporal media inversions around the question of entropy: from cinema to architecture to cinema, in a perfect spiral of media effects.

This spiral is vividly illustrated in *2001* itself, in the "stargate" sequence that marks an implosion, a radical cut ushered in by the monolith. After this cut we literally witness the "rebirth" of an astronaut, the organization man who has exchanged his gray business suit for an orange space suit and, implicitly, the letters IBM for NASA. The dizzying sequence of blurred images running first horizontally and then vertically along two sides of a narrow slot in the solar system was actually made by filming at close range photographs of architectural drawings, op-art paintings, wiring diagrams, and computer schematics projected at high speed.[24] This was Kepes in reverse. Instead of acting as organizing regulators, these second-generation technological patterns, sweeping past in a phantasmagoric blur, become agents of a disequilbrium so radical that it holds humanity at its mercy.

Douglas Trumbull, the special effects designer on *2001* responsible for the sequence, reminds us that this hole in the solar system was originally to be marked by a hole or slot in one of Jupiter's moons, which was eventually replaced by Kubrick with the black slab.[25] So to enter into this cut—the hole in space that is all black boxes, including Saarinen's—is not to rush headlong into some "posthuman" future, current mythology notwithstanding. Instead, it involves traveling backward into an irreversible history. As we have already seen at CBS, there is nothing behind the surfaces of the black

7.8
Stanley Kubrick, dir., *2001: A Space Odyssey*, 1968. "Stargate" sequence. © Turner Entertainment Co. An AOL Time Warner Company. All rights reserved.

Hallucinations

box but more surfaces, a discovery also made by Eliot Noyes when he tried to expose the insides of the information machines to view, only to be frustrated by the patterned disarray of their circuits—the same circuits that Trumbull and Kubrick rush past the viewer so fast that even a "vision in motion" cannot decode their psychedelic patterns.

If, at the end of the 1960s, it became fashionable to attend screenings of *2001* while under the influence of hallucinogens, we might finally recall the hallucinogenic, supernatural spaces mapped and explored by Thomas Pynchon in *Gravity's Rainbow* (1973), a novel that can be said to inhabit the unconscious of the organizational complex. Friedrich Kittler notes that Pynchon's novel "is essentially assembled from documentary sources, many of which—circuit diagrams, differential equations, corporate contracts, and organizational plans—are textualized for the first time."[26] Examining the novel's paranoid linkages between technology, erotics, and the Allied and Axis military-industrial apparatus, Kittler notes: "A thorough study of the files always reveals the conspiracy behind apparent coincidences."[27] Pynchon's space is a space in which "paranoia is knowledge itself"—a space in which, according to one of the novel's many undercover agents, "the world's gone insane, with information come to be the only real medium of exchange."[28]

As Kittler observes, under these conditions, "when the symbolic of signs, numbers and letters determine so-called reality, then gathering the traces becomes the paranoid's primary duty."[29] And so we arrive at where we began, with the last of six "Proverbs for Paranoids" proffered in the novel, which reminds us that "If there is something comforting—religious, if you want—about paranoia, there is still also anti-paranoia, where nothing is connected to anything, a condition not many of us can bear for long."[30] Traces of anti-paranoia are discernible in the novel's own tendency toward entropy, in what Kittler calls its "increasing mixture of characters, organizations, and fronts." This tendency is, according to Kittler, what make *Gravity's Rainbow* more a film than a novel, "because it offers up for inspection the progressive disintegration of the negentropy of the military-industrial complex." Its nonlinear temporality requires that "the constant and simultaneous presence of all episodes as such tends towards the state of forgettability that allows no room for the linear chains of cause and effect."[31] Even the stimulus-response, input-output causalities of behaviorism are exhausted, "a signal to the chief behavioralist in the text that 'reality is not reversible.' It could only end if 'rockets dismantle, the entire film runs backward.'"[32]

So too in cinema. *"The people are missing."*[33] That absence above all else is what, according to Deleuze, defines the political cinema of the postwar period, a "minor" cinema of "other" peoples affiliated with the "minor literature" mobilized by Franz Kafka against the despotic bureaucracies earlier in the century.[34] This same absence of "the people" is to be found in the "spaces we no longer know how to describe" that constitute the ground for the reinvention of the image Deleuze finds in postwar cinema in general.[35] Again there is memory, "the strange faculty which puts into immediate contact the outside and the inside, the people's business and private business, the people who are missing and the I who is absent, a membrane, a double becoming."[36] If—in however limited a sense—it can be said that Pynchon is to the postwar military-industrial complex what Kafka was to the modern bureaucratic state, then Walter Benjamin's famous call for the politicization of the artwork in the age of its technical reproducibility must be translated into the recognition that, as Kittler says of Tyrone Slothrop, Pynchon's GI protagonist (whose postwar tag, we might add, could easily read GM), an individual "escapes the 'operational paranoia' of the intelligence agent only to the extent to which it seizes him at the personal level."[37] That is, the personal becomes political precisely to the extent that subjectivity—both individual and collective—is interpolated into a media-induced hallucination.

So to run our film backward and project these hallucinations in other media—Cage, Smithson, Kubrick, Pynchon—onto architecture is to extend our map back outward, into the "spaces we no longer know how to describe," the spaces of the organizational complex. The transaction is authorized by the exchangeability of media that is the hallmark of this complex. And its effect is to remind us that architecture's overcodings within the power-knowledge continuum are measurable precisely as a function of such exchanges. Elsewhere Kittler observes: "Modulation, transformation, synchronization; delay, memory, transposition; scrambling, scanning, mapping—a total connection of all media on a digital base erases the notion of the medium itself. Instead of hooking up technologies to people, absolute knowledge can run as an endless loop."[38]

But our response should not be an attempt to restore "humanity" to its former place within the loop, as was sought by the conjunction of architecture and the organizational complex after the Second World War, when mechanization took command. Our response should be to interrogate that conjunction itself, seeking the "operational paranoias" internalized within it. Its overdetermined strivings for organicity, its desperate invocations of the "human," were nothing less than instruments, launch codes for the passage into a regime of generalized microphysical control. But it also contains another and perhaps more salutary set of codes. For if the analysis I have attempted here has demonstrated anything, it is that paranoia and anti-paranoia, organization and entropy, meet on the infinitesimally thin surfaces that encode the memories, and the futures, of a humanity lost in the hallucinatory glow of an iridescent, radioactive mirror.

Notes

Introduction

1. Siegfried Kracauer, "The Mass Ornament," in *The Mass Ornament: Weimar Essays,* trans. Thomas Y. Levin (Cambridge, Mass.: Harvard University Press, 1995), 74–86.

2. Gilles Deleuze, "Postscript on Control Societies," in *Negotiations, 1972–1990,* trans. Martin Joughin (New York: Columbia University Press, 1995), 177–182. See also William H. Whyte Jr., *The Organization Man* (New York: Simon and Schuster, 1956).

3. Max Horkheimer and Theodor W. Adorno, "The Culture Industry: Enlightenment as Mass Deception," in *Dialectic of Enlightenment,* trans. John Cumming (New York: Continuum, 1972), 120–167.

4. Manfredo Tafuri and Francesco Dal Co, "The Activity of the Masters after World War II," chap. 17 in *Modern Architecture,* trans. Robert Erich Wolf (New York: Electa/Rizzoli, 1986), 2: 309–314. Siegfried Kracauer's phrase is from "Pictorial Deluge," *Trans/formation* 1, no. 1 (1950): 52–53.

5. K. Michael Hays, "Odysseus and the Oarsmen, or, Mies's Abstraction Once Again," in *The Presence of Mies,* ed. Detlef Mertins (New York: Princeton Architectural Press, 1994), 234–247, and "Abstractions Appearance (Seagram Building)," in *Autonomy and Ideology: Positioning an Avant-Garde in America,* ed. R. E. Somol (New York: Monacelli Press, 1997), 276–291.

6. On the "differential specificity" of television, see Samuel Weber, "Television, Set and Screen," in *Mass Mediauras: Form, Technics, Media* (Stanford: Stanford University Press, 1996), 108–128. I have argued for a mass-mediatic reading of the curtain wall in "Atrocities. Or, Curtain Wall as Mass Medium," *Perspecta* 32 (2001): 66–75.

7. Paul Baran, "On Distributed Communications: Introduction to Distributed Communications Network," RAND Corporation memorandum RM3420-PR, August 1964 (originally written ca. 1961). Available online at <http://rand.org/publications/RM/RM3420/> (accessed August 2002); cited in Peter Galison, "War against the Center," *Grey Room,* no. 4 (summer 2001): 26–27, 33 n. 40.

8. On Mies's organicism, see Detlef Mertins, "Architectures of Becoming: Mies van der Rohe and the Avant-Garde," in *Mies in Berlin,* ed. Terence Riley and Barry Bergdoll (New York: Museum of Modern Art, 2001), 106–133, and "Living in a Jungle: Mies, Organic Architecture, and the Art of City Building," in *Mies in America,* ed. Phyllis Lambert (New York: Harry N. Abrams, 2001), 590–641. On biological models in modern architecture in general, see Peter Collins, "The Biological Analogy," chap. 14 in *Changing Ideals in Modern Architecture, 1750–1950* (London: Faber and Faber, 1965), 149–158.

9. The most nuanced of such arguments is to be found in Manfredo Tafuri and Francesco Dal Co's treatment of what they call an international "architecture of bureaucracy" in "The International Panorama in the Fifties and Sixties," in *Modern Architecture,* 2: 339–356. For Tafuri and Dal Co, such works as Gordon Bunshaft's Union Carbide Building or Chase Manhattan Bank headquarters stand in contrast to the heroic "silence" of Mies: "What is tragic in the Seagram Building is repeated as a norm in these in the form of farce" (312).

10. Friedrich A. Kittler, *Discourse Networks, 1800/1900,* trans. Michael Metteer with Chris Cullens (Stanford: Stanford University Press, 1990), esp. "Afterword to the Second Printing," 369–372. Kittler defines a "discourse network" as a "network of technologies and institutions that allow a given culture to select, store, and process relevant data" (369).

11. On the "network" as a discursive figure in planning and design during the 1960s, see Mark Wigley, "Network Fever," *Grey Room,* no. 4 (summer 2001): 82–122.

12. See Donna Haraway, "A Cyborg Manifesto: Science, Technology and Socialist-Feminism in the Late Twentieth Century," in *Simians, Cyborgs, and Women: The Reinvention of Nature* (New York: Routledge, 1991), 149–181 (first published as "Manifesto for Cyborgs: Science, Technology, and Socialist Feminism in the 1980s," *Socialist Review,* no. 80 [1985]: 65–108).

13. Martin, "Atrocities," passim.

1

The Organizational Complex

1. Norbert Wiener, *Cybernetics; or, Control and Communication in the Animal and the Machine* (Cambridge, Mass.: Technology Press, 1948), 191.

2. Ibid., 49–50, 54–55.

3. Among the most important of these studies of the new epoch are Jacques Ellul, *The Technological Society,* trans. John Wilkinson (New York: Alfred A. Knopf, 1964); Alain Touraine, *The Post-Industrial Society; Tomorrow's Social History: Classes, Conflicts, and Culture in the Programmed Society,* trans. Leonard F. X. Mayhew (New York: Random House, 1971); and Daniel Bell, *The Coming of Post-Industrial Society: A Venture in Social Forecasting* (New York: Basic Books, 1973). For a history of technological and managerial control systems, see also James R. Beniger, *The Control Revolution: Technological and Economic Origins of the Information Society* (Cambridge, Mass.: Harvard University Press, 1986).

4. Gilles Deleuze, in conversation with Antonio Negri, "Control and Becoming," in Deleuze, *Negotiations, 1972–1990,* trans. Martin Joughin (New York: Columbia University Press, 1995), 175. Anson Rabinbach has characterized a similar shift in the historical definition of work, from an energetic conversion of labor power to linguistic simulation, in slightly different terms, in "The Biopolitics of Work," in *Biopolitics: The Politics of the Body, Race, and Nature,* ed. Agnes Heller and Sonja Puntscher Riekmann (Aldershot: Avebury, 1996), 95–111.

   Deleuze's periodization—from sovereign societies to disciplinary societies to control societies—itself belongs to an intellectual tradition sensitive to historical discontinuity, ranging from the "epistemological ruptures" identified by Gaston Bachelard, to the foundational status of "error" in the work of Georges Canguilhem, to the analytics of discursive redistribution carried out by Michel Foucault. Deleuze's schema is especially reliant on the Foucauldian *episteme,* or "the total set of relations that unite, at a given period, the discursive practices that give rise to epistemological figures, sciences, and possibly formalized systems" (Foucault, *The Archaeology of Knowledge,* trans. A. M. Sheridan Smith [London: Tavistock, 1972], 191). It repeats Foucault's identification of a radical break separating the "classical age" (the mid-seventeenth through the eighteenth century) from the disciplinary ordering systems of the nineteenth century, and then again from that future conditional moment when, according to Foucault, "man would be erased, like a face drawn in sand at the edge of the sea" (Foucault, *The Order of Things: An Archaeology of the Human Sciences* [London: Tavistock, 1970], 387).

5. Anson Rabinbach, *The Human Motor: Energy, Fatigue, and the Origins of Modernity* (Berkeley: University of California Press, 1990), 117.

6. In the words of François Jacob:

If respiration is always a combustion, each living being, whatever its form and habitat, must be able to obtain oxygen. It must obtain fuel for food, carry it to the place of combustion, reject the waste matter and control its temperature—in short, combine accurately a whole series of operations. The lungs, the stomach, the heart or the kidneys can no longer be considered independently. A living being is no longer a simple association of organs, each working autonomously. It becomes a whole whose parts are interdependent, each performing a particular function for the common good. (*The Logic of Life: A History of Heredity,* trans. Betty E. Spillmann [New York: Pantheon, 1973], 83)

Jacob devotes an entire chapter to the history of "organization" in biology (chap. 2, "Organization," 74–129).

7. Ibid., 100–111.

8. Gilles Deleuze, *Foucault,* trans. Séan Hand (Minneapolis: University of Minnesota Press, 1988), 127.

9. Jacob, *The Logic of Life,* 111.

10. Georges Canguilhem, "Knowledge and the Living: Science and Life," in *A Vital Rationalist: Selected Writings from Georges Canguilhem,* ed. François Delaporte, trans. Arthur Goldhammer (New York: Zone Books, 1994), 300, 302.

11. Gilles Deleuze, "Postscript on Control Societies," in *Negotiations,* 178–179.

12. Herbert Marshall McLuhan to Norbert Wiener, 28 March 1951, MC22, box 3, folder 135, Norbert Wiener Papers, Massachusetts Institute of Technology, Institute Archives and Special Collections. McLuhan even goes so far as to venture an analogy between Wiener's description of the capacity of an electron valve (or vacuum tube) to amplify information constructed of small units through feedback and the poetic techniques of Joyce, Mallarmé, and Eliot. Finally, McLuhan tells Wiener of a proposed project for the study of communication, inspired by Karl Deutsch's discussion of communication and education.

13. Sigfried Giedion to Norbert Wiener, 22 February 1950, box 3, folder 112, Norbert Wiener Papers, MIT.

14. As Sigfried Giedion put it, "With unbelievable speed atomic energy sprang from the worksheets and the laboratories into reality, playing 'phantastic tricks' and threatening human culture with annihilation" (*Mechanization Takes Command: A Contribution to Anonymous History* [New York: W. W. Norton, 1948], 717).

15. Ibid., 718–719. Giedion cites Walter B. Cannon's *Bodily Changes in Pain, Hunger, Fear, and Rage* (1929), as well as J. N. Langley's *Autonomic Nervous System* (1921) and *Holism and Evolution,* published in 1926 by the nationalist field marshal and prime minister of South Africa, Jan Christian Smuts.

16. Walter B. Cannon, *The Wisdom of the Body* (New York: W. W. Norton, 1932), 287–306.

17. Wiener, *Cybernetics,* 6.

18. See Peter Galison, "The Ontology of the Enemy: Norbert Wiener and the Cybernetic Vision," *Critical Inquiry* 21, no. 1 (autumn 1994): 228–266. In particular, Galison explores the sociocultural dimensions of Wiener's early work on what Wiener called the "antiaircraft (AA) predictor" in terms of the projection of an image of a "servomechanical enemy" (233) as a

prototype for an agonistic account of the human relation with an unknowable environment—which Galison ultimately compares to postmodern critiques of cybernetic control systems.

19. Wiener, *Cybernetics,* 141–142.

20. During the 1930s, László Moholy-Nagy came into contact with the evolutionary humanism of the biologist Julian Huxley, who argued that the capacity for rational thought enabled humanity to intervene in its own biological development—a project acted out in Huxley's advocacy of eugenic population management policies in Great Britain. Where in *The New Vision* (1928) Moholy-Nagy saw the evolution of an enhanced visual faculty as a more or less inevitable aftereffect of realizing an avant-gardist aesthetic revolution, in *Vision in Motion* (1947) and in his pedagogical initiatives in Chicago he attempted to institutionalize a new human type through direct appeal to interdisciplinary, humanistic principles of rational self-actualization (also propagated at the same time at the University of Chicago by Robert M. Hutchins and others). I discuss this subject more fully in chapter 2.

21. See Sigfried Giedion, "The Nineteenth Century and the Capturing of Movement," "The Appearance of Scientific Management," and "Scientific Management and Contemporary Art," in *Mechanization Takes Command,* 17–30, 96–101, 101–113.

22. Gyorgy Kepes, *Language of Vision* (Chicago: Paul Theobald, 1944), 12.

23. In the same letter, Marshall McLuhan writes that "running through some papers on Sigfried Giedion, especially his *Space, Time and Architecture* and *Mechanization Takes Command,* I realized what a tremendous debt I owe him in my work" (letter to Kamala Bhatia, 6 April 1971, Marshall McLuhan Papers, National Archives of Canada, Ottawa). This letter is cited in Philip Marchand, *Marshall McLuhan: The Medium and the Messenger* (New York: Ticknor and Fields, 1989), 69.

24. Herbert Marshall McLuhan, *The Mechanical Bride: Folklore of Industrial Man* (New York: Vanguard Press, 1951), v.

25. Norbert Wiener, *The Human Use of Human Beings: Cybernetics and Society,* 2nd ed. (Garden City, N.Y.: Doubleday, 1954), 39.

26. Ibid., 57.

27. Ibid., 129.

28. Ibid., 130–131.

29. Ibid., 132–133.

30. Deleuze, "Postscript on Control Societies," 180.

31. Foucault, "Different Spaces," trans. Robert Hurley, in *Aesthetics, Method, and Epistemology,* ed. James O. Faubion, vol. 2 of *Essential Works of Foucault, 1954–1985* (New York: New Press, 1998), 176. The text was presented as a lecture to the Architectural Studies Circle on 14 March 1967, and first published in *Architecture, Mouvement, Continuité* in October 1984.

32. On the architectural reception of Foucault's text and related works, see Daniel Defert, "Foucault, Space, and the Architects," in *Politics, Poetics: Documenta X, the Book* (Ostfildern-Ruit: Cantz, 1997), 274–283.

33. Foucault, "Different Spaces," 177.

34. One outgrowth of generalizing cybernetic principles to apply to both machines and organisms is the "sociobiological synthesis" formalized by, among others, Edmund O. Wilson in his *Insect Societies* (1971) and his *Sociobiology, the New Synthesis* (1975). See Donna J. Haraway, "The High Cost of Information in Post-World War II Evolutionary Biology: Ergonomics, Semiotics, and the Sociobiology of Communication Systems," *Philosophical Forum* 13, nos. 2–3 (spring 1981–82): 244–278.

35. Gilles Deleuze, "Desire and Pleasure," trans. Daniel W. Smith, in *Foucault and His Interlocutors,* ed. Arnold I. Davidson (Chicago: University of Chicago Press, 1997), 189.

36. Wiener, *The Human Use of Human Beings,* 185–186.

37. Ibid., 129.

38. "How U.S. Cities Can Prepare for Atomic War: M.I.T. Professors Suggest a Bold Plan to Prevent Panic and Limit Destruction," *Life,* 18 December 1950, 76–84. The article is a sign of early public awareness of cybernetics, evidenced also in a *Time* cover story earlier the same year on advances in computing (*Time,* 23 January 1950, 54–60).

39. Norbert Wiener, Karl W. Deutsch, and Giorgio de Santillana, "Cities that Survive the Bomb," 10, undated draft, box 12, folder 638, Norbert Wiener Papers, MIT.

40. Norbert Wiener, Karl W. Deutsch, and Giorgio de Santillana, "The Planners Evaluate Their Plan," *Life,* 18 December 1950, 85.

41. Proposals for urban decentralization to defend against nuclear attack may be found, for example, in Ralph E. Lapp, *Must We Hide?* (Cambridge, Mass.: Addison-Wesley Press, 1949). Ludwig Hilberseimer, in diagramming the geographic range of a hydrogen bomb (*The Nature of Cities* [Chicago: Paul Theobald, 1955], 282–283), also cites an article by Lapp, "Civil Defense Faces New Peril," *Bulletin of the Atomic Scientists* 10, no. 9 (November 1954): 349–351. See as well the special issue on civil defense, *Bulletin of the Atomic Scientists* 6, nos. 8–9 (August–September 1950), especially the contributions by Lapp ("The Strategy of Civil Defense," 241–243) and the planner Tracy B. Augur ("Dispersal Is Good Business," 244–245). Both Lapp and Augur also published articles on decentralization as defense in this influential journal during the 1940s. Augur had been president of the American Institute of Planners and a consultant on the planning of Oak Ridge. Lapp was a physicist working for the military and had worked on the Manhattan Project in Chicago.

For a general history of post–World War II civil defense strategies in the United States, see Allan M. Winkler, "A Forty-Year History of Civil Defense," *Bulletin of the Atomic Scientists* 40, no. 6 (June–July 1984); 16–22, as well as idem, *Life under a Cloud: American Anxiety about the Atom* (New York: Oxford University Press, 1993); Paul Boyer, *By the Bomb's Early Light: American Thought and Culture at the Dawn of the Atomic Age* (Chapel Hill: University of North Carolina Press, 1985); and Guy Oakes, *The Imaginary War: Civil Defense and American Cold War*

Culture (New York: Oxford University Press, 1994). Peter Galison has also traced a mimetic internalization of planning strategies developed in Germany to resist Allied bombing during the war in the networked, decentralized postwar civil defense plans for American cities and the industries they support, as evidence of what he calls "a new, bizarre, and yet pervasive species of Lacanian mirroring" associated with postmodernist decentering; see "War against the Center," *Grey Room,* no. 4 (summer 2001): 6–33.

42. Cited in Norbert Wiener, *The Human Use of Human Beings; Cybernetics and Society* (Boston: Houghton Mifflin, 1950), 207; 2nd ed., 178–179.

43. In December 1945, a number of atomic scientists involved in the Manhattan Project launched the *Bulletin of the Atomic Scientists,* intended to raise public and scientific awareness of the dangers of atomic energy; its sponsors included Albert Einstein, J. Robert Oppenheimer, and Edward Teller. See Winkler, *Life under a Cloud,* 39–40.

44. Dwight D. Eisenhower, "Farewell Radio and Television Address to the American People, January 17, 1961," in *Public Papers of the President of the United States, Dwight D. Eisenhower, 1960–61* (Washington, D.C.: U.S. Government Printing Office, 1961), 1035–1040.

45. See Stuart W. Leslie, *The Cold War and American Science: The Military-Industrial-Academic Complex at MIT and Stanford* (New York: Columbia University Press, 1993), 24–25.

46. For scholarly treatment of the military-industrial complex, see Leslie, *The Cold War and American Science;* Seymour Melman, *Pentagon Capitalism: The Political Economy of War* (New York: McGraw-Hill, 1970); Carroll W. Pursell Jr., ed., *The Military-Industrial Complex* (New York: Harper and Row, 1972); Stephen Rosen, ed., *Testing the Theory of the Military-Industrial Complex* (Lexington, Mass.: D.C. Heath, 1973); Paul A. C. Koistinen, *The Military-Industrial Complex: A Historical Perspective* (New York: Praeger, 1980); David F. Noble, *Forces of Production: A Social History of Industrial Automation* (New York: Alfred A. Knopf, 1984); and Gregg B. Walker, David A. Bella, and Steven J. Sprecher, eds., *The Military-Industrial Complex: Eisenhower's Warning Three Decades Later* (New York: Peter Lang, 1992).

47. C. Wright Mills, *The Power Elite* (New York: Oxford University Press, 1956).

48. Talcott Parsons, *Structure and Process in Modern Societies* (Glencoe, Ill.: Free Press, 1960), 199–225.

49. Ibid., 275. On the "communicative complex," see 266–275.

50. Karl W. Deutsch, *The Nerves of Government: Models of Political Communication and Control* (Glencoe, Ill.: Free Press, 1963), ix. Deutsch cites Wiener extensively in pt. 2 of the book, "Cybernetics: New Models in Communication and Control," in which one chapter is titled "A Simple Cybernetic Model" (75–97).

51. Ibid., 39–50.

52. Ibid., 124.

53. By the late 1960s a systems approach had also begun to influence scholarship on the military-industrial complex. As one scholar puts it, "the key to understanding the complex is to see it as a system, and to realize that it is only as part of this system that the individual ex-

amples of its operations make any sense at all" (Pursell, introduction to part 1, "The Military-Industrial Complex in Theory and Fact," in *The Military-Industrial Complex,* 13). On the debates regarding the existence of the military-industrial complex, see Marc Pilisuk and Thomas Hayden, "Is There a Military-Industrial Complex Which Prevents Peace? Consensus and Countervailing Power in Pluralistic Systems," *Journal of Social Issues* 21, no. 3 (July 1965): 67–117, which is partially reprinted in Pursell's collection (51–80).

54. In *The Postmodern Condition: A Report on Knowledge,* trans. Geoffrey Bennington and Brian Massumi (Minneapolis: University of Minnesota Press, 1984), Jean-François Lyotard sharply criticizes the systems theory of Niklas Luhmann, who draws heavily on the work of Parsons (also cited by Lyotard). Lyotard locates the totalizing drive of the systems approach not only in the relative closure of the "system" (what he calls its "unicity") but also in the univocality of the criterion—optimum performativity—uncritically assumed as the system's goal (see 11–12, 61–62).

55. The colonel is quoted in Noble, *Forces of Production,* 52. For a history of SAGE, see Paul N. Edwards, *The Closed World: Computers and the Politics of Discourse in Cold War America* (Cambridge, Mass.: MIT Press, 1996), 75–111.

56. For documentation and analysis of interdisciplinary conferences on cybernetics sponsored by the Josiah R. Macy, Jr. Foundation, see Steve J. Heims, *The Cybernetics Group* (Cambridge, Mass.: MIT Press, 1991). On Wiener's skepticism regarding the applicability of cybernetics to the "human sciences," see 28–30, as well as Heims, *John von Neumann and Norbert Wiener: From Mathematics to the Technologies of Life and Death* (Cambridge, Mass.: MIT Press, 1980). On the dissemination of cybernetic thought in the biological sciences, see Lily E. Kay, "Cybernetics, Information, Life: The Emergence of Scriptural Representations of Heredity," *Configurations* 5, no. 1 (winter 1997): 23–91.

57. Richard Neutra to Norbert Wiener, 25 January 1954, box 4, folder 186, Norbert Wiener Papers, MIT.

58. Richard Neutra, *Survival through Design* (New York: Oxford University Press, 1954), 317, 327.

59. Richard Neutra, "Inner and Outer Landscape," in *The New Landscape in Art and Science,* by Gyorgy Kepes (Chicago: Paul Theobald, 1956), 84. On Neutra's domestic architecture as a corresponding psychophysiological instrument, see Sylvia Lavin, "Open the Box: Richard Neutra and the Psychology of the Domestic Environment," *Assemblage,* no. 40 (December 1999): 6–25.

60. Sigfried Giedion, "Universalism and the Enlargement of Outlook," and Walter Gropius, "Reorientation," in Kepes, *The New Landscape in Art and Science,* 92–93, 94–97. Kepes (328) quotes a definition of a (feedback-based) "circular process" from *The Transaction of Cybernetics,* Eighth Conference (n.p.: Josiah R. Macy, Jr. Foundation, 1951).

61. Norbert Wiener, "Pure Patterns in a Natural World," in Kepes, *The New Landscape in Art and Science,* 274–276.

62. Gyorgy Kepes to Norbert Wiener, 1 August 1951, box 3, folder 141, Norbert Wiener Papers, MIT; Wiener to Kepes, 9 September 1951, Gyorgy Kepes Papers, Archives of American Art,

Washington, D.C. The quote is in a letter from Kepes to Wiener, 27 September 1951, box 3, folder 141, Norbert Wiener Papers, MIT.

63. Kepes, *The New Landscape in Art and Science,* 328.

64. See Jacob, *The Logic of Life,* 267–286, as well as Donna Haraway, *Crystals, Fabrics, and Fields: Metaphors of Organicism in Twentieth-Century Developmental Biology* (New Haven: Yale University Press, 1976), and Kay, "Cybernetics, Information, Life," 32–49.

65. American Telephone and Telegraph Corporation, *AT&T Corporation Annual Report, 1958,* inside front cover.

66. American Telephone and Telegraph Corporation, *AT&T Corporation Annual Report, 1961,* 19.

2

Pattern-Seeing

1. Gyorgy Kepes, *The New Landscape in Art and Science* (Chicago: Paul Theobald, 1956), 206.

2. Ibid., 204.

3. Ibid., 371.

4. In this chapter I will refer only to Kepes's writings and pedagogy. In addition to a career as a distinguished teacher and a painter of some note, Kepes engaged in a number of collaborations with architects, including mural designs with Carl Koch & Associates in the late 1940s and 1950s, glass windows for the Church of the Redeemer in Baltimore by Pietro Belluschi in 1959, a light mural in the Manhattan offices of KLM the same year, and other such works into the 1960s. Kepes also worked on exhibition designs from the 1940s through the 1960s, and resumed painting in the early 1950s after an extended hiatus. For a partial chronology of this work, see Judith Wechsler, *Gyorgy Kepes: The MIT Years, 1945–1977* (Cambridge, Mass.: MIT Press, 1978), 87–98. Wechsler also sketches Kepes's biography (7–19).

5. The diagram, in which the Bauhaus curriculum is figured as a series of concentric circles converging on "Building Design," is part an exposition of the school's pedagogy published as Walter Gropius, *Idee und Aufbau des Staatlichen Bauhauses Weimar* (Munich: Bauhausverlag, 1923); it is partially translated as "The Theory and Organization of the Bauhaus," in *Bauhaus: Weimar/Dessau, 1919–1928,* ed. Gropius, Herbert Bayer, and Ise Gropius (New York: Museum of Modern Art, 1938), 20–29.

6. Gropius declared: "We want to create a clear, organic architecture, whose inner logic will be radiant and naked, unencumbered by lying facades and trickeries; we want an architecture adapted to our world of machines, radios and fast motor cars, an architecture whose function is clearly recognizable in the relation of its forms" ("The Theory and Organization of the Bauhaus," 29). Detlef Mertins has explored aspects of early twentieth-century organicism in

Germany in "Transparencies Yet to Come: Sigfried Giedion and the Prehistory of Architectural Modernity" (Ph.D. diss., Princeton University, 1996). Mertins points out that as early as 1931 Giedion, following Moholy-Nagy, was promoting the aesthetic potential of aerial views, microscopy, and the X ray (79).

7. By 1923 Lucia Moholy had become an assistant to Hermann Eckner, a professional photographer working in Weimar who was occasionally employed to photograph Bauhaus student work for publicity and prototypes for industry. On Bauhaus photography, see Rosalind Krauss, "Jump over the Bauhaus," *October*, no. 15 (winter 1980): 103–110. Krauss considers the Bauhaus photographers' shared self-consciousness concerning the experience of being photographed, and the reflexive role played by traces of the photographic apparatus in the images themselves. See also Suzanne E. Pastor, "Photography at the Bauhaus," *Archive*, no. 21 (March 1985): 5–26, for documentation. In the context of the debilitating inflation that peaked in 1923, the turn of the Bauhaus toward industry and mass production was also a turn toward a more advanced publicity apparatus. Thus the Bauhaus exhibition of 1923 and the accompanying catalogue—*Staatliches Bauhaus in Weimar, 1919–1923*—are evidence both of the early production of the school and, as the most ambitious publicity event staged by Gropius to that point, of the new imperatives it faced.

The event was also the occasion for Lucia Moholy to assume the role of Bauhaus photographer and unofficial public relations consultant. She went on to document systematically the production of the Bauhaus, while remaining the only professionally trained photographer there until the arrival of Walter Peterhans. For a brief account of Lucia Moholy's involvement with the Bauhaus exhibition and subsequent publications, see Rolf Sachsse, "Notes on Lucia Moholy," in *Photography at the Bauhaus,* ed. Jeannine Fiedler (Cambridge, Mass.: MIT Press, 1990), 25.

8. László Moholy-Nagy, "Production Reproduction," in *Painting, Photography, Film* (London: Lund Humphries, 1969), 30–31 (originally published as *Malerei, Fotographie, Film* [Munich: Bauhausbücher, 1925]). The problem of production vs. reproduction was also connected to Moholy-Nagy and Moholy's experiments with photograms, the direct traces left by objects and light on photosensitive paper. Similar work was being done simultaneously by other artists as well. In their case, Lucia Moholy recollects: "I clearly remember how it [the idea of the photogram] came about. During a stroll in the Rhön Mountains in the summer of 1922 we discussed the problems rising from the antithesis Production versus Reproduction. This gradually led us to implement our conclusions by making photograms, having had no previous knowledge of any steps taken by Schad, Man Ray and Lissitzky" (*Marginalien zu Moholy-Nagy: Dokumentarische Ungreimtheiten/Moholy-Nagy, Marginal Notes: Documentary Absurdities* [Krefeld: Scherpe Verlag, 1972], 59).

9. In Moholy-Nagy's words: "Art attempts to establish far-reaching *new relationships* between the known and the as yet unknown optical, acoustical and other functional phenomena so that these are absorbed in increasing abundance by the functional apparatus" ("Production Reproduction," 30; emphasis in original).

10. By advocating that the photographer manipulate the environment to produce "light phenomena (moments from light-displays) *which we ourselves have composed* (with contrivances of mirrors or lenses, transparent crystals, liquids, etc.)," and adding that "[w]e may

regard *astronomical, x-ray* and lightning photographs all as forerunners of this type of composition," Moholy-Nagy makes it clear that the new photography all but requires a proto-architecture of "mirrors," "lenses," and "light displays," an architecture whose effects were foreshadowed by such enhancements of human vision as X-ray and telescopic photography (ibid., 31; emphases in original). Here and in the references to Moholy-Nagy that follow we can discern a variation on what Jonathan Crary has identified as the production of a new kind of "observer" during the middle of the nineteenth century. For Crary this is an observer whose mobile, contingent, and variable vision engages reciprocally with a kinetic optics expressed in such devices as the phenakistiscope (see *Techniques of the Observer: On Vision and Modernity in the Nineteenth Century* [Cambridge, Mass.: MIT Press, 1990], esp. chap. 4, "Techniques of the Observer," 97–136). Crary (112) also cites Walter Benjamin's comment that in the nineteenth century "technology has subjected the human sensorium to a complex kind of training" (Benjamin, *Charles Baudelaire: A Lyric Poet in the Era of High Capitalism,* trans. Harry Zohn [London: NLB, 1973], 126). Significantly, Benjamin on several occasions referred to Moholy-Nagy in his discussions of photography, most famously in the "Small History of Photography" by declaring, "'The illiteracy of the future,' someone has said, 'will be ignorance not of reading or writing, but of photography.' But must not a photographer who cannot read his own pictures be no less counted an illiterate?" ("A Small History of Photography," in *One-Way Street, and Other Writings,* trans. Edmund Jephcott and Kingsley Shorter [London: NLB, 1979], 256). This essay was originally published in German in *Literarische Welt* 7 (1931), in three separate installments.

11. "The newly invented optical and technical instruments offer the optical creator valuable suggestions; among other things they give us light painting side by side with painting in pigment, kinetic painting side by side with static. (Moving light displays side by side with easel-painting, instead of frescoes—films in all dimensions; outside the film theatre, too, of course.)" (Moholy-Nagy, introduction to *Painting, Photography, Film,* 9.)

12. László Moholy-Nagy, sketch for *Dynamic of the Metropolis* (1921–1922), in *Painting, Photography, Film,* 124–137.

13. The developmental sequence in *The New Vision* and its predecessor in *Painting, Photography, Film* may be compared to a series of transpositions between different media tracked by Friedrich A. Kittler in *Discourse Networks, 1800/1900,* trans. Michael Metteer with Chris Cullens (Stanford: Stanford University Press, 1990). Kittler's thesis is that literary production at these two moments is part of two different communications networks assembled from different media. In describing the literary effects of communication between typewriters, phonographs, telegraphs, and films in the "discourse network of 1900," Kittler notes: "The system of 1900 could spare itself the effort to spare muscular energy because it undertook to create substitutions for the central nervous system itself" (296–297). Moholy-Nagy's progressive media substitutions may be understood as an extension of this undertaking, which eventually led back to the human nervous system and an effort to reorganize vision.

14. László Moholy-Nagy, *The New Vision: From Material to Architecture,* trans. Daphne M. Hoffmann (New York: Brewer, Warren, and Putnam, 1932), 204. Detlef Mertins has noted connections between Moholy-Nagy's search for an architecture of transparent dynamism associated with this new optic and the early experiments in glass conducted by Ludwig Mies van der

Rohe, especially the "Glass Room" Mies designed with Lilly Reich at the Werkbund exhibition of 1927 (Mertins, "Architectures of Becoming: Mies van der Rohe and the Avant-Garde," in *Mies in Berlin,* ed. Terence Riley and Barry Bergdoll [New York: Museum of Modern Art, 2001], 129).

15. Moholy-Nagy and Kepes had been collaborating on stage design and experimental cinema in Berlin since 1930, when Kepes, who was active in the same avant-gardist circles in Budapest as Moholy-Nagy had been, wrote asking to work with him. On the relationship between Moholy-Nagy and Kepes, see Sibyl Moholy-Nagy, *Moholy-Nagy: Experiment in Totality* (Cambridge, Mass.: MIT Press, 1950), 62.

16. Kepes, in an interview with the archivist Robert Brown in 1972–1973, Brown, transcript of taperecorded interview with Gyorgy Kepes, March 1972–January 1973, uncatalogued, 9–10, Gyorgy Kepes Papers, Archives of American Art (henceforth AAA), Washington, D.C. In the interview, Kepes also indicates his early interest in studying architecture (4). Note: All citations of the Kepes Papers refer to their indexing at the time my research was completed. The bulk of the papers have since been microfilmed and reorganized.

17. On Moholy-Nagy's contact with Julian Huxley in London, see Sibyl Moholy-Magy, *Moholy-Nagy: Experiment in Totality,* 135–137.

18. Brown-Kepes interview, 10, Kepes Papers, AAA. Kepes later referred to what he took to be the scientists' shared project as a "unity of life," an unwillingness to separate scientific work from "human commitment."

19. Although Kepes did not begin reading the literature on Gestalt psychology until the 1940s, this early exposure coincided with what he called his first "excitement in the visual records of science," when a physicist friend working in the metallurgy department at the Kaiser Wilhelm Institute showed him photographs of the surfaces of metals. Thus already in Berlin in the early 1930s, several years after Moholy-Nagy's departure from the Bauhaus, the conditions that underlay Kepes's project of integrating art and science into a larger, social whole through the agency of images were partially in place (ibid., 9–10).

20. Other members of the Theoretical Biology Club included J. D. Bernal and Lancelot Law Whyte. Bernal was a crystallographer with communist allegiances who was later to write *The Social Function of Science* (1939), a compendium of what he considered to be the potential social benefits and menaces of modern science. Whyte was a mathematical physicist turned biologist who later became active in connecting artistic and scientific concepts in England. Donna Haraway has characterized this group as a "paradigm community," which saw the consolidation of a new, paradigmatic organicism in biology that overturned the basic premises of earlier mechanisms and vitalisms; see Donna Jeanne Haraway, *Crystals, Fabrics, and Fields: Metaphors of Organicism in Twentieth-Century Developmental Biology* (New Haven: Yale University Press, 1976), 1–33.

21. On the role of concepts drawn from Gestalt psychology in twentieth-century organicist biology, see Haraway, *Crystals, Fabrics, and Fields,* 129–130. The Austrian biologist Ludwig von Bertalanffy gave the name "general system theory" to his own effort to articulate systemic biological behavior in logico-mathematical terms. According to von Bertalanffy, general system theory offered modern science a general theory of organization, an account of "structural

uniformities" or "isomorphic traces of order" at different hierarchical levels, in response to the biological problem of describing organized complexity (*General System Theory: Foundations, Developments, Applications* [New York: George Braziller, 1968], 30–49). The position of von Bertalanffy within the overall field of organicist biologists is also documented by Haraway (*Crystals, Fabrics, and Fields,* 38).

22. Haraway's book on biological visualization takes as its premise the significant role played by images, which she refers to as "metaphors," in the development of these ideas. She examines the discourse of Needham and his colleagues together with that of his American predecessor Ross G. Harrison and of Paul Weiss, who in the 1920s was responsible for transferring early systems theory from engineering and carrying the "field" concept from modern physics into developmental biology. To illustrate the centrality accorded to the problem of visualization in organicist biology, Haraway quotes Needham: "When we consider the fact that the protoplasm of the living cell is undoubtedly polyphasic, containing, as it were, globules within globules, each separate kind with its own organization and potentialities which it cannot overpass, we are able to visualize the immense complexity which the simplest unit of life must have within it" (*Crystals, Fabrics, and Fields,* 130).

23. Ibid., 190; emphasis added.

24. In 1960 Gyorgy Kepes published an article by Paul Weiss titled "Organic Form: Scientific and Aesthetic Aspects," in *The Visual Arts Today,* a special issue of *Daedalus* guest-edited by Kepes (89, no. 1 [winter 1960]: 177–190). An essay by Conrad Waddington, titled "The Modular Principle and Biological Form," appeared in *Module, Proportion, Symmetry, Rhythm,* ed. Kepes (New York: George Braziller, 1966), 20–37.

25. Significantly, Haraway refers to the thesis of Philip C. Ritterbush, in *The Art of Organic Forms* (Washington, D.C.: Smithsonian Institution Press, 1968), that the history of biology is characterized by research that proceeds from an initially aesthetic notion toward its concretization in scientific knowledge. However, as she reads Ritterbush, "the metaphor of organic form became progressively powerful as it became more concrete, never losing its nature as metaphor" (Haraway, *Crystals, Fabrics, and Fields,* 12). Ritterbush proceeds from Goethe's understanding of nature as almost exclusively visual, through an idealist morphology central to Romanticism and the influence of German *Naturphilosophie* on anatomists and biologists during the late eighteenth and early nineteenth centuries. He also carries this analysis forward into the late nineteenth and early twentieth centuries, as he examines Ernst Haeckel's profusely illustrated *Art Forms in Nature* (1899–1904). Haeckel believed that the internal characteristics of organisms could be inferred from their external form, and he altered (i.e., idealized) his drawings to exaggerate the symmetries and other geometric regularities of the organisms he catalogued, in accordance with a belief in the inherently geometrical nature of organic form (Ritterbush, *The Art of Organic Forms,* 69). Ritterbush's thesis reflects a notion of the relatedness of modernist abstraction and organic form that was common at the time he was writing thanks in no small measure to figures such as Kepes and other interpreters of abstract painting (including Alfred H. Barr and Lawrence Alloway, to whose work Ritterbush refers).

26. Correspondence between László Moholy-Nagy and the Association for Arts and Industries, Chicago, is reproduced by Sibyl Moholy-Nagy in *Moholy-Nagy: Experiment in Totality,*

140–141: the quotations are from the initial cable to Moholy-Nagy dated 6 June 1937 and a letter dated 29 May 1937.

27. According to Charles W. Morris, in the New Bauhaus prospectus, "Moholy-Nagy knew of the interest of Rudolf Carnap and myself in the unity of science movement. He once remarked to us that his interest went a stage farther: his concern was with the unity of life. It was his belief that all cultural phalanxes at any time moved abreast, though often ignorant of their common cultural front. Certain it is that the integration and interpenetration of the characteristic human activities of the artist, scientist, and technologist is a crying need of our time. The problem is a general problem of all education which aims to be of vital contemporary significance." (Charles W. Morris, "The Contribution of Science to the Designer's Task," from the New Bauhaus prospectus, 1937–1938, reprinted in *The Bauhaus: Weimar, Dessau, Berlin, Chicago,* by Hans M. Wingler, [trans. Wolfgang Jabs and Basil Gilbert], ed. Joseph Stein [Cambridge, Mass.: MIT Press, 1969], 195.) See also Sibyl Moholy-Nagy, *Moholy-Nagy: Experiment in Totality,* 153.

28. Richard A. Fiordo, *Charles Morris and the Criticism of Discourse* (Bloomington: Indiana University Press, 1977), 1–11. It is said that Morris decided to devote his career to the study of signs while waiting in a car for Moholy-Nagy (6). James Sloan Allen has shown the links between the pedagogy of the New Bauhaus, the notion of a unified scientific discourse (comparable here to the unified aesthetic discourse advanced through the succession of media in the *Vorkurs*), and the pragmatic positivism of such thinkers as Morris and John Dewey, both of whom publicly supported the New Bauhaus (Allen, *The Romance of Commerce and Culture: Capitalism, Modernism, and the Chicago-Aspen Crusade for Cultural Reform* [Chicago: University of Chicago Press, 1983], 60). Lloyd C. Engelbrecht, in "The Association of Arts and Industries: Background and Origins of the Bauhaus Movement in Chicago" ([Ph.D. diss., University of Chicago, 1973], 286–288), notes that Morris was introduced to Moholy-Nagy by Rudolf Carnap, a leader in the Unity of Science movement also teaching at the University of Chicago. Morris's course and those taught by the University of Chicago scientists Carl Eckhart and Ralph Gerard (discussed later in this chapter) were mandatory. Kepes speaks of his contacts with Morris, Gerard, and Eckhart in the Brown-Kepes interview, passim, Kepes Papers, AAA.

29. New Bauhaus prospectus, 1937, 4, Getty Center for the History of Art and the Humanities, Special Collections, Santa Monica, Calif.

30. In their popular exposition of mechanistic biology, Wells and Huxley also describe organisms, including humans, as "combustion engines," thereby comparing them to automobiles. See H. G. Wells, with Julian Huxley and G. P. Wells, *The Science of Life* (New York: Doubleday, 1934), 1469; on eugenics, see 1468–1472; on the body as a combustion engine, see 30–31.

31. In Brown's interview from 1972–1973, Kepes speaks of being threatened by an Association of Arts and Industries trustee with blacklisting if he didn't cooperate in the effort to form a new school without Moholy-Nagy (Brown-Kepes interview, 19, Kepes Papers, AAA).

32. Ralph Gerard was an original participant in the cybernetics conferences sponsored by the Josiah J. Macy, Jr. Foundation beginning in 1946. Interestingly, Gerard was among the more cautious of the group's members in finding broad applications in cybernetic research. See Steve J. Heims, *The Cybernetics Group* (Cambridge, Mass.: MIT Press, 1991), 29.

33. "School of Design in Chicago," prospectus, n.d., 11, Getty Center for the History of Art and the Humanities, Research Library.

34. László Moholy-Nagy, *The New Vision: Fundamentals of Design, Painting, Sculpture, Architecture,* trans. Daphne M. Hoffmann, rev. and enlarged ed. (New York: W. W. Norton, 1938). This edition was the first in an anticipated series of New Bauhaus Books, to be edited by Moholy-Nagy and Gropius. Its publication coincided with an exhibition at the Museum of Modern Art devoted to the Bauhaus and with the release of *Bauhaus: Weimar/Dessau, 1919–1928,* the exhibition catalogue edited by Walter Gropius, Herbert Bayer, and Ise Gropius.

35. Also added to the American editions of *The New Vision* were excerpts from "Light Architecture"; in that essay, published in London in 1936, Moholy-Nagy proposes that three-dimensional figures or environments made solely of light are the logical extension of his earlier work in other media. In its original edition, *The New Vision* had juxtaposed photographs of Naum Gabo's kinetic sculptures with an image of a brightly lit revolving merry-go-round. According to Moholy-Nagy, the virtual solids produced by the accumulated photographic afterimages of a rapidly moving reflective or luminous object embodied a state of "kinetic equipoise." As representatives of this ultimate stage in the evolution of sculpture, Moholy-Nagy considered them to be dematerializations of the "biotechnical elements," the building blocks of nature resembling the rods, cones, and spheres set forth in 1920 by the biologist Raoul Francé. Like the reflections emanating from his *Light Space Modulator* of 1932–1938, these building blocks were no longer solids but rather were new bodies composed solely of light; their anatomy can be grasped only through a photographic vision capable of breaking down motion into a series of afterimages, and then compiling these into a spatiotemporal sequence.

36. László Moholy-Nagy, *Vision in Motion* (Chicago: Paul Theobald, 1947), 28.

37. Moholy-Nagy illustrates his account by citing Margaret Mead's celebration of the kinesthetic interconnectedness of art and society in the rituals of "primitive" cultures; in contrast, in modernity artist and society are alienated, and "everybody suffers" from lack of meaning. Moholy-Nagy quotes the anthropologist:

[T]he art of primitive culture seen now as the whole ritual, the symbolic expression of the meaning of life, appeals to all the senses, through the eyes and ears, to the smell of incense, the kinaesthetisia of genuflection and kneeling or swaying to the passing procession. . . . [I]n primitive societies the artist is not a separate person, having no immediate close relationship to the economic processes and everyday experience of his society. The concept of the artist who sets himself apart, or only becomes an artist because his life history has set him apart, is almost wholly lacking[.] (*Vision in Motion,* 26)

38. Ibid., 14. Moholy-Nagy is quoting Julian Huxley from *Evolution: The Modern Synthesis* (London: George Allen and Unwin, 1942), 574.

39. Moholy-Nagy, *Vision in Motion,* 20.

40. Ibid., 52–54.

41. Ibid., 113.

42. The relationship between Walter Paepcke and modernism, from the advertising campaign of the Container Corporation of America to the founding of the Aspen design conferences (including his relationship with Moholy-Nagy and the Institute of Design), is chronicled by James Sloan Allen in *The Romance of Commerce and Culture.*

43. Paepcke continued to solicit financial support and design commissions for the institute, often making the argument that the school could repay industry by supplying the means to redesign products in accordance with market pressures. He wrote to one potential donor that "there is no question in anyone's mind, that in the postwar era practically all civilian products, whether they are refrigerators, automobiles, Mixmasters, or cooking utensils, are going to be designed in an attractive and streamlined way" (quoted in Allen, *The Romance of Commerce and Culture,* 68).

44. At the School of Design Kepes ran the "light workshop," which was described in the school's catalogue as bringing "a thorough revaluation of the advertising art" ("School of Design in Chicago," prospectus, 7). In 1939 he also taught a course in the Art Director's Club of Chicago called "Visual Fundamentals," which he would later develop into *Language of Vision.*

45. Gyorgy Kepes, *Language of Vision* (Chicago: Paul Theobald, 1944), 45.

46. John L. Scott, "Civilian Camouflage Goes into Action," *Civilian Defense* 1, no. 2 (June 1942): 7–11, 33–34; illustration, 8. A copy of this article is available in box 3, Kepes Papers, AAA.

47. "Outline of the Camouflage Course at the School of Design in Chicago 1941–1942," box 4, Kepes Papers, AAA.

48. Kepes, *Language of Vision,* 16; emphasis added.

49. Ibid., 12.

50. Ibid., 13.

51. Marshall McLuhan's essay "The Emperor's Old Clothes" was included in *The Man-Made Object,* ed. Gyorgy Kepes (New York: George Braziller, 1966), 90–95.

52. Kepes, *Language of Vision,* 13.

53. In his 1972–1973 interview with Brown, Kepes recalls the "fashion" for his book among general semanticists (Brown-Kepes interview, 24, Kepes Papers, AAA). A year later, S. I. Hayakawa published *Language in Action: A Guide to Accurate Thinking, Reading, and Writing* (New York: Harcourt, Brace, 1945). General semantics had loose affinities with the Unity of Science movement and roots in the pseudo-scientific teachings of Alfred Korzybski, especially as found in *Science and Sanity: An Introduction to Non-Aristotelian Systems and General Semantics* (Lancaster, Pa.: Science Press, 1933). See Charlotte S. Read, "General Semantics," in *Bridging Worlds through General Semantics: Selections from the First Forty Years of "Et cetera," 1943–1983,* ed. Mary Morain (San Francisco: International Society for General Semantics, 1984), 63–72.

54. Charles Morris, *Signs, Language and Behavior* (New York: Prentice-Hall, 1946), 2; see passim. Clark L. Hull was instrumental in developing a "performance"-oriented theory of behavior based on a logical system. See Robert S. Woodworth and Mary R. Sheehan, *Contemporary Schools of Psychology* (New York: Ronald Press, 1964), 141–149.

55. See Peter Galison, "The Ontology of the Enemy: Norbert Wiener and the Cybernetic Vision," *Critical Inquiry* 21, no. 1 (autumn 1994): 228–266. Galison makes the case for understanding the cybernetic treatment of the "other" as a "black box," which was embodied in Wiener's wartime antiaircraft experiments, in terms of the stimulus-response schema of behavioral psychology. See also Arturo Rosenblueth, Julian Bigelow, and Norbert Wiener, "Behavior, Purpose, and Teleology," *Philosophy of Science* 10, no. 1 (January 1943): 18–24.

56. Charles Morris, *Signification and Significance: A Study of the Relations of Signs and Values* (Cambridge, Mass.: MIT Press, 1964), 62–64.

57. Here is Kepes: *"The only farsighted way of visually approaching the customer is to consider the eye of the customer. . . .* To look from a high mountain or a tall skyscraper or to see the architecture with a rich space articulation offers to us an intense aesthetical satisfaction. To take the eye as the customer, it is first necessary to satisfy its basic needs of spatial experience." ("The Task of Visual Advertising," in *Gyorgy Kepes,* exhibition pamphlet, n.d., 10; emphasis in original. A copy is available in box 11, Kepes Papers, AAA.)

58. During this period, possibly in part because he needed to define his role within the architectural curriculum, Kepes made numerous course notes in which he worked out his pedagogy for an academic environment distinctly different from that of the Bauhaus-inspired workshops he ran in Chicago. Among the first of these explicitly addressing the problem of architectural education was a page most likely written in response to overtures from MIT. Here, Kepes locates architecture in a "blind alley" between the (regressive) Beaux-Arts education and the "material fetish" of functionalism. Consistent with *Language of Vision,* his notes argue for a "reorganization" effected through a "sense of organic relatedness" and "cultural meaning" in visual form. "Plastic organization," supplemented by a series of visual terms of reference, is enlisted as the primary agent in this restorative process (Kepes, undated notes, box 3, Kepes Papers, AAA).

59. In the MIT catalogue for 1946–1947, Kepes's course "Visual Fundamentals" was described as a study of "[t]he structure of two dimensional picture surfaces. The elements: point, line, shape, value, form, texture. Their organization: balance, dynamic equilibrium, tension, rhythm, proportion, etc." Likewise, the second course, "Light and Color," was described as "[r]esearch into the organization of light and color in two and three dimensions. Studies in light modulation with cameraless photography, light modulators, light and shadow boxes. Space organization with light" (*Massachusetts Institute of Technology Bulletin* 81, no. 4 [June 1946]: 99). On the prewar reception of Bauhaus discourse in the United States, see Margret Kentgens-Craig, *The Bauhaus and America: First Contacts, 1919–1936,* trans. Lynette Widder (Cambridge, Mass.: MIT Press, 1999).

60. Kepes to Sibyl Moholy-Nagy, 8 September 1948 (emphasis added), box 1, Kepes Papers, AAA.

61. Excerpts from Kepes's presentation were published in *Arts and Architecture,* the magazine that had initiated the Case Study Houses program in Los Angeles three years earlier. The conference, held on 5 and 6 March 1947 at Princeton University, is documented in *Planning Man's Physical Environment* (Princeton: Princeton University, 1947). Other participants included Sigfried Giedion, Walter Gropius, Alvar Aalto, Frank Lloyd Wright, William Wurster, George

Howe, and Robert Moses. Among the invited guests in attendance were Philip Johnson, Ludwig Mies van der Rohe, and Richard Neutra. A second, more comprehensive publication with revised contributions appeared two years later as Thomas H. Creighton, ed., *Building for Modern Man: A Symposium* (Princeton: Princeton University Press, 1949).

62. Gyorgy Kepes, "Gyorgy Kepes," *Arts and Architecture* 64, no. 5 (May 1947): 25. It is possible that Kepes was aware of Georg Lukács's notion of "second nature," for he had already read the Hungarian philosopher's early work as a student in the 1910s. In 1920, in *The Theory of the Novel,* Lukács criticized the metropolitan world of objects as a reified, dead nature evacuated of meaning. For Lukács, "The second nature, the nature of man-made structures, has no lyrical substantiality; its forms are too rigid to adapt themselves to the symbol-creating moment; . . . it is a charnel-house of long-dead interiorities" (*The Theory of the Novel,* trans. Anna Bostock [Cambridge, Mass.: MIT Press, 1971], 63–64). Reference is made to a "Lukács book" in correspondence between Kepes and the sociobiologist Edmund Wilson on 25 October and 1 November 1965, box 1, Kepes Papers, AAA.

In a set of notes that most likely date from this same period, Kepes summarizes his diagnosis as "form = function: image = form," and adds a prescription: "image building" (undated notes, box 2, Kepes Papers, AAA). These and other notes referred to later are handwritten, apparently as an outline for a lecture or text.

63. Kepes, "Gyorgy Kepes," 25. The expression "new symbolic form" is almost certainly an allusion to Erwin Panofsky, whose essay "Perspective as Symbolic Form" (1927) is listed in Kepes's personal bibliographic notes under its original German title.

64. Sigfried Giedion, "Notes on the Ames Demonstrations: Art and Perception," *Trans/formation: Arts, Communication, Environment* 1, no. 1 (1950): 8. Kepes, who was a consulting editor for *Trans/formation,* possessed a copy of this text.

65. In his own contribution to *Trans/formation,* Adelbert Ames listed two primary conclusions:

> 1) The processes that underlie our perception of our immediate external world and those that underlie our perception of social relationships are fundamentally the same.
>
> 2) The insights gained in the study of visual sensation can serve as indispensable leads to better understanding and more effective hand-ling of the complexities of social relationships. ("Sensations, Their Nature and Origin," *Trans/formation: Arts, Communication, Environment* 1, no. 1 [1950]: 12)

66. Adelbert Ames Jr. to Kepes, 4 April 1947, box 1, Kepes Papers, AAA. Kepes had to postpone a visit to Ames's Dartmouth Eye Institute in Hanover, N.H., planned for that month, but correspondence from Ames indicates that both Alexander Dorner and Serge Chermayeff did visit the institute then (Ames to Kepes, 30 April 1947, ibid.).

67. Erwin Schrödinger, a Nobel laureate in physics, was the author of *What Is Life?* (Cambridge: Cambridge University Press, 1944). On Schrödinger's role in the development of information-based models of the organism, see Evelyn Fox Keller, *Refiguring Life: Metaphors of Twentieth-Century Biology* (New York: Columbia University Press, 1995), esp. 45–47, 66–78. The Dartmouth team was, in Ames's words, attempting "an integration of our disclosures on the origin and nature of perception with Schroedinger's material" (Ames to Kepes, 4 April 1947, box 1, Kepes Papers, AAA).

In 1948 Kepes published a two-part article titled "Form and Motion" in *Arts and Architecture.* Here he reiterates the diagnosis of the generalized "formlessness" with which he had become preoccupied, invoking the biological figure of the "organizer," a cell "charged with forms, as an electric battery is charged with energy," as a model for rebuilding the disintegrated whole ("Form and Motion," part 1, *Arts and Architecture* 65 [July 1948]: 26–28; for part 2, see 66 [August 1948]: 26, 52–53). Ames had been given a manuscript of this text (which was originally presented as a lecture at the Institute of Design in Chicago on 23 October 1947) several months earlier by the president of Dartmouth College, and he wrote to Kepes that he was "especially impressed by the close similarity of the development of your line of thought and that which is emerging here." He also indicated that the Hanover Institute was developing another set of demonstrations on the perception of motion (Ames to Kepes, 15 March 1948, box 1, Kepes Papers, AAA).

68. These citations are from a series of undated handwritten bibliographic lists headed "Visual Fundamentals" and "Education of Vision" (box 2, Kepes Papers, AAA). These lists almost certainly date from the late 1940s: no titles were published later than 1947, and Kepes tended to keep up with current literature in his fields of interest.

69. This quotation appears in a series of handwritten notes by Kepes under the heading "Education of Vision" (box 2, Kepes Papers, AAA).

70. Kepes, handwritten notes, box 4, Kepes Papers, AAA.

71. *The New Landscape,* exhibition brochure, 19 February to 8 March 1951, Massachusetts Institute of Technology, box 3, Kepes Papers, AAA.

72. Sigfried Giedion, *Space, Time and Architecture: The Growth of a New Tradition* (Cambridge, Mass.: Harvard University Press, 1941), 574–578. On the history of scientific photography, see Jon Darius, *Beyond Vision* (New York: Oxford University Press, 1984); he also reproduces Harold Edgerton's photograph of the explosion (96).

73. Sigfried Giedion, *Mechanization Takes Command: A Contribution to Anonymous History* (New York: Oxford University Press, 1948), 246.

74. Sigfried Giedion to Kepes, 27 August 1951, box 1, Kepes Papers, AAA.

75. Walter Gropius to Kepes, 17 April 1952, microfilm, Kepes Papers, AAA.

76. D'Arcy Wentworth Thompson, *On Growth and Form,* new ed. (Cambridge: Cambridge University Press, 1942); Giedion and Gropius are referring to Lancelot Law Whyte, ed., *Aspects of Form* (London: Lund Humphries, 1951). The exhibition *Growth and Form,* proposed by future Independent Group members Nigel Henderson and Richard Hamilton and designed by Hamilton, consisted of scientific photographs illustrating natural phenomena at all scales, in-

stalled and projected as an encompassing environment at the ICA (see Anne Massey, *The Independent Group: Modernism and Mass Culture in Britain, 1945–1959* [New York: Manchester University Press, 1995], 42–45). Kepes sent Whyte a copy of *The New Landscape in Art and Science* in 1957, to which Whyte responded with effusive praise (Whyte to Kepes, 7 March 1957, box 1, Kepes Papers, AAA). In his preface to Whyte's book, the ICA director Herbert Read noted: "The increasing significance given to form or pattern in various branches of science has suggested the possibility of a certain parallelism, if not identity, in the structures of natural phenomena and of authentic works of art" (editorial preface to Whyte, ed., *Aspects of Form*, xxi).

77. Lancelot Law Whyte, "Editorial Preface to the 1968 Edition," in *Aspects of Form,* ed. Whyte 2nd ed. (London: Lund Humphries, 1968), x; emphasis in original.

78. Kepes, *The New Landscape in Art and Science,* 17.

79. For example, Kepes comments:

> From every source there come warnings of menace in our lack of regulation. The wild oscillations of art so characteristic of our age are not accidental; they describe the conditions of our life. Current history calls upon us to adjust ourselves to change faster than men have ever had to adjust themselves in the past. Each new phase of development has intensified the continuing struggle between old and new. The driving forces of change must meet enough resistance from us that we are not rent apart. They must receive enough accommodation from us so that we can continue to function and grow within our environment. But how much is enough? How far can we go? In what direction? This basic indecision is carried into every outer and inner process. Will mechanization crush individuality and spontaneity? Must one specialize in specific directions, leaving all others undeveloped? How can both individual and common interest be protected? (ibid., 326)

80. Herbert Marshall McLuhan, *The Mechanical Bride: Folklore of Industrial Man* (New York: Vanguard Press, 1951), v.

81. Kepes, *The New Landscape in Art and Science,* 344–355. A film documenting the construction of Eero Saarinen's Kresge Auditorium at MIT (completed in 1955) can be found among the material in the Kepes Papers, AAA.

82. On Kepes's organicist project as developed in the Vision + Value series, see Reinhold Martin, "Organicism's Other," *Grey Room,* no. 4 (summer 2001): 34–51.

83. Marcel Breuer to Kepes 27 March 1962, microfilm, Kepes Papers, AAA. Breuer, a fellow Hungarian, had designed a summer house for Kepes and his family in Wellfleet, Mass., on Cape Cod in 1949, identical to the one he built for himself at the same time.

84. On the invitation of Johnson E. Fairchild, director of the Division of Adult Education, Kepes gave a public lecture at the Cooper Union for the Advancement of Science and Art on 24 November 1958 (Fairchild to Kepes, 7 May 1958, box 1, Kepes Papers, AAA). Kepes, "Cooper Union" (lecture manuscript), 21 ff., Kepes Papers, AAA.

85. Gyorgy Kepes, introduction to *The Visual Arts Today,* 10. The aesthetic forces of the form-less (*l'informe,* after Georges Bataille) have been catalogued and analyzed by Yve-Alain Bois and Rosalind Krauss with respect to modern painting and sculpture. Significantly, "entropy" is among them (Bois and Krauss, *Formless: A User's Guide* [New York: Zone Books, 1998], 169–231). On Mies's organicism, see Detlef Mertins, "Living in a Jungle: Mies, Organic Architecture, and the Art of City Building," in *Mies in America,* ed. Phyllis Lambert (New York: Harry N. Abrams, 2001), 590–641.

86. Manfredo Tafuri and Francesco Dal Co, and after them K. Michael Hays, have produced the most provocative analyses of the "silence" attributed by many commentators to Mies's Sea-gram Building. See Manfredo Tafuri and Francesco Dal Co, *Modern Architecture,* trans. Robert Erich Wolf (New York: Electa/Rizzoli, 1986), 2:309–314; and K. Michael Hays, "Odysseus and the Oarsmen, or, Mies's Abstraction Once Again," in *The Presence of Mies,* ed. Detlef Mertins (New York: Princeton Architectural Press, 1994), 234–247, and "Abstraction's Appearance (Seagram Building)," in *Autonomy and Ideology: Positioning an Avant-Garde in America,* ed. R. E. Somol (New York: Monacelli Press, 1997), 276–291. In all cases, the silence that these and other au-thors see in the nonfigural grid of Mies's curtain wall is taken as a "negative" property, in the sense of the dialectical role assigned by Theodor W. Adorno to the autonomous artwork of art in his *Aesthetic Theory* (1970). Hays modifies Tafuri and Dal Co's analysis to allow this "negative dialectics" to encompass the sublimation of mass-cultural techniques in the billboardlike sur-face of Seagram's front facade. Similarly, for Rosalind Krauss, "the grid announces, among other things, modern art's will to silence, its hostility to literature, to narrative, to discourse" (Krauss, "Grids," in *The Originality of the Avant-Garde and Other Modernist Myths* [Cambridge, Mass.: MIT Press, 1985], 9). For an alternative reading that draws on the discourse of John Cage and the specificities of a postwar neo-avant-garde, see Branden W. Joseph, "John Cage and the Architecture of Silence," *October,* no. 81 (summer 1997): 81–104.

87. Kepes, *The New Landscape in Art and Science,* 327. Kepes argues that such oscillations and the instability they produce are subject to regulation by laws of proportion and symmetry common to both art and science, driven by rhythms of feedback and auto-regulation associ-ated with cybernetic processes:

Scientific and technical knowledge have given us an unprecedented opportunity to understand certain aspects of proportioning. Our knowledge of biological regulation has become a model for under-standing other phenomena. From thermostats to guided missiles, there are a growing number of automatic control systems based upon symmetry and proportion which help us to understand how men stand upright without toppling, how the human heart beats, why our economic system endures slumps and booms. Automatic-control de-vices and self-regulating mechanisms not only have become impor-tant in our economic and social life but also have philosophical and symbolic implications of the utmost significance. (328)

88. Marshall McLuhan, "Preface to the Third Printing," in *Understanding Media: The Extensions of Man* (New York: McGraw-Hill, 1964), vii.

3

The Physiognomy of the Office

1. Gyorgy Kepes, undated notes, box 3, Gyorgy Kepes Papers, Archives of American Art (AAA), Washington, D.C.

2. Heinz Werner, "On Physiognomic Perception," in *The New Landscape in Art and Science,* by Gyorgy Kepes (Chicago: Paul Theobald, 1956), 280–283.

3. "High Rise Office Buildings," *Progressive Architecture* 38, no. 6 (June 1957): 159. Sullivan's text, which was first published in *Lippincott's,* March 1896, appears later in the issue as Louis Sullivan, "The Tall Office Building Artistically Considered" (204–206).

4. Horatio Greenough, *Form and Function: Remarks on Art, Design, and Architecture,* ed. Harold A. Small (Berkeley: University of California Press, 1947), 71ff. For a contextualization of Greenough, his sources, and Sullivan within organicist discourse, see Joseph Rykwert, "Organic and Mechanical," *Res* 22 (autumn 1992): 11–18, and Peter Collins, "The Biological Analogy," chap. 14 in *Changing Ideals in Modern Architecture* (London: Faber and Faber, 1965), 149–158.

5. Greenough, *Form and Function,* 116–118; quotations, 116–117, 118.

6. Sullivan, "The Tall Building Artistically Considered," 204.

7. The French novelist Paul Bourget, quoted by Montgomery Schuyler in 1895 (referring to the work of Dankmar Adler and Sullivan), as subsequently quoted by Colin Rowe in "Chicago Frame," in *The Mathematics of the Ideal Villa and Other Essays* (Cambridge, Mass.: MIT Press, 1976), 102. Rowe's essay was first published in *The Architectural Review* in 1956. Sullivan himself refers to the office building as the "joint product of the speculator, the engineer, the builder" (Sullivan, "The Tall Office Building Artistically Considered," 204). See also Sullivan, *The Autobiography of an Idea* (New York: W. W. Norton, 1922), 314.

8. Rowe, "Chicago Frame," 103.

9. Colin Rowe, "Neo-'Classicism' and Modern Architecture I," and "Neo-'Classicism' and Modern Architecture II," in *The Mathematics of the Ideal Villa,* 119–138, 139–158. Both essays were written in 1956–1957.

10. Louis Sullivan, "The *Chicago Tribune* Competition," *Architectural Record* 53, no. 2 (February 1923): 152. This passage is cited by Manfredo Tafuri in "The Disenchanted Mountain: The Skyscraper and the City," in *The American City: From the Civil War to the New Deal,* by Giorgio Ciucci et al., trans. Barbara L. La Penta (Cambridge, Mass.: MIT Press, 1979), 418.

11. Tafuri, "The Disenchanted Mountain," 419.

12. Ibid., 396.

13. Stanford Anderson cites Behrens's own account of the Mannesmann project: "one must know and comprehend the organic structure of a great administrative body, the functional

importance of its different members for each other, and its nervous system, in order to be able to create a healthy body for this complicated organism" (*Peter Behrens and a New Architecture for the Twentieth Century* [Cambridge, Mass.: MIT Press, 2000], 194). On Behrens's flexible planning approach, see 144–203.

14. Tafuri, "The Disenchanted Mountain," 418.

15. In a typical declaration, Warren D. Bruner observes: "The best modern practice is to leave all floors undivided as rented" ("Office Layouts for Tenants," *Architectural Forum* 52, no. 6 [June 1930]: 906). Bruner describes the process of fitting out office interiors: "The space is sold by a broker or renting agent, and a tentative layout of the space for the prospective tenant is a valuable assistance in closing the transaction. These tentative and final layouts are made by the architect, the renting agent, or a layout specialist" (906). The same issue of *Architectural Forum* also contains detailed information on the technical, economic, and aesthetic terms under which commercial office buildings were being produced at the time; see Albert Kahn, "Designing Modern Office Buildings" (775–777); Arthur Loomis Harmon, "The Design of Office Buildings" (819–820); James B. Newman, "Factors in Office Building Planning" (881–890); and C. F. Palmer, "Office Buildings from an Investment Standpoint" (891–896).

16. From 1933 to 1934, the popular Broadway revue *As Thousands Cheer* featured a skit in which John D. Rockefeller Jr. played a joke on his father, John D. Rockefeller, by presenting him with a model of Rockefeller Center, which was understood at the time to be a failing investment. By the fall of 1934, it was reported that the enterprise had reversed its financial fortunes. See "A Phenomenon of Exploitation," *Architectural Forum* 61, no. 4 (October 1934): 292–298.

17. Sigfried Giedion, *Space, Time and Architecture: The Growth of a New Tradition* (Cambridge, Mass.: Harvard University Press, 1941), 578, 573; Edgerton photograph; 577.

18. On the history of the "slab"-type office building, from Rockefeller Center to the United Nations to Lever House, see Winston Weisman, "Slab Buildings," *Architectural Review* 111, no. 662 (February 1952): 119–124. William Jordy also traces the architecture of the RCA Building to Hood's Daily News Building of 1930, whose vertically striated elevation he describes as producing "[m]uch more a graphic than an architectural effect" (*American Buildings and Their Architects: The Impact of European Modernism in the Mid–Twentieth Century* [Garden City, N.Y.: Doubleday, 1972], 64).

19. During the design phase of the project, Raymond Hood observed that this and all other planning decisions in Rockefeller Center were made on a "cost and return" basis:

In the 66-story tower, which we refer to as Building No. 9, we have worked out a scheme that is likely to have an important bearing on all future commercial office buildings. Grouped in the center are the elevators, and the service, and surrounding them on each floor we have stretched the 27 ft. of lighted space that experience has proved is the maximum to be allowed to provide adequate light an air to all parts of the building. Although many a building has been planned on this principle, we have carried the principle to its logical conclusion. As each elevator shaft ended, we cut the building back to maintain the same 27 ft. from the core of the building to the exterior walls. By so doing, we have eliminated every dark corner; there is not a single point in the rentable area of the building that is more than 27 ft. away from a window. (Hood, "The Design of Rockefeller City," *Architectural Forum* 16, no. 1 [January 1932]: 5)

20. On the changing standards for optimally rentable office space depths up to 1930, see Palmer, "Office Buildings from an Investment Standpoint," 892.

21. Jordy, *American Buildings and Their Architects,* 68–71. Hood's Daily News Building of 1930 had also employed the window-pier-window vertically striped facade. In the RCA building, columns spaced at 27′ 6″ intervals are wrapped in a shell of alternating vertical glazing strips and solid piers. The piers containing columns measure 6′ 3″ wide, the intermediate piers are 3′ 6″ wide, and the continuous vertically aligned windows (spaced between bronze spandrels at floor and ceiling) are 4′ 9″ wide. As documented in an *Architectural Record* study of office fenestration done with the assistance of Harrison's then-partner Max Abramowitz in 1955, the result was a wide range of possibilities for office sizes at the perimeter, with a minimum office width of 8 feet—just wide enough to accommodate the necessary furniture and circulation. The *Record* study inventoried the range of possibilities: "The C-to-C [center to center] module is then about 9 ft., each typical division having one window, and one radiator. The extra dividend, however, comes in the ability to put the partition at any point between windows, so that any given office may have any desired width—8, 9, 10, 11, 12, 13, 14, 15, 16, or 17 ft." It also noted that "[t]he architectural staffs for Rockefeller Center carried the minimum office idea into a scheme since considered a classic in this regard" ("The Disciplines of Fenestration: A Study Prepared with the Assistance of Max Abramowitz, Harrison & Abramowitz, Architects," in "Building Types Study No. 221: Office Buildings; Fenestration," *Architectural Record* 117, no. 4 [April 1955]: 201).

22. Jordy, *American Buildings and Their Architects,* 68–71.

23. L. Andrew Reinhard and Henry Hofmeister, "New Trends in Office Design," *Architectural Record* 97, no. 3 (March 1945): 99.

24. Ibid., 100; emphasis added.

25. The most thorough analysis of the legacy of the Hawthorne Experiments is to be found in Richard Gillespie, *Manufacturing Knowledge: A History of the Hawthorne Experiments* (New York: Cambridge University Press, 1991). See also Anson Rabinbach, "Science, Work, and Worktime," *International Labor and Working Class History,* no. 43 (spring 1993): 48–64. It is Gillespie's contention that because Mayo and his colleagues overlaid a specific interpretation onto the empirical results of the experiments, those results were mistaken as evidence of a correlation between a sense of participation in the corporate whole and productivity. See especially Elton Mayo, *The Human Problems of an Industrial Civilization* (New York: Macmillan, 1933), and Fritz Roethlisberger and William Dickson, *Management and the Worker* (Cambridge, Mass.: Harvard University Press, 1939).

26. As Robert Wood Johnson, chairman of Johnson & Johnson Corporation, put it in an important report published in the *Harvard Business Review*: "No problem is greater or more urgent than that of establishing sound, cooperative relations between workers and management" ("Human Relations in Modern Business," *Harvard Business Review* 27, no. 5 [September 1949]: 521). The *Harvard Business Review* was a major conduit for disseminating human relations doctrine and related aspects of organizational theory during the 1950s, and it succinctly delineates how these ideas passed into conventional wisdom among America's corporate elite. See also, for example, William Foote Whyte, "Human Relations Theory—A Progress Report," *Harvard Business Review* 34, no. 5 (September–October 1956): 125–132, and Fritz J. Roethlisberger, ed., *Human Relations: Rare, Medium, or Well-Done?* (Cambridge, Mass.: President and Fellows of Harvard College, 1954). On organizational performance as a function of group participation, see Rensis Likert, "Measuring Organizational Performance," *Harvard Business Review* 36, no. 2 (March–April 1958): 41–49.

In 1949 a survey published by the *Harvard Business Review* on the reading habits of executives also found that the largest number of titles listed by the executives questioned belonged to the general heading of industrial and personnel management. Not surprisingly, prominent among these were Mayo's *Human Problems of an Industrial Civilization* and Roethlisberger and Dickson's *Management and the Worker*. See Edward C. Bursk and Donald T. Clark, "Reading Habits of Business Executives," *Harvard Business Review* 27, no. 3 (May 1949): 330–345.

27. James R. Beniger, *The Control Revolution: Technological Origins of the Information Society* (Cambridge, Mass.: Harvard University Press, 1986). See also James Burnham, *The Managerial Revolution: What Is Happening in the World* (New York: John Day, 1941), and Alfred D. Chandler Jr., *The Visible Hand: The Managerial Revolution in American Business* (Cambridge, Mass.: Harvard University Press, Belknap Press, 1977).

28. Barbara S. Heyl, "The Harvard 'Pareto Circle,'" *Journal of the History of Behavioral Sciences* 4, no. 4 (October 1968): 333. The effect of Pareto's ideas on Elton Mayo is vividly illustrated by the concluding lines of Mayo's book:

The chief difficulty of our time is the breakdown of the social codes that formerly disciplined us to effective working together. For the non-logic of a social code the logic of understanding—biological and social—has not been substituted. The situation is as if Pareto's circulation of the *élite* had been fatally interrupted—the consequence, social disequilibrium. We have too few administrators alert to the fact that it is a human social and not an economic problem which they face. The universities of the world are admirably equipped for the discovery and training of the specialist in science; but they have not begun to think about the discovery and training of the new administrator." (*The Human Problems of an Industrial Civilization*, 188)

29. Heyl, "The Harvard 'Pareto Circle,'" 325–326. See also Steven J. Cross and William R. Albury, "Walter B. Cannon, L. J. Henderson, and the Organic Analogy," *Osiris* 3 (1987): 165–192.

30. On the Larkin Building's central atrium as a "hearth" for the "Larkin family," see Neil Levine, *The Architecture of Frank Lloyd Wright* (Princeton: Princeton University Press, 1996), 38.

31. There exist numerous precedents for the glazed "curtain wall" as I use the term in this chapter. Among those most often cited are Van der Vlugt and Brinkman's Van Nelle factory (1929) in Rotterdam, and Le Corbusier's Cité de Refuge (1933) in Paris. Both possess large glazed facades that, however, rest between structural members, rather than hanging from them in the manner of a "curtain." A more convincing technical precedent in the United States is Willis Polk's Hallidie Building in San Francisco, completed in 1918.

32. As the *Architectural Record* study on fenestration cited above put it, "the width of partitions takes off space enough that two modules make the minimum office a trifle small" ("The Disciplines of Fenestration," 201).

33. Richard Roth, "High Rise Down to Earth," *Progressive Architecture* 38, no. 6 (June 1957): 197.

34. Roth made his argument two years after "The Disciplines of Fenestration," which focused on the work of Harrison & Abramowitz and came to markedly different conclusions. While firms such as Emery Roth & Sons and Kahn & Jacobs produced dozens of office buildings of the types described by Roth, Harrison & Abramowitz continued to explore the window-pier-window layout after 1945. In buildings such as the US Rubber Building at Rockefeller Center and the Mellon–US Steel and Alcoa Buildings, both in Pittsburgh, piers between windows varied from a minimum 1' 5" (Alcoa, with its aluminum paneled exterior), and 4' 1" (US Rubber). As the *Architectural Record* study noted, the essential difference between this system and that of continuous glazing "lies in the rigidity of the module, assuming that any partitioning is done only at a mullion or some other interruption to the glass." Significantly, the study also identified modular, gridded interiors, and curtain walls with the rigors of corporate identity:

> One important development since the twenties is the increasing number of office buildings for single occupancy, most of them away from the pressure of high land values. In such cases industrial management tends to have its own ideas of office arrangements and dimensions, ranging from no private offices at all, or no windows at all, up to full glass walls and 12-ft. office widths. Sometimes it is important for organization and standardization that the company management enforce a standard width without exception: frequently it is desirable that there be no physical possibility of variation. Thus the discipline of the module might be desirable, and the appropriate module can be based on office requirements. ("The Disciplines of Fenestration," 201)

By the mid-1950s, efforts to standardize and coordinate the dimensions of construction materials and assemblies had been under way for some time in the United States. The most common point of reference was the experiment in "modular coordination" performed in Great Britain in the Hertfordshire school construction program in the late 1940s and early 1950s. On that program, see Ezra D. Ehrenkrantz and John D. Kay, "Flexibility through Standardization,"

Progressive Architecture 38, no. 7 (July 1957): 105–115. An early advocate of modular construction products in the United States during the first half of the century was the builder Albert Farwell Bemis.

35. Kepes, *The New Landscape in Art and Science,* 334; quoted in "Modular Assembly," *Progressive Architecture* 38, no. 11 (November 1957): 119.

36. *Curtain Walls of Stainless Steel Construction* (Princeton: School of Architecture, Princeton University, 1955) was prepared for the Committee of Stainless Steel Producers, American Iron and Steel Institute. According to the report, "The wall of a building is analogous to the skin of the body which is not just a covering but an active and important organ of the body" (12).

37. Ibid.; quotation from the 1956 ABRI conference in "Syntax: The Contribution of the Curtain Wall to a New Vernacular," Ian McCallum, ed., *Machine Made America,* special issue of *Architectural Review* 121, no. 724 (May 1957): 299.

38. Quoted in "Syntax," 299. The curtain wall classifications appear on pp. 299–300.

39. Robert W. McLaughlin, quoted in "Syntax," 308.

40. Ibid., 307.

41. "Lever House: Spacious, Efficient, and Washable," *Business Week,* 3 May 1952, 76–78.

42. In the words of Lewis Mumford: "For a company whose main products are soap and detergents, that little handicap of the sealed windows is a heaven-sent opportunity, for what could better dramatize its business than a squad of cleaners operating in the chariot, like the deus ex machina of Greek tragedy, and capturing the eye of the passerby as they performed their daily duties?" (quoted in Alex Herrera, *Lever House, 390 Park Avenue, Borough of Manhattan* [New York: Landmarks Preservation Commission, 1982], 8). On Lever House, see also "Miniature Skyscraper," *Architectural Forum* 92, no. 6 (June 1950): 85–89; "Lever House Complete," *Architectural Forum* 96, no. 6 (June 1952): 107–111; "New York's Blue Glass Tower," *Contract Interiors* 112, no. 1 (August 1952): 58–65, 152–154.

43. On Behrens's work over several decades for the Allgemeine Elektricitäts-Gesellschaft (AEG), see Anderson, *Peter Behrens and a New Architecture for the Twentieth Century;* on the turbine factory itself, see 129–145.

44. Following the school's move to Dessau in 1925, the Bauhaus Corporation was formed to handle the sale of Bauhaus prototypes to industry.

45. "Syntax," 296.

46. On Bunshaft's own identification with his corporate clients, see Reinhold Martin, "The Bunshaft Tapes: A Preliminary Report," *Journal of Architectural Education* 54, no. 2 (November 2000): 80–87.

47. Randall is quoted in "Inland's Steel Showcase," *Architectural Forum* 108, no. 4 (April 1958): 89. The company building committee is quoted in "19 Office Floors without Columns," *Architectural Forum* 102, no. 5 (May 1955): 116.

48. "19 Office Floors without Columns," 116.

49. "19 Office Floors without Columns," 115.

50. By 1957 Skidmore, Owings & Merrill was "an architect-engineer organization with four semi-autonomous offices located across the United States, engaged on projects in all parts of the world" (William E. Hartmann, "S.O.M. Organization," *Bauen und Wohnen* 11, no. 4 [April 1957]: 114). Hartmann describes the firm's "organization in depth," with partners backed up by associate partners and participating associates, in detail, including an organization chart. See also in the same issue Sigfried Giedion, "The Experiment of S.O.M." (113–114).

51. Editors of Architectural Forum, "A Memorandum to 194X Architects," in "The New House of 194X," *Architectural Forum* 77, no. 3 (September 1942): 66.

52. Louis Skidmore, Nathaniel A. Owings, and John O. Merrill, "Flexible Space," in "The New House 194X," 101–103.

53. Ibid., 100.

54. R. Buckminster Fuller's "Mechanical Wing," first published in the October 1940 issue of *The Architectural Forum,* is reproduced in Robert W. Marks, *The Dymaxion World of Buckminster Fuller* (Carbondale: Southern Illinois University Press, 1960), 108.

55. Fuller's "Dymaxion Deployment Unit" is documented in Marks, *The Dymaxion World of Buckminster Fuller,* 110–119. See also Beatriz Colomina, "DDU at MOMA," *Any,* no. 17 (1997): 48–53.

56. Skidmore, Owings, and Merrill, "Flexible Space," 100.

57. Again the architects' statement confirmed the conceptual nature of the division: "The social functions of the home—dining, playing, lounging, and studying—are allowed a greater individuality by virtue of the standardization of the biological and mechanical elements. The social functions, vastly affected by climate, income, and personal taste, are untouched by this standardization. Prefabrication methods are adaptable to the living space, but local whims may govern" (Eero Saarinen and Oliver Lundquist, quoted in "Designs for Postwar Living," *California Arts and Architecture* 60 [August 1943]: 29).

58. I. M. Pei and E. H. Duhart describe their scheme as follows: "[W]ith various time-saving devices at our disposal, the kitchen is no longer to be designed as the housewife's perpetual environment. Rather, it is an efficient work space which will allow her to do her daily work easily and well. The result is more leisure for her and emphatically brings us to a new conception—our 'home room.' This is a space for living, a space for family life" (quoted in ibid., 33).

59. Charles Eames, John Entenza, and Herbert Matter argue, "It is the kitchen, the bathroom, the bedroom, the utility and storage units that will profit most by the industrialized system of prefabrication. Here the activities of all men are much the same in the use of these basic household utilities, which properly designed and engineered will accommodate the over-all family function and offer facilities and conveniences impossible to the individual's most ambitious preferences." But they suggest further that again, "It is in the living-recreational areas that variation becomes a matter of personal preference where the family desires in terms of differences in activities must be considered. The accommodation of this difference in family activity is perfectly feasible and will be a natural part of the study of the industrialized house" ("What Is a House?" *Arts and Architecture* 61 [July 1944]: 35). They describe the architect of the "prefabricated house" as "1. The Student of Human Behavior; 2. The Scientist; 3. The Economist; 4. The Industrial Designer." And like the architects of corporate buildings, the architect of

the house was expected to reduce family life to the "most simple common denominator with scientific precision, redirect capital, and put it all on the assembly line," in accordance with the formula set by the marketplace: price is directly proportionate to service (33).

60. Eero Saarinen, "Demountable Space," advertisement for the United States Gypsum Co., in *Architectural Forum* 76, no. 3 (March 1942): 156–160.

61. Eames, Entenza, and Matter's "What Is a House?" is accompanied by eight quotations from Fuller on the mass production of shelter.

62. On the Chase Manhattan Bank project as the center of a large-scale urban master plan, see Nathaniel Alexander Owings, *The Spaces in Between: An Architect's Journey* (Boston: Houghton Mifflin, 1973), 162–168. On the Chase building, see also "Tower with a Front Yard," *Architectural Forum* 106, no. 4 (April 1957): 110–115, and "Chase Manhattan's New Home," *Contract Interiors* 121, no. 2 (September 1961): 112–117.

63. On the DLMA and the influence of the Chase Manhattan master plan on the World Trade Center, see Eric Darnton, *Divided We Stand: A Biography of New York's World Trade Center* (New York: Basic Books, 1999), 71–73, 83, 93–96, and Owings, *The Spaces in Between,* 168. See also Reinhold Martin, "One or More," *Grey Room,* no. 7 (spring 2002): 114–123. In "The Disenchanted Mountain," Tafuri invokes both the Chase Manhattan Bank plan and the World Trade Center as projects that "at best ... aim at a localization of integrated functions," but fail to reintegrate the city itself (487ff.).

64. Owings, *The Spaces in Between,* 166, 167–168.

65. Tafuri, "The Disenchanted Mountain," 503.

66. "Tower with a Front Yard," 112.

67. Ibid.

68. *SOM News,* no. 20 (15 October 1956); a copy is available in the Gordon Bunshaft Papers, Avery Art and Architecture Library Archives, Columbia University. See also "Union Carbide's Shaft of Steel," *Architectural Forum* 113, no. 5 (November 1960): 114–121, and "The Current Pacesetter," *Architectural Record* 128, no. 5 (November 1960): 155–162. On the development of a commercial district along Park Avenue during the 1950s, see Jane Jacobs, "New York's Office Boom," *Architectural Forum* 106, no. 3 (March 1957): 104–113.

69. "SOM's Details of Distinction," *Architectural Forum* 112, no. 6 (June 1960): 124–129.

70. *The Salaried Masses* is the title of English translation of *Die Angestellten* (1929), Siegfried Kracauer's portrait of the white-collar worker in Weimar Germany that was based on a series of informal interviews (*The Salaried Masses: Duty and Distraction in Weimar Germany,* trans. Quintin Hoare [London: Verso, 1998]). While Kracauer was conducting his interviews in Berlin, Elton Mayo and his team of industrial psychologists were conducting interviews of their own at the Hawthorne Works of the Western Electric Company in Chicago. Unlike Kracauer, who had set out to cast "the light of publicity on the public condition of salaried employees" (29), Mayo and his colleagues saw their interviews as instruments of a new managerialism: "The interview must be considered as revealing a personality—its history, its attitudes, its merits, and defects. But how to advance beyond the mere revelation, how to develop from a knowl-

edge-of-acquaintance of persons to a knowledge-about persons and a method of control—these questions became urgent" (Mayo, *The Human Problems of an Industrial Civilization*, 101).

71. C. Wright Mills, *White Collar: The American Middle Classes* (New York: Oxford University Press, 1951), 189–212, 233–235; quotations, 233.

72. Theodor W. Adorno, "Television and the Patterns of Mass Culture," in *Mass Culture: The Popular Arts in America,* ed. Bernard Rosenberg and David M. White (New York: Free Press, 1957), 485. Adorno's treatment of television here as "a medium of undreamed of psychological control" (476) is related to the critique he developed with Max Horkheimer in *Dialectic of Enlightenment,* trans. John Cummings (New York: Herder and Herder, 1972; originally published as *Dialektik der Aufklärung* [New York: Social Studies Association, 1944]), most explicitly in chap. 4, "The Culture Industry: Enlightenment as Mass Deception" (120–167).

73. David Riesman, with Reuel Denney and Nathan Glazer, *The Lonely Crowd: A Study of the Changing American Character* (New Haven: Yale University Press, 1950). Adorno ("Television and the Patterns of Mass Culture") quotes from Riesman's preface: "the conformity of earlier generations of Americans of the type I term 'inner-directed' was mainly assured by their internalization of adult authority. The middle-class urban American of today, the 'other-directed,' is, by contrast, in a characterological sense more the product of his peers—that is, in sociological terms, his 'peer-groups,' the other kids at school or in the block" (Riesman, v; Adorno, 477). According to Riesman, societies dependent on "inner-direction" (as distinct from the "tradition-directed" societies of the Middle Ages and of non-Western cultures) are historically transitional, in that internalized values regulated by what Riesman calls a "psychological gyroscope" are destabilized with the rapid growth of surplus capital and consumerism, rendering the gyroscopic "control" (Riesman's term) insufficiently flexible (6–19). For Riesman, "*What is common to all other-directeds is that their contemporaries are the source of direction for the individual—either those known to him or those with whom he is indirectly acquainted, through friends and through the mass media*" (22). So the internal "gyroscope" is externalized in what Riesman describes, appropriately enough for the servomechanical logic implicit in his characterizations, as an exchange of "signals" with others (22).

74. William H. Whyte Jr., *The Organization Man* (New York: Simon and Schuster, 1956), 44. Whyte identifies the "organization man" with human relations, as follows:

> Human relations can mean a lot of things—as one critic defines it, it is any study called human relations to escape the discipline of established theory in the appropriate field. But, generally speaking, most human-relations doctrine is pointed to the vision of Mayo, and this reinforces what many people are already very well prepared to believe. Particularly the organization man. Who is the hero of human relations? In the older ideology, it was the top leader who was venerated. In human relations it is the organization man, and thus the quasi-religious overtones with which he gratefully endows it. (ibid.)

75. Ibid., 68.

76. Ibid., 404.

77. Jean-François Lyotard makes the same point, citing both Riesman and Whyte as well as Herbert Marcuse as part of his general indictment of the totalizing imperatives of performance-based systems models of society: "Administrative procedures should make individuals 'want' what the system needs in order to perform well" (*The Postmodern Condition: A Report on Knowledge,* trans. Geoff Bennington and Brian Massumi [Minneapolis: University of Minnesota Press, 1984], 62, 216 n. 101).

78. The economy of "home" and "work," and of the "housewife" and the "organization man," is vividly illustrated in two 1954 films used by Whyte to exemplify an ethic of corporate conformity disseminated through the mass media, *Woman's World* and *Executive Suite.* The first follows the process by which a company president selects among men to be promoted, basing his decision on their wives. Two candidates are eventually ruled out—one because of his excessive attention to wife and family, the other because of his utter indifference to his wife (see Whyte, *The Organization Man,* 261).

The overt misogyny of *Woman's World* (left more or less untouched by Whyte) is internalized in *Executive Suite,* in which board members of a furniture company vie for the presidency after the sudden death of the top executive. All aspects of the corporation are represented: management, production, design, accounts, outside stockholders, the founder's family, an executive secretary. A dynamic young designer—who is shown designing Eames furniture—with a supportive wife eventually triumphs (261–263, 76).

In each case, the corporation lays claim on the organization man's devotion, in one instance with the help of a dutiful wife; in the other, despite her. As these films demonstrate, and as Whyte keenly observes, home and work thus depend on one another as regulatory mechanisms. In that sense, no matter where his loyalties ultimately lie, the organization man is at home—providing that the other components of the system, including the housewife, occupy their proper places.

4
Organic Style

1. The photograph of the General Motors Technical Center through an automobile windshield accompanies Lawrence Alloway, "City Notes," *Architectural Design* 29, no. 1 (January 1959): 34. Its caption reads: "GM Tech Centre seen through wide windscreen, an echo of cinema techniques."

2. Charles Eames, John Entenza, and Herbert Matter, "What Is a House?" *Arts and Architecture* 61 (July 1944): 35.

3. Le Corbusier, *Towards a New Architecture,* trans. Frederick Etchells (London: Butterworth, 1987), 137–138.

4. In 1955 Reyner Banham also published "The New Brutalists" in *Architectural Review,* reprinted in *A Critic Writes: Essays by Reyner Banham,* ed. Mary Banham (Berkeley: University of California Press, 1996), 7–15; the essay concentrates primarily on the work of Alison and Peter Smithson.

5. Banham, "Vehicles of Desire," in *A Critic Writes,* 3. The essay was originally published in *Art,* 1 September 1955.

6. Ibid., 4–5.

7. Ibid., 5.

8. *Industrial Design* is quoted in ibid.

9. General Motors Corporation, "Summary of the Architecture of the General Motors Technical Center," 14, unpublished typescript, Eero Saarinen Papers, group no. 593, Sterling Memorial Library (SML), Manuscripts and Archives, Yale University.

10. This and the following quotations are from Harlow H. Curtice, transcript of speech given at the dedication of the General Motors Technical Center, 16 May 1956, 1–2, historic files, General Motors Technical Center Design Library, Warren, Mich.

11. As Eero Saarinen privately observed, "I have until recently had a reputation as being one of the best younger architects. The publication of the General Motors Technical Center put me about half way between that category and the category of being 'successful' with big business and industry" (Saarinen, to Astrid Sampe, undated letter, Eero Saarinen Papers, Cranbrook Academy Archives, Cranbrook Academy of Art, Bloomfield Hills, Mich.).

12. Reyner Banham, "The Fear of Eero's Mana," *Arts Magazine* 36, no. 5 (February 1962): 72.

13. Cranston Jones, "Interview with Mies van der Rohe," 24 November 1958, 3, box 2, Gyorgy Kepes Papers, Archives of American Art (AAA), Washington, D.C. Mies also makes a reference to Kepes's painting in the interview.

14. Kevin Roche, interview with the author, 24 July 1996.

15. Jones, "Interview with Mies van der Rohe," 2.

16. Henry Ford's characterization of the Model T circa 1912 is cited in Allan Nevins, with Frank Ernest Hill, *Ford: The Times, the Man, the Company* (New York: Charles Scribner's Sons, 1954), 452.

17. The institutionalization of planned obsolescence at General Motors was also accompanied by substantial changes in the organizational structure of the company. The most notable change was an increasing degree of decentralization, prompted by the necessity for local penetration into markets that needed to be constantly prepared (with traveling auto shows called "Motoramas," for example) for the upcoming changes and tested in advance for their response. This model has since become the basis of Arthur J. Kuhn's hypotheses linking Sloan's thinking with the later feedback-driven control systems of cybernetics; see *GM Passes Ford, 1918–1938: Designing the General Motors Performance-Control System* (University Park: Pennsylvania State University Press, 1986).

Kuhn's thesis—which contains heavily technocratic overtones—is that the use of a proto-cybernetic "performance-control system" led in the 1930s to General Motors' overtaking Ford—which retained its rigidly pyramidal management model until a reorganization in the late 1940s—as market leader. He begins his comparison of Sloan's approach to the cybernetic notion of "steersmanship" by quoting him as describing GM's success in "devis[ing] scientific means of administration and control" to prepare management "to alter the course of this ship of ours promptly and effectively" when needed (4). Sloan's account of the development of these techniques can be found in Alfred P. Sloan Jr., *My Years with General Motors* (Garden City, N.Y.: Doubleday, 1963). See also Ed Cray, *Chrome Colossus: General Motors and Its Times* (New York: McGraw-Hill, 1980). The full range of pathologies associated with so-called organizational cybernetics—here derived from Kuhn's analysis of General Motors—are exhibited in Kuhn, *Organizational Cybernetics and Business Policy: System Design for Performance Control* (University Park: Pennsylvania State University Press, 1986).

18. Along with styling came the concern that its variety in product would be pushed toward uniformity by the requirements of standardization or the hand of a single designer. Thus already in 1927 Sloan's director of sales had warned: "Several people have expressed the fear that if the art and color end of our business would be dominated by one personality, it might possibly be that in the future all General Motors cars would more or less resemble each other" (B. G. Koethe, quoted in Sloan, *My Years with General Motors,* 271).

19. Sloan, *My Years with General Motors,* 308.

20. Many such efforts at product redesign successfully contributed to their manufacturers' recovery from the Depression, as they reinvented the commodity as an integral part of an overall corporate image. In addition to cars, trains, and buses, the streamliners designed aerodynamic pencil sharpeners, stoves, refrigerators, vacuum cleaners, radios, and furniture. Norman Bel Geddes, for one, redesigned an entire line of gas stoves for the Standard Gas Equipment Corporation, standardizing the parts and combining them into four different models. He developed a method of combining these interchangeable parts clad in sheet metal by applying what he called the "principle of skyscraper construction," in which the external cladding is suspended from the steel frame, thus relieving the skin of its structural role and affording it greater resilience during assembly and shipping. According to Geddes, the clean lines and rounded white surfaces of the object accounted for its style, while also accommodating it to the rigorous requirements of use and production. For a description of the stove's redesign, see Geddes, *Horizons* (Boston: Little, Brown, 1932), 250–258; quotation, 256.

21. Jeffrey L. Meickle, *Twentieth Century Limited: Industrial Design in America, 1925–1939* (Philadelphia: Temple University Press, 1979), 201. Eero Saarinen's role is confirmed by Peter C. Papademetriou in "In Search of a Modern American Architecture: The Saarinens after Cranbrook," in his catalog *Kleinhans Music Hall: The Saarinens in Buffalo, 1940—A Streamline Vision* (Buffalo, N.Y.: Burchfield Art Center, Buffalo State College, 1990), n.p.

22. Also displayed at the General Motors exhibit were the streamlined diesel locomotives that the company had developed when it bought out the industry during the Depression, as well as the streamlined refrigerators produced by its Frigidaire division (*Futurama,* visitors' guide, 1939). For an analysis of the architecture of Futurama and the 1939–1940 New York World's Fair, see Rosemarie Haag Bletter, "The 'Laissez-Fair,' Good Taste, and Money Trees," in

Remembering the Future: The New York World's Fair from 1939–1964, by Bletter et al. (New York: Rizzoli, 1989), 105–135.

23. Geddes defines streamlining as follows: "An object is streamlined when its exterior surface is so designed that upon passing through a fluid such as water or air the object creates the least disturbance in the fluid in the form of eddies or partial vacua tending to produce resistance" (*Horizons,* 45). Donald J. Bush proposes the connection between Geddes and D'Arcy Wentworth Thompson in *The Streamlined Decade* (New York: George Braziller, 1975); he cites a passage added to the 1942 edition of D'Arcy Thompson's *On Growth and Form* describing a stream's ability to mold bodies with its flow as evidence of an implied influence on Geddes's illustration, ignoring the discrepancy in the publication dates (8). D'Arcy Thompson's expanded references to streamlining may in part reflect the popularization of the idea in the years after the 1917 first edition. By including Harold Edgerton's famous stroboscopic photograph of a drop of milk, he shows his familiarity with the 1930s cult of movement. See D'Arcy Wentworth Thompson, *On Growth and Form,* 2nd ed. (Cambridge: Cambridge University Press, 1942).

24. Geddes, *Horizons,* 50–51.

25. Harley J. Earl, "Always in the Future," in General Motors Corporation, *Styling: The Look of Things* (1955), brochure produced by the General Motors Public Relations Staff, with the Cooperation of the General Motors Styling Staff, 11; copy available in historic files, General Motors Technical Center Design Library.

In *Vision in Motion,* a book with which Earl or his colleagues were probably familiar, László Moholy-Nagy had quoted D'Arcy Thompson's description of the streamlined form of a swimming fur seal: "No creature shows more perfect streamlining than a fur seal swimming. Every curve is a continuous curve, the very ears and eyeslits and whiskers falling into the scheme, and the flippers folding close against the body" (D'Arcy Thompson, *On Growth and Form;* quoted in Moholy-Nagy, *Vision in Motion* [Chicago: Paul Theobald, 1947], 53).

26. General Motors Corp., *Styling,* 39.

27. As early as 1934, future "Junior Miesian" Philip Johnson—then a purveyor of the "International Style"—condemned both streamlining and styling for their superficiality: "Besides the French decorative movement in the '20s there developed in America a desire for 'styling' objects for advertising. Styling a commercial object gives it more 'eye-appeal' and therefore helps sales. Principles such as 'streamlining' often receive homage out of all proportion to their applicability" (Johnson, in *Machine Art,* by Alfred H. Barr Jr. and Johnson [New York: Museum of Modern Art, 1934], 8–9). Johnson's co-curator Alfred Barr rehearsed the organicist equation of form and function, adding:

> The beauty of the machine art in so far as it is a mere by-product of its function may seem a meagre and even trivial kind of beauty. But this is not necessarily so. The beauty of all natural objects is also a by-product—the helix of a snail's shell (and a steel coil), the graduated feathering of a bird's wing (and the leaves of a laminated spring), the rabbit's footprints in the snow (and the track of non-skid tires), the elegance of fruit (and of incandescent bulbs). (4)

28. The brochure cites Kepes's *Language of Vision* in a footnote appended to the following text:

As with any means of communication, the art of design has its own language—sometimes called the language of vision.
    This special language has only four basic symbols: line, plane, form, and surface quality (which includes value, color and texture).
    Any visual organization or design, regardless of how complicated or spectacular, is the result of blending these four visual ingredients. (General Motors Corp., *Styling,* 15)

29. As Mies said in his 1938 inaugural address as director of the Armour Institute of Technology (one of the schools that merged in 1940 to create IIT), "we shall emphasize the organic principle of order that makes the parts meaningful and measurable while determining their relationship to the whole" (Ludwig Mies van der Rohe, "Inaugural Address as Director at Armour Institute of Technology (1938)," in *The Artless Word: Mies van der Rohe on the Building Art,* by Fritz Neumeyer, trans. Mark Jarzombek [Cambridge, Mass.: MIT Press, 1991], 317). Although Mies's "organic principle" probably belongs more to an Augustinian concept of order than to biological purposefulness, his continued research into the primacy of structure preserves the tradition of Viollet-le-Duc with all of its biological allusions intact. Neumeyer argues that Mies's statement must be read solely in terms of the philosophy of Romano Guardini and of St. Augustine, whom Mies cites in ending his speech. Earlier on, however, Neuemeyer remarks on Mies's allegiance to Viollet-le-Duc, noting that Mies had copied Viollet's declaration that "[t]oute forme, qui n'est pas ordonnée par le structure, doit être repoussé" (70).

30. After winning second place in the *Chicago Tribune* tower competition and receiving $20,000 in prize money, Eliel Saarinen emigrated from Finland to the United States with his family: his wife Loja, daughter Pipsan (Eva-Lisa), and son Eero, all of whom had intimately participated in the architectural and crafts culture at Hvitträsk, the family compound in Kirkkonummi, outside Helsinki. In 1923 they settled in Ann Arbor, where Saarinen had received an invitation to teach at the University of Michigan. While still in Finland, Saarinen generated a speculative design for the development of the Chicago lakefront, including the area in which the *Tribune* tower site was located; in 1924 Saarinen produced a similar scheme for the development of the riverfront area of Detroit. On relations between Saarinen's urbanism and his architecture, see Manfredo Tafuri, "The Disenchanted Mountain: The Skyscraper and the City," in *The American City: From the Civil War to the New Deal,* by Giorgio Ciucci et al., trans. Barbara L. La Penta (Cambridge, Mass.: MIT Press, 1979), 421–431.

31. In addition to the first General Motors scheme, begun three years after the conclusion of their work at Cranbrook, the Saarinen office produced a number of master plans throughout the 1940s in a generally modern idiom: a 1945 project for Antioch College, a 1946–1947 master plan for Drake University, and a 1947 project for a Detroit Civic Center whose large, organizing central space repeats that at General Motors (minus the lake) designed the year before. The momentum of these projects carried forward, after the elder Saarinen's death in 1950,

into the organicist imperatives that guided Eero Saarinen's own contributions to the exurban landscape in the 1950s.

32. Intimations of the postwar corporate project of addressing social integration to the common individual are present in Eliel Saarinen's foreword, as he appeals here (and again in the book's concluding lines) to the "people of towns and cities themselves" for their participation in the revitalization of cities. Hence his history of the growth, maturity, and decay of the "urban community" is written from what he calls a "layman's standpoint," as Saarinen announces that "I have endeavored to explain the physical order of the urban community much in the same manner as one understands organic order in any living organism" (*The City: Its Growth, Its Decay, Its Future* [New York: Reinhold Publishing, 1943], x).

33. Ibid., 143.

34. Saarinen calls for "the dispersion of the present compactness into concentrated units, such as centers, suburbs, satellite townships, and like community units; and furthermore it must aim at the organization of these units into '*functional concentrations of related activities*'" (ibid., 151; emphasis in original).

35. Ibid., 163.

36. Ibid., 164, 170.

37. Ibid., 171.

38. Kepes's broad view of the rather narrow topic so successfully preempted Saarinen's own efforts to widen the arena beyond a discussion of graphic techniques that Saarinen jokingly asked the audience to "please ignore everything that Kepes said" so that he too could have his say (Eero Saarinen, in "Architectural Lettering Symposium," tape 1 of 2, Gyorgy Kepes Papers, AAA). Philip Johnson also participated in the symposium.

39. Gyorgy Kepes and Kevin Lynch, "Draft Proposal to the Rockefeller Foundation for Perceptual Form in the City," 4 December 1953, box 2, Kepes Papers, AAA.

40. Gyorgy Kepes, in "Architectural Lettering Symposium," tape 1 of 2. Such a modified sensorium was exactly the focus of the Rockefeller proposal, which hypothesized that the form of the urban environment was a potential source of "psychological satisfaction," derived from an "organization in the environment allowing the inhabitant to sense the whole," the legibility of urban functions, and a controlled range of sensory stimulation. Kepes and Lynch set out their assumptions regarding the impact of the urban environment on emotional life, based on the presence or absence of "a certain unity, connectedness, or organization," a legibility of part and whole, and a range of sensory stimulation ("Draft Proposal to the Rockefeller Foundation for Perceptual Form in the City"). The progress and aims of the project are documented further with documents dated 22 March 1955, 24 March 1955, and 5 May 1955 and in "Proposal for a Study of Meaning in the Cityscape" (n.d., box 3, Kepes Papers, AAA), as well as in a series of uncatalogued notes.

41. Kevin Lynch, *The Image of the City* (Cambridge, Mass.: MIT Press, 1960), vi.

42. Lynch defines a highly imageable city as "one that could be apprehended over time as a pattern of high continuity with many distinctive parts clearly interconnected" (ibid., 10).

43. Ibid., 12.

44. Gyorgy Kepes and Kevin Lynch, "Summary of Accomplishments: Research Project on the Perceptual Form of the City," ca. 1959, 8, box 4, Kepes Papers, AAA.

45. Ibid., 9.

46. President Dwight D. Eisenhower, quoted in Kenneth T. Jackson, *Crabgrass Frontier: The Suburbanization of the United States* (New York: Oxford University Press, 1985), 249. Jackson gives a useful summary of the Interstate Highway Act of 1956 and its aftermath (248–251). On the design of early highways, the discourse surrounding them, and their implementation of networking strategies, see Keller Easterling, *Organization Space: Landscapes, Highways, and Houses in America* (Cambridge, Mass.: MIT Press, 1999), 74–121.

47. General Motors was not the only automobile company to patronize modern architecture. In 1957 a new headquarters for the Ford Motor Company designed by Skidmore, Owings & Merrill in Dearborn, Mich.—like GM's headquarters, outside Detroit—was completed. Again the image of flexible modularity dominated. The entire plan was on a 4' 8" module. According to SOM partner J. Walter Severinghaus, "this flexibility of office arrangement has already proved advantageous in making office layouts conform to administrative organizational changes" (quoted in "Ford's 'Home Office,'" *Progressive Architecture* 38, no. 6 [June 1957]: 183).

48. Strengthening a sense of manifest destiny had been the overt agenda of the General Motors "Highways and Horizons"/Futurama exhibit as it projected a "city of 1960," designed by Norman Bel Geddes and connected to other cities by the highways that Geddes would celebrate in *Magic Motorways* (New York: Random House, 1940). In *The American Technological Sublime* (Cambridge, Mass.: MIT Press, 1994), David E. Nye points out that Geddes was also invited by President Franklin D. Roosevelt to the White House to discuss the feasibility of building the highways envisioned in Futurama (218).

49. On General Motors' logistics of product differentiation, see Kuhn, *GM Passes Ford, 1918–1938*, 82–95. In *Chrome Colossus,* Ed Cray gives the following account:

Taking advantage of computers newly introduced to production, computers that could tabulate and keep track of a virtually infinite number of possibilities while directing production lines, General Motors introduced ever more body styles into its automobile lines and ever more combinations of trim and engine. By 1957, the company was offering seventy-five body styles—in two-doors, four-doors, station wagons, soft-top and hard-top convertibles—and no less than 450 trim combinations that might be affixed to the three basic bodies the corporation manufactured. (363)

50. Peter F. Drucker, *Concept of the Corporation* (New York: John Day, 1946), 74.

51. Ibid., 47.

52. Curtice, transcript of speech given at the dedication of the General Motors Technical Center, 3.

53. Drucker, *Concept of the Corporation,* 157–158. On the Hawthorne experiments, discussed in chapter 3 above, see Richard Gillespie, *Manufacturing Knowledge: A History of the Hawthorne Experiments* (Cambridge: Cambridge University Press, 1991), a work reviewed by Anson Rabinbach, "Science, Work, and Worktime," *International Labor and Working Class History,* no. 43 (spring 1993): 48–64. By historicizing the project, Gillespie demystifies the myth of the discovery of "human factors" attributed to the experiments by writers like Drucker.

54. Sloan, *My Years with General Motors,* 309.

55. In the words of Harley J. Earl, "the stylist's role on the team of advanced creative thinkers at the Technical Center is significant, for it is his lot to arouse in that all-important person, the customer, a flair for fashion through skillful application of the elements of design—line, plane, form, and surface quality" ("Styling in General Motors," *General Motors Engineering Journal* 3, no. 3 [May–June 1956]: 78).

56. In a pamphlet introducing the scheme, Kettering described the Technical Center as conceived primarily to help organize the various aspects of General Motors' long-range planning apparatus into a centralized system capable of delivering coordinated technical and styling policy to the company's decentralized operations and administration network. Kettering also emphasized its role as a quasi-educational institution for GM's employees; potential future employees could be equipped to work in industry by an in-house educational service that would work together with the General Motors Institute, a formal educational facility run by the company. See General Motors Corporation, "Tomorrow's Challenge," pamphlet, n.d., Eero Saarinen Papers, SML.

57. In 1944 Saarinen was responsible for the planning, layout, and production of charts for a document titled "Army Personnel Control," which presented graphically the work of an ad hoc committee appointed to improve reporting and accounting procedures for personnel and troop control (U.S. Army, "Army Personnel Control," and letter from Lt. Gen. Joseph T. McNarney to Saarinen, Eero Saarinen Papers, SML). By the late 1940s, Eliel Saarinen had handed control of the office to his son. For a useful overview of Eero Saarinen's career, see Peter Papademetriou, "Coming of Age: Eero Saarinen and Modern American Architecture," *Perspecta,* no. 21 (1984): 116–143. See also Walter McQuade, "Eero Saarinen, a Complete Architect," *Architectural Forum* 116 (April 1962): 102–119, and Allan Temko, *Eero Saarinen* (New York: George Braziller, 1962). By 1956, the year the General Motors Technical Center was complete, Eero Saarinen was the subject of a cover story in *Time* ("The Maturing Modern," *Time,* 2 July 1956, 50–57).

58. On the work of Albert Kahn in Detroit—its affinities with Saarinen's project and relation to Fordist notions of productivity and function—see Terry Smith, "Architecture and Mass Production: The Functionalism Question," chap. 2 in *Making the Modern: Industry, Art, and Design in America* (Chicago: University of Chicago Press, 1993), 51–92. Precisely because he remains lodged in a Fordist notion of mechanical functionality (as well as a functional/symbolic opposition that does not recognize the "functionality" of images in the postwar period) and refers Saarinen to Kahn in a relatively unmediated fashion, Smith misreads the General Motors Technical Center. He wrongly judges that "Saarinen's is a 'factory aesthetic' because it depends on formal transference, on allusion. In the terms of reference of the first phase of

modernity, the Machine Age, it is symbolic rather than functional. But the terms change by the 1950s: perhaps all becomes symbolic in corporate architecture; even the 'actually functional' exists mainly as historical quotation" (91).

59. Banham, "The Fear of Eero's Mana," 73.

60. Early on in the design process, a team of stylists under Earl produced their own version of the styling building: a cross-shaped building with one side curved. Saarinen responded by assigning his entire office to the project to produce alternatives. In his presentation to Earl, Saarinen characterized his new version of the building as only a "minor" modification of Earl's and was authorized to proceed (Mark Jaruszewicz, a former associate of Saarinen, in the recorded proceedings of the Saarinen/Swanson Office Reunion, Cranbrook Academy, 1995, tape 137, Cranbrook Academy Archives).

61. Eero Saarinen, "General Motors Technical Center," unpublished typescript, 2, Eero Saarinen Papers, SML.

62. Eero Saarinen, "General Motors Technical Center," in *Eero Saarinen on His Work,* ed. Aline B. Saarinen (New Haven: Yale University Press, 1962), 24.

63. Saarinen, "General Motors Technical Center," 2, Eero Saarinen Papers, SML. When a GM document compared the differentiation of the five main clusters of buildings in the complex to the differentiation of the company's five automotive divisions, it exposed the manifest affinity between the flexible, individuated unity of the corporate organism and the image of organic unity imparted by the architecture (General Motors Corporation, "Summary of the Architecture of General Motors Technical Center," unpublished typescript, 10, Eero Saarinen Papers, SML).

64. Saarinen, "General Motors Technical Center," 2–3, Eero Saarinen Papers, SML. As Saarinen was to write (based on experience) of a similar approach to the planning of university campuses, this was an "aesthetics of the whole organism" ("Campus Planning: The Unique World of the University," *Architectural Record* 128, no. 5 [November 1960]: 128).

65. Saarinen, "General Motors Technical Center," 1, Eero Saarinen Papers, SML. Cranston Jones cites Saarinen's assertion that the Technical Center campus is best viewed from a convertible moving at 30 miles per hour in *Architecture Today and Tomorrow* (New York: McGraw-Hill, 1961), 142.

66. This transposition is underscored by the slightly earlier efforts of László Moholy-Nagy at the New Bauhaus in Chicago to evolve a "vision in motion" adapted to the disorienting visual effects of speed. Moholy-Nagy's preoccupation with the body in motion is evident in aspects of the work of Charles and Ray Eames, Saarinen's friends and occasional collaborators. While teaching at Cranbrook and in contact with Saarinen, Charles Eames frequently visited Chicago to consult with Moholy-Nagy. See R. Craig Miller, "Interior Design and Furniture," in *Design in America: The Cranbrook Vision, 1925–1950,* by Robert Judson Clark et al. (New York: Abrams, in association with the Detroit Institute of Arts and the Metropolitan Museum of Art, 1983), 109.

67. Kevin Roche, interview with the author. The Saarinen office was designing another domed auditorium on another campus at the same time as the GM styling dome. This was

the domed Kresge Auditorium at the Massachusetts Institute of Technology, which was completed in 1955. A number of design options were tried and rejected there as well, including a Buckminster Fuller–style geodesic dome.

68. General Motors Corporation, "Summary of the Architecture of General Motors Technical Center," 14; Saarinen, "General Motors Technical Center," 5, Eero Saarinen Papers, SML.

69. John McAndrew, "First Look at the General Motors Technical Center," *Art in America* 44, no. 2 (spring 1956): 29.

70. General Motors Corporation, "Architectural Notes on the Styling Section of the General Motors Technical Center," unpublished typescript, 6, Eero Saarinen Papers, SML.

71. The persistence of the figural water tower and the styling dome indicates that this shift toward integrated modularity is anything but pure; more evidence is found in the repeated appearance of organicist figures in Saarinen's later work, such as the Ingalls hockey rink at Yale, the Trans World Airlines terminal at Idlewild (now JFK) Airport, and the skeletal terminal at Dulles International Airport in Washington, D.C. But the General Motors Technical Center was nevertheless an important model for the numerous exurban corporate campuses built throughout the United States during the 1950s and into the 1960s. Two of the most visible of these, in which traces of the horizontal, modular organization of Saarinen's project are evident, are the Connecticut General Life Insurance Company Headquarters in Bloomfield, Conn., completed in 1958, and the United States Air Force Academy in Colorado Springs, Colo., begun in 1954 and completed in 1960, both of which were designed by Skidmore, Owings & Merrill.

In the former, designed by Gordon Bunshaft—the headquarters of a major life insurance company relocated to the suburbs from nearby Hartford—the column-free, modular planning being practiced at that time by SOM in urban curtain wall skyscrapers was flattened into a low, compact campus plan, with the primary structure organized around four courtyards (designed by sculptor Isamu Noguchi) and laid out on a 6-foot module based on a unit of 48 square feet per clerk. Here, the flows of a flexible workforce were explicitly identified with a productivity oriented toward information rather than goods. See "Rural Insurance Plant," *Architectural Forum* 101, no. 3 (September 1954): 104.

At the U.S. Air Force Academy, whose design was supervised by Walter Netsch, sleek surfaces were mobilized as regulators of a low, linear pedestrian campus lifted one level above the automotive ground plane. The two SOM projects were celebrated by the Museum of Modern Art as "small cities in themselves" whose "rational organization" emphasized the advantages of coordinated planning in the "disordered urban scene" (Museum of Modern Art, *Buildings for Business and Government* [New York: Museum of Modern Art, 1957], 7). Saarinen was a candidate for the Air Force commission but had to settle for a seat on the board of architectural consultants. It is noteworthy that Walter Dorwin Teague Associates chose to color code the cadets' rooms at the academy to distinguish between each class. They also systematically indexed each modulation of standardized equipment and furnishings according to a thirteen-digit IBM code (see "Furnishing for Fifty Years," *Industrial Design* 5, no. 4 [April 1958]: 28–37). I am grateful to Hyun Tae Jung for calling this fact to my attention. The details of the planning, design, and cultural context of the Air Force Academy in Colorado Springs, including Saarinen's role in the project, are given in Robert Bruegmann, *Modernism at*

Mid-Century: The Architecture of the United States Air Force Academy (Chicago: University of Chicago Press, 1994).

5

Computer Architectures

1. Gyorgy Kepes, *The New Landscape in Art and Science* (Chicago: Paul Theobald, 1956), 173.

2. International Business Machines Corporation, "IBM: People . . . Products . . . Progress," 1955, cover, 1, IBM Rochester files, Olmsted County Historical Society, Rochester, Minn.

3. "P/A News Survey, Saarinen Uses Curtain Wall ⁵/₁₆" Thick," *Progressive Architecture* 38, no. 6 (June 1957): 57. Dinkeloo's reply was published in the "Views" section of *Progressive Architecture* 38, no. 9 (September 1957): 14.

4. Details on the IBM wall are also published in "Factories Planned for People," *Architectural Forum* 109, no. 4 (October 1958): 142, and "Usine et Bureaux de l'IBM, Rochester, Minnesota, États-Unis," *L'Architecture d'aujourd'hui* 30, no. 85 (September 1959): 24.

5. According to Saarinen's associate Kevin Roche, "the idea was that now that we have this panel, with porcelain and everything, why not make a pattern out of it? We had about a hundred different patterns. We simply selected this one" (interview with the author, 24 July 1996).

6. Eero Saarinen, "International Business Machines, Rochester, Minnesota," December 1958, 3, Manuscript Group no. 593, Eero Saarinen Papers, Sterling Memorial Library (SML), Manuscripts and Archives, Yale University.

7. Thomas J. Watson Jr. and Peter Petre, *Father, Son, and Co.: My Life at IBM and Beyond* (New York: Bantam Books, 1990), 253–254. IBM organization charts from 1956 to 1976 are published in Emerson W. Pugh, Lyle R. Johnson, and John R. Palmer, appendix E of *IBM's 360 and Early 370 Systems* (Cambridge, Mass.: MIT Press, 1991), 651–670.

8. Emerson W. Pugh, *Building IBM: Shaping an Industry and Its Technology* (Cambridge, Mass.: MIT Press, 1995), 263–265. The first (1956) phase of administrative reorganization at IBM is documented in *A New Plan for Corporate Organization Is Announced,* special issue of *IBM Business Machines* 39, no. 19 (28 December 1956): 2–13. Saarinen's Rochester plant was designed to service the newly created Data Processing Division.

9. Watson and Petre, *Father, Son, and Co.,* 257.

10. In the reorganization, top executives were shuffled to produce a corporate management committee reporting to Watson. It comprised the heads of the IBM World Trade Corporation; the Military, Time, and Special Engineering Products Group; the Electric Typewriter and Supplies Group; and two newly formed divisions, the Corporate Staff and the Data Processing Division. The basis of this structure was product type: each product division was equipped with

its own manufacturing, sales, and service functions. See also "A New Plan for Corporate Organization Is Announced," 2. The reorganization was described in detail to IBM employees in this article, complete with comprehensive organization charts featuring photographs of each executive (2–13).

11. To these comments Watson adds: "We were a computer company, not a punch card company; we were firmly in the 1950s, not the 1920s; we were leaders in a new field that would shape the future" (Watson and Petre, *Father, Son, and Co.,* 257).

12. Again here the correspondence with Gilles Deleuze's outline of a "control society" is more than schematic. For Deleuze,

> Disciplinary societies have two poles: signatures standing for *individuals,* and numbers or places in a register standing for their position in a *mass.* Disciplines see no incompatibility at all between these two aspects, and their power both amasses and individuates, that is, it fashions those over whom it's exerted into a body of people and molds the individuality of each member of that body.... In control societies, on the other hand, the key thing is no longer a signature or a number but a code: codes are *passwords,* whereas disciplinary societies are ruled (when it comes to integration or resistance) by *precepts* [*mots d'ordres:* watchwords, directives]. ("Postscript on Control Societies," in *Negotiations, 1972–1990,* trans. Martin Joughin [New York: Columbia University Press], 179–180)

The command "Think" functioned as a watchword at IBM under Thomas J. Watson Sr., but it did not disappear with the decentralization of power under his son. It became instead a routine protocol against which the relative "humanity" of the company's machines was tested, and a password into the human-machine assemblage.

13. Watson and Petre, *Father, Son, and Co.,* 258.

14. Watson describes being struck by a display of typewriters in a Fifth Avenue shop window: "They were on stands with rolls of paper in them for anybody's use. They were in different colors and very attractively designed. (In those days you could have an IBM typewriter in any color as long as it was black, as Henry Ford said about his 'Tin Lizzie.') I went into the shop and also found attractive, modern furniture in striking colors with a kind of collectiveness. The name plate over the door was Olivetti" (Thomas J. Watson Jr., "Good Design Is Good Business," in *The Art of Design Management: Design in American Business,* Tiffany Lectures [New York: Tiffany, 1975], 57–58). On the state of Olivetti's comprehensive design program during the early and mid-1950s, see "Olivetti," *Architectural Forum* 97 (November 1952): 116–121, and Georgina Masson, "Olivetti: The Creation of a House Style," *Architectural Review* 121 (June 1957): 431–439.

The Olivetti program, which also included active patronage of architecture and architectural discourse, was closely tied to the community-oriented humanistic social project of the company's president, Adriano Olivetti. Masson summarizes his position: "For him the present crisis is due to the fact that man is a misfit in the modern world, which has now become a kind of Frankenstein monster that its creator is no longer able to control in order to fulfil the basic needs of society" (432). A distinct feature of the 1954 Olivetti showroom, designed by Banfi, Belgiojoso, Peressutti & Rogers (BBPR), was the individual typewriters displayed on marble stands, where they could be tested by customers. A selection of these had also been exhibited at the Museum of Modern Art in 1952, and the Museum bulletin observed: "It is not only the esthetic quality of these achievements that is remarkable. More important as a lesson in our industrial world of today is the organization of all the visual aspects of an industry, unified under a single high standard of taste" ("Olivetti: Design in Industry," *Museum of Modern Art Bulletin* 20, no. 1 [fall 1952]: 3). Bernard Huet and Georges Teyssot were subsequently to identify the stakes, in a dossier in *L'Architecture d'aujourd'hui* dedicated to Olivetti, which they edited. Huet and Teyssot conclude their opening statement: "A. Olivetti probably did not suspect himself that he was thus repositioning architecture in a new art market. The large American firms (IBM, Lever, Johnson, Seagram) had quickly understood the lesson: Henceforth, architects serve to fashion the 'corporate image.' For architecture, this is without a doubt one of the last chances for survival in the capitalist system" (Huet and Teyssot, "Politique industrielle et architecture: le cas Olivetti," *L'Architecture d'aujourd'hui,* no. 188 [December 1976]: 1; translation by author).

15. Watson, "Good Design Is Good Business," 58.

16. As Paul Rand put it in retrospect, "The design of the IBM logo, like any design problem, is one of integrating form and substance—of making three familiar letters of the alphabet look different, attractive, memorable, and adaptable to an infinite number of applications" (*Design, Form, and Chaos* [New Haven: Yale University Press, 1993], 116).

17. Ibid., 56.

18. Jessica Helfand, *Paul Rand: American Modernist* (New York: William Drenttel, 1998), 32–33. On Rand's meeting with Le Corbusier, see 45.

19. Paul Rand did more than aid the graphic encryption of corporate identity. His effort to reconcile the interests of business with those of society through art is clearly evident in "Advertisement: Ad Vivum or Ad Hominem?," a contribution that he and his wife, Ann Rand, made to *The Visual Arts Today,* ed. Gyorgy Kepes, a special issue of *Daedalus* (89, no. 1 [winter 1960]), 127–135. The article begins by expressing dismay at a "barrage" of disorienting sensory experiences. Assertions are made in favor of individual choice (analogous to that exerted by the artist), and against a mechanistic determinism based on earlier technological models that have been superseded by the programmability (and thus controllability) of the "simulation machine" (or computer). Significantly, the Rands go on to conclude that "From a long-range standpoint, the interests of business and art are not opposed" (135).

20. William H. Whyte Jr., *The Organization Man* (New York: Simon and Schuster, 1956), 131–132.

21. One of those who quoted this phrase from Watson Sr. was Albert L. Williams, executive vice president of IBM, as he explained IBM's decision to locate its plant in Rochester in a speech given to the local business community on 24 February 1956. (Williams, "Why Rochester?" 3, IBM Archives, Somers, N.Y.).

22. Watson, "Good Design Is Good Business," 63.

23. "Good Design . . . IBM's Silent Salesman," *IBM Business Machines* 46, no. 5 (August 1963): 16–19.

24. Williams, "Why Rochester?" 2–3.

25. "Policy on Employees Has Human Touch," *Everybody's Business* (Rochester Chamber of Commerce), February 1956, 7; a copy is available in the Olmsted County Historical Society, Rochester, Minn.

26. Ibid. A later paraphrase of the chamber of commerce report is to be found in "Human Relations Important to IBM," *Rochester Post-Bulletin,* 27 September 1958, 29.

27. "IBM Plant Designed for Two Objectives," *Rochester Post-Bulletin,* 27 September 1958, 25–26. Very similar statements appear in Saarinen, "International Business Machines, Rochester, Minnesota," 3.

28. Saarinen, "International Business Machines, Rochester, Minnesota," 2.

29. "IBM Plant Designed for Two Objectives," 25.

30. "IBM's New Industrial Campus," *Architectural Forum* 108, no. 6 (June 1958): 106. Watson characterized the San Jose plant as "a set of low-slung H-shaped buildings in the new 'campus' style" (Watson and Petre, *Father, Son, and Co.,* 261).

31. Noyes's first commission as design consultant was to redesign the ground-floor showroom of IBM's world headquarters on Madison Avenue and 57th Street. At the time it housed IBM's Defense Calculator (the IBM 701)—in Watson's words, "a set of drab gray cabinets"—next to a marble and brass salon full of business machines. The space was renamed the "Data Processing Center" and equipped with new 702 machine, set against a red wall with spare finishes and Rand's new IBM logo in large gray type. Like the Selective Sequence Electronic Calculator (SSEC) and the 701 that preceded it, the 702 was a working machine—customers could rent computer time and perform their calculations in public. For Watson's account of the redesign of the space, see Watson and Petre, *Father, Son, and Co.,* 259–260; quotation, 259. A later facility designed by Noyes for IBM in Los Angeles bears a striking resemblance to the famous IBM punched card. Noyes was also later to design a fully internalized real-time "telecomputing center" for Westinghouse Corporation. I am grateful to John Harwood for bringing this latter project to my attention.

32. Writing in 1959 about Noyes's work for IBM, the critic Hugh B. Johnston observed that "Noyes has promoted an architectural treatment of machine masses. . . . He has coached the various designers to bank significant interior elements behind glass, wherever they are visually coherent, and to articulate the operational elements on the machine surface." Johnston goes on to quote Noyes: "'Before, there was no expression of structure,' said Noyes. 'But these machines should not be like a ranch house. They should be like a Mies house'" (Johnston, "From Old IBM to New IBM," *Industrial Design* 4, no. 3 [March 1957]: 52).

33. Arthur Gregor, "IBM Develops Its Random-Access Memory Accounting Machine," *Industrial Design* 4, no. 3 (March 1957): 53.

34. Eliot Noyes, quoted in Johnston, "From Old IBM to New IBM," 48. Efforts to expose the interiors of machines apparently didn't always work out. For the IBM 608 transistorized calculator, Noyes and Sundberg-Ferar first tried an all-glass front; but because the printed circuits it

revealed exhibited an insufficient degree of "visual coherence," only the magnetic-core memory and a small piece of the bank of printed circuits were exposed (51).

35. Watson, "Good Design Is Good Business," 59.

36. According to a 1963 account of the IBM design program, color was also consciously identified with gender: "The cerise and gray packages for typewriter ribbons and carbon paper, for example, acknowledge the fact that most typewriter users are women" ("Good Design . . . IBM's Silent Salesman," 18).

37. Watson and Petre, *Father, Son, and Co.,* 260.

38. The appearance and role of the "white room," with white floors and ceilings and a white vinyl floor, in a prefabricated building constructed in Poughkeepsie in the 1960s, were described by James La Due, a designer manager at IBM who worked with Noyes during that decade, in an interview with the author on 6 June 1998. The white room can be seen in photographs of IBM machines from the period.

39. Alan M. Turing, "Computing Machinery and Intelligence," *Mind* 14 (1950); reprinted in *The Mind's I: Fantasies and Reflections on Self and Soul,* ed. Douglas R. Hofstadter and Daniel C. Dennett (New York: Basic Books, 1981), 53–67. In a near-parody of the Turing test, the RAMAC was installed at the American Pavilion at the Brussels World's Fair of 1958. Visitors to the fair could take up the role of Turing's "interrogator" and pose questions to "Professor RAMAC," who would answer in any one of ten languages. See Paul E. Ceruzzi, *A History of Modern Computing* (Cambridge, Mass.: MIT Press, 1998), 70.

40. Watson and Petre, *Father, Son, and Co.,* 259.

41. Pugh, *Building IBM,* 142–143.

42. Thomas J. Watson Jr., "Plant Dedication Ceremonies, Rochester, Minnesota, September 30, 1958," 2, IBM Archives.

43. "We Build Brains for Defense," *IBM Business Machines* 37, no. 14 (1 July 1954): 10.

44. Ibid., 3.

45. On connections between von Neumann's research and IBM's machines, see Emerson W. Pugh, *Memories That Shaped an Industry: Decisions Leading to IBM System/360* (Cambridge, Mass.: MIT Press, 1984), 14. See also Pugh, *Building IBM,* 142–143. There Pugh notes parallels between von Neumann's neurological terminology, which implicitly compares humans and information-processing machines, and the use of the term *computer* (with its previously human referent) in the name of the Electronic Numerical Integrator and Computer (ENIAC), constructed in 1946 by Presper Eckert and John Mauchly with von Neumann's collaboration at the University of Pennsylvania's Moore School of Electrical Engineering.

46. There are competing claims to the title of originator of the stored program computer. In 1945 work on such a machine was begun by the mathematicians Presper Eckert and John Mauchly at the Moore School at the University of Pennsylvania on the EDVAC under contract with the U.S. Army. Before actually documenting the initial EDVAC concepts, Eckert and Mauchly were joined by von Neumann, whose "First Draft of a Report on the EDVAC" (1945)

first outlined the logical structure of stored program computers. See Herman H. Goldstine, *The Computer from Pascal to von Neumann* (Princeton: Princeton University Press, 1972), 184–210, and Stan Augarten, *Bit by Bit: An Illustrated History of Computers* (New York: Ticknor and Fields, 1984), 136–141. On the designation of this concept as "von Neumann architecture," see Paul N. Edwards, *The Closed World: Computers and the Politics of Discourse in Cold War America* (Cambridge, Mass.: MIT Press, 1996), 51, and Ceruzzi, *A History of Modern Computing,* 23–24.

47. The term *architecture* is used to refer to system design in L. R. Johnson, "A Description of Stretch," IBM Research Report, 10 December 1959; cited in Charles J. Bashe, Lyle R. Johnson, John H. Palmer, and Emerson W. Pugh, *IBM's Early Computers* (Cambridge, Mass.: MIT Press, 1986), 610 n. 64.

48. Frederick P. Brooks Jr., "Architectural Philosophy," in *Planning a Computer System: Project Stretch,* ed. Werner Buchholz (New York: McGraw-Hill, 1962), 5. This passage is also partially quoted in Bashe et al., *IBM's Early Computers,* 610 n. 64.

49. Brooks, "Architectural Philosophy," 5.

50. A detailed account of the history and design of the IBM System/360 is available in Pugh, Johnson, and Palmer, *IBM's 360 and Early 370 Systems;* see esp. chap. 3, "A Unified Product Line" (113–174). The design team leader, Frederick P. Brooks Jr., "had recognized during his 1959–1960 soujourn in research ... that [the word *architecture*] might be useful in distinguishing overt (user-related) aspects of a computer's design from the inescapable welter of design detail" (Pugh, Johnson, and Palmer, *IBM's 360 and Early 370 Systems,* 137; see also above, nn. 47, 48). A range of compatibility problems were addressed at the level of software, of hardware, and of interface, including the machines' volumes and skins. By the mid-1960s, standard "box sizes" and coordinated color palettes had been developed for companywide application (James La Due, former IBM design manager, interview with the author, 22 June 1998).

In addition to its commercial success, the System/360 also played a crucial role in eliminating the boundary separating computers designed for science from those designed for business, owing to its variable size and flexibility. It also encouraged customers to remain a part of the IBM "family" (and thus remain identified with its image) over time, since, according to Pugh, Johnson, and Palmer, "Full compatibility among processors helped to preserve the customer's growing investment in programs. Modularity in devices, coupled with standard interfaces, permitted customers to configure systems that matched their needs and then to readily reconfigure as their needs changed" (174).

51. Watson, "Good Design Is Good Business," 60.

52. Ibid., 60–61.

53. Eliot Noyes, quoted in Scott Kelly, "Curator of Corporate Character ... Eliot Noyes and Associates," *Industrial Design* 13, no. 1 (June 1966): 43.

54. Leslie J. Comrie, "Babbage's Dream Come True," *Nature* 158 (1946): 568. Comrie's description is also quoted by Saarinen's friends Charles and Ray Eames, in *A Computer Perspective* (Cambridge, Mass.: Harvard University Press, 1973), 123, a work published to accompany an IBM exhibition designed by the Eameses.

Drawing on the press release, the 7 August 1944 edition of the *New York Herald Tribune* referred to the ASCC as a "super brain," while the *New York Times* called it an "algebra machine" (Bashe et al., *IBM's Early Computers,* 30).

55. According to the company historian Emerson Pugh, IBM's Selective Sequence Electronic Calculator "was the first operational computer to satisfy the modern definition of a stored program computer" (*Building IBM,* 136). Other historians, however, credit the Manchester University Mark I, on technical grounds. Both machines were completed in 1948 (the IBM SSEC ran its first program six months earlier than the Mark I). But the SSEC was an electromechanical device with only a small amount of programmable memory, and it still relied largely on plugboards and tape for its instructions. The Manchester Mark I was fully electronic and significantly more versatile (Augarten, *Bit by Bit,* 148, 189; Michael R. Williams, *A History of Computing Technology* [Englewood Cliffs, N.J.: Prentice-Hall, 1985], 325). See also Paul N. Edwards, *The Closed World: Computers and the Politics of Discourse in Cold War America* (Cambridge, Mass.: MIT Press, 1996), 378 n. 19.

56. Bashe et al., *IBM's Early Computers,* 52–53. The ASCC's control tape is a version of the hypothetical protosoftware described by Alan Turing in 1936. In Turing's system, a tape of infinite length is scanned by a "computing machine," whose behavior, or output, is altered by the input; see Turing, "On Computable Numbers, with an Application to the Entscheidungsproblem," *Proceedings of the London Mathematical Society (2)* 42 (1936–1937): 230–265.

57. John von Neumann, *The Computer and the Brain* (New Haven: Yale University Press, 1958), 11–21.

58. In a volume edited by Gyorgy Kepes, the physicist and Manhattan Project veteran Philip Morrison used a series of photographs of the circuitry of System/360 computers at different scales to illustrate the modularity of all written knowledge (Morrison, "The Modularity of Knowing," in *Module, Proportion, Symmetry, Rhythm,* ed. Kepes [New York: George Braziller, 1966], 7–12).

59. Two items published in *Business Week* in the 1980s—"Big Blue Hints That This Wine May Be a Bit Off-Color" (14 November 1988, 1204) and a report on IBM's acquisition of Opel "No. 1's Awesome Strategy" (8 June 1981, 84)—suggest that the nickname "Big Blue" originates from the pervasiveness of IBM's blue computers, which began in the 1960s. According to the IBM archivist Robert Godfrey, this explanation is also generally accepted within the company, and it is most likely that the System/360—which was available in several colors, including blue—initiated the association. According to James La Due, who worked at IBM Poughkeepsie and Kingston with Noyes through the 1950s and 1960s as a manager of an IBM design group, the first use of a blue accent on the predominantly gray IBM machines appeared on the 729 tape drive (ca. 1955), a decision that La Due discussed with Noyes (interview with the author). A similar blue later became known as "IBM blue" or "SMS blue" (SMS = Standard Modular System); the latter designation referred to the 29$^{1}/_{2}$" cubes that formed the basic design unit of the later modular machines (beginning with the System/360). During the 1960s these colored elements were studied and discussed with Noyes in the white room at Poughkeepsie.

60. Roche, interview with the author.

61. Norbert Wiener, *Cybernetics; or, Control and Communication in the Animal and the Machine* (Cambridge, Mass.: Technology Press, 1948), 193. The book's concluding chapter is titled "Information, Language, and Society."

62. "Deep Blue" was the name of a supercomputer designed by a group of scientists working in the IBM Thomas J. Watson Research Center and elsewhere, beginning in 1990. In 1997 the machine won a six-game match with world chess champion Garry Kasparov. A synopsis of Deep Blue's history can be found at IBM's website, "Kasparov vs. Deep Blue: The Rematch," 11 May 1997 <www.research.ibm.com/deepblue> (accessed August 2002).

6

The Topologies of Knowledge

1. For representative laboratory buildings designed and constructed during and after the Second World War, see "Firestone Research Laboratory" [Voorhees, Walker, Foley & Smith], *Architectural Record* 98, no. 5 (November 1945): 82–97; "General Motors Technical Center: To Unite Science with Its Application" [Saarinen & Swanson], in ibid., 98–103; "Research Laboratory for Hoffmann-La Roche Inc., Nutley, N.J." [Fellheimer & Wagner], in ibid., 105–111; "Research and Manufacture Combined under One Roof" [Johns-Manville Corp. Research Center, Shreve, Lamb, & Harmon], in ibid., 112–113; "University Lab" [Georgia School of Technology, Bush-Brown & Gailey], in ibid., 114–115; "Industrial Group on the Campus Plan" [General Electric "Electronics Park," Giffels & Valet, Inc.], in ibid., 116–117; Charles Haines, "Planning the Scientific Laboratory," *Architectural Record* 108, no. 1 (July 1950): 107–122; Edwin F. Pike, "Purposes, Objectives, Common Denominators," in ibid., 202–205; "*Architectural Record* Building Types Study No. 226: Laboratories for Industry," *Architectural Record* 118, no. 3 (September 1955): 201; Harold C. Bernhard, "An Analysis of Several Laboratory Plot Plans," in ibid., 215–217; William B. Foxhall, "*Architectural Record* Building Types Study No. 300: Industrial Buildings," *Architectural Record* 130, no. 6 (November 1961): 169; "Campus Plan for a Five-Building Research Center" [Parke, Davis & Co.; Skidmore, Owings & Merrill], in ibid., 170–175; "Expansibility and Flexibility on a Modular Plan" [Koppers Company, Inc., Voorhees, Walker, Smith, Smith & Haines], in ibid., 176–179; and *Laboratories: Voorhees, Walker, Smith, Smith, and Haines, Architects* (New York: Voorhees, Walker, Smith, Smith, and Haines, 1961).

2. "The New Landscape," exhibition brochure, 19 February to 8 March 1951, Massachusetts Institute of Technology, box 3, Kepes Papers, Archives of American Art, Washington, D.C.

3. In 1914 the General Electric Company built an "experimental laboratory" at Nela Park, outside Cleveland, Ohio. The new campus was described by one architectural critic as a "university of industry," planned around courtyards borrowed from Oxford University fused with the landscaping of a British manor house. See Georges Teyssot, "The American Lawn: Surface of

Everyday Life," in *The American Lawn,* ed. Teyssot (New York: Princeton Architectural Press; Montreal: Canadian Centre for Architecture, 1999), 26.

4. Leonard S. Reich, *The Making of American Industrial Research: Science and Business at GE and Bell, 1876–1926* (New York: Cambridge University Press, 1985), 242, 252.

5. The National Research Council was set up during the First World War to coordinate the participation of American science in the war effort. During the 1920s, it and other such organizations continued to aid the philanthropic foundations and commercial corporations interested in supporting specific types of university research. On the NRC, see Roger L. Geiger, *To Advance Knowledge: The Growth of American Research Universities, 1900–1940* (New York: Oxford University Press, 1986), 94–109. On the role of foundations and corporations in American research universities in the 1920s and 1930s, see chap. 4, "Foundations and University Research" (140–173) and chap. 5, "The Privately Funded University Research System" (174–245). On New Deal policies and university research, see 255–264.

6. United States Office of Scientific Research and Development, *Science, the Endless Frontier: A Report to the President* (Washington, D.C.: U.S. Government Printing Office, 1945). Vannevar Bush was the author of the report.

7. Secretaries of War and Navy, joint letter to the National Academy of Sciences, cited in ibid., 12. See also Paul N. Edwards, *The Closed World: Computers and the Politics of Discourse in Cold War America* (Cambridge, Mass.: MIT Press, 1996), 58–59, Geiger, *To Advance Knowledge,* 264–267, and Stuart W. Leslie, *The Cold War and American Science: The Military-Industrial-Academic Complex at MIT and Stanford* (New York: Columbia University Press, 1993), 6–7.

8. Edwards, *The Closed World,* 59–60, 380 n. 39.

9. On the goal-oriented organization of the Manhattan Project, see Lillian Hoddeson, "Mission Change in the Large Laboratory: The Los Alamos Implosion Program, 1943–1945," in *Big Science: The Growth of Large-Scale Research,* ed. Peter Galison and Bruce Hevly (Stanford: Stanford University Press, 1992), 265–289.

10. Leslie, *The Cold War and American Science,* 8.

11. On the emergence of so-called big science in the laboratories of the military-industrial-academic complex, see the essays in Galison and Hevly, eds., *Big Science.*

12. Leslie, *The Cold War and American Science,* 6.

13. Hoddeson, "Mission Change in the Large Laboratory."

14. Charles J. Bashe, Lyle R. Johnson, John H. Palmer, and Emerson W. Pugh, *IBM's Early Computers* (Cambridge, Mass.: MIT Press, 1986), 523–524. The description of the reorganization of the IBM research program given in the text is based on chap. 13, "Research" (523–570).

15. Robert W. Marks, *The Dymaxion World of Buckminster Fuller* (Carbondale: Southern Illinois University Press, 1960), 203–204.

16. Edwards, *The Closed World,* 106.

17. Robert R. Everett, Charles A. Zraket, and Herbert D. Benington, "SAGE—A Data-Processing System for Air Defense," *Annals of the History of Computing* 5, no. 4 (October 1983): 335–336.

On the history of SAGE, see also in the same issue (a special issue devoted to SAGE) John F. Jacobs, "SAGE Overview" (323–329); Morton M. Astrahan and John F. Jacobs, "History of the Design of the SAGE Computer—The AN/FSQ-7" (340–349); C. Robert Wieser, "The Cape Cod System" (362–369), and "A Perspective on SAGE: Discussion" (375–398). See also Edwards, *The Closed World*, 75–112, and Bashe et al., *IBM's Early Computers*, 240–248.

18. Astrahan and Jacobs, "History of the Design of the SAGE Computer—The AN/FSQ-7," 342.

19. Edwards, *The Closed World*, 76–79.

20. Bashe et al., *IBM's Early Computers*, 231.

21. Edwards, *The Closed World*, 96.

22. IBM Yorktown Heights, tube #11, "Building Types; IBM Research Center," 20 December 1956, Eero Saarinen Papers, Sterling Memorial Library (SML), Manuscripts and Archives, Yale University.

23. Eero Saarinen, "Campus Planning: The Unique World of the University," *Architectural Record* 128, no. 5 (November 1960): 127, 128.

24. Ibid., 130.

25. The awarding of the Bell Laboratories contract to Saarinen on 7 April 1957 was announced in "Expansion of Holmdel Location Under Study," *Bell Laboratories Record* 35 (May 1957): 174; a copy is available in the AT&T Archives, Warren, N.J. Saarinen's desk calendar in 1957 also documents appointments related to the project: 8 May 1957, "Bell Tell boss"; 29 July 1957, "Tentative meeting with Bell people here"; 8–9 August 1957, "Bell Lab people here"; 15 August 1957, "Bell"; Eero Saarinen Papers, SML, Manuscript Group no. 593, series 7, box 11. According to a Bell Laboratories press release, the company had presented Saarinen with a list of eight criteria to guide the design of the new building:

> 1. Maximum flexibility in the use of space for good office and laboratories.
>
> 2. Centrally located common service facilities such as library, medical, personnel, restaurant, auditorium, reproduction and other facilities.
>
> 3. Flexibility to make changes in laboratories, with minimum interruption of work.
>
> 4. Minimum traffic past offices and labs.
>
> 5. Central air conditioning.
>
> 6. Minimum distance from parking lots to buildings.
>
> 7. Road system to eliminate pedestrian traffic across roads and to keep traffic problems on public roads to a minimum.
>
> 8. Construction and operating costs as low as possible. ("Features of the Holmdel Laboratory," press release, Bell Telephone Laboratories, 5 December 1966, 2, AT&T Archives)

Further details are given in "Construction Highlights of Bell Laboratories' New Development Center at Holmdel, N.J.," press release, Bell Telephone Laboratories, 26 September 1962, AT&T Archives.

26. Eero Saarinen invokes the Murray Hill facility as a point of departure, in "Statement about Bell Telephone Laboratories for Holmdel, N.J.," 8 April 1959, Eero Saarinen Papers, SML.

27. "Bell Laboratories at Holmdel Has Long, Distinguished History," press release, Bell Telephone Laboratories, N.Y., 24 September 1962, 2, AT&T Archives. On Karl Jansky's early work at the Holmdel site that detected extraterrestrial radio frequencies see also Jeremy Bernstein, *Three Degrees above Zero: Bell Labs in the Information Age* (New York: Charles Scribner's Sons, 1984) 191–193.

28. In 1960 voice signals were transmitted via Echo, a high-altitude plastic balloon launched by NASA, between Holmdel and a Bell Laboratories station in California; this first communication by "satellite" laid the groundwork for AT&T's 1962 Telstar satellite, which demonstrated the feasibility of long-distance telecommunication via orbiting satellite (Prescott C. Mabon, *Mission Communications: The Story of Bell Laboratories* [Murray Hill, N.J.: Bell Telephone Laboratories, 1975], 71, 176).

29. Ibid., 180.

30. Don Graf, *Convenience for Research: Buildings for the Bell Telephone Laboratory, Inc., Murray Hill, New Jersey; Voorhees, Walker, Foley, and Smith* (New York: Voorhees, Walker, Foley, and Smith, 1944), 11.

31. Mabon, *Mission Communications,* 10.

32. Eero Saarinen, "Statement on IBM (Thomas J. Watson Research Center) Yorktown, New York," 17 April 1961, 1, Eero Saarinen Papers, SML.

33. Ibid., 2.

34. Ibid.

35. Max Horkheimer and Theodor W. Adorno, *Dialectic of Enlightenment,* trans. John Cumming (New York: Herder and Herder, 1972), 158.

36. WECO (Western Electric Company), tube #8, five undated and unsigned sketches, Eero Saarinen Papers, SML.

37. By 1957 Vincent Scully had noted the classicizing tendency in Johnson and Saarinen in "Modern Architecture: Toward a Redefinition of Style," *Perspecta,* no. 4 (1957): 4–11. Sarah Williams Goldhagen has recently shown the connection to Kahn in *Louis Kahn's Situated Modernism* (New Haven: Yale University Press, 2001), 146–147.

38. Dan Kiley, "Bell Labs, Internal court," SK-5, 25 April 1958, tube #8, Eero Saarinen Papers, SML.

39. Anthony Vidler, "Bell Laboratory," *Architectural Design* 37, no. 7 (August 1967): 355. Vidler also observes: "Eero Saarinen's Bell Telephone Laboratory takes its place between radar installations and a Nike X missile base as the third elegant piece of equipment to be deployed in

the fields of Holmdel, New Jersey." During the Second World War, Bell Laboratories made major contributions to the development of Allied radar systems, and beginning in 1945 the company developed the NIKE series of surface-to-air missiles and accompanying radar, computers, and guidance units (Mabon, *Mission Communications,* 179).

40. Kevin Roche, interview with the author, 24 July 1996.

41. Eero Saarinen & Associates, "International Business Machines Research Center, Yorktown, New York," set of plans, sections, and elevations, 28 March 1958, misc. tube, "IBM Research," Eero Saarinen Papers, SML.

42. Saarinen, "Statement on IBM (Thomas J. Watson Research Center) Yorktown, New York," 2. Saarinen's text was later published in Eero Saarinen, *Eero Saarinen on His Work,* ed. Aline Saarinen (New Haven: Yale University Press, 1962), 70–71.

43. Detailed contemporaneous publications of the IBM Thomas J. Watson Research Center include "Unique Cross-Curve Plan for IBM Research Center," *Architectural Record* 130, no. 1 (July 1961): 137–146; "Research in the Round," *Architectural Forum* 114, no. 6 (June 1961): 80–85; "Research Centre, Yorktown, N.Y.," *Architect and Building News* 221, no. 26 (27 June 1962): 923–926; and "Centre de recherches I.B.M. Yorktown Heights, États-Unis" *L'Architecture d'aujourd'hui* 33, no. 100 (February 1962): 48–53.

44. Betsy Brown, "Scientists Designing Machines for Space Age Housed in Giant New IBM Research Center," *Patent Trader* (Mount Kisco, N.Y.), 2 March 1961. The idea that the cool-to-warm colored spectrum was designed to mimic the seasonal color changes visible in the surrounding landscape outdoors was part of the folklore about the building that spread among its inhabitants (Phil Summers, site historian, IBM Thomas J. Watson Research Center, Yorktown Heights, N.Y., conversation with the author, 18 February 1998).

45. Some of the markings on the stones remain visible, but no copies of the site map to which the stones are indexed are now available (Summers, conversation with the author).

46. Thomas J. Watson Jr., in "Proceedings: Annual Meeting of Stockholders of the International Business Machines Corporation," at the Thomas J. Watson Research Center, Yorktown, New York, 25 April 1961, 4; recorded and transcribed by the Master Reporting Company, Inc., New York, IBM Archives, Somers, N.Y.

47. International Business Machines Corp., "IBM: The Thomas J. Watson Research Center," undated brochure, 5. A copy is available in the IBM Archives.

48. Ibid.

49. James B. Fisk, "The Bell Telephone Laboratories," in *The Organisation of Research Establishments,* ed. John Cockroft (Cambridge: Cambridge University Press, 1965), 210. Fisk goes on to list the research laboratories devoted to the physical sciences at Bell Laboratories: the Physical Research Laboratory, the Semiconducter Research laboratory, the Solid State Electronics Research Laboratory, the Metallurgical Laboratory, and the Chemical Laboratory (210–211). In an aside, he also mentions "a modest but interesting research activity on interpersonal and intra group relations which aims toward ways of improving human communication, learning, and effectiveness" (212). Fisk's text was written in 1962, the year the Holmdel facility opened.

50. Bell Telephone Laboratories, "Bell Telephone Laboratories at Holmdel," undated brochure, n.p.

51. Fisk, "The Bell Telephone Laboratories," 198.

52. A Bell Laboratories document, prepared in 1966 for a visit of Western Electric Company executives, details how Saarinen's building fulfilled the design criteria presented to him by his client at the outset (see above, n. 25). For example, the criterion of "minimum interruption of work" for building changes is addressed by the service spines: "All service work can be done in the nearly 5′ wide service cores without disturbing the occupants of a laboratory or office during change-overs or introduction of new equipment" ("Notes on the Holmdel Laboratory Building," 1966, 2, AT&T Archives).

53. Saarinen's stipulation—as presented in 1959 to Kinney Vacuum Coatings of Pennsauken, N.J., the manufacturers of the mirrored glass—is recorded by George L. Dienes, "Birth of a Design Trend," *Glass Digest,* July 1970; a copy is available in AT&T Archives. See also "Two Acres of Glass Enclose Lab," *Engineering News Record* 168, no. 6 (8 February 1962): 25; "Mirrored Block Takes Shape," *Engineering News Record* 174, no. 23 (10 June 1965): 27; and "Saarinen's Looking Glass Wall," *Progressive Architecture* 40 (January 1967): 38. The clear laminated glass is coated with an aluminum film. The manufacturer was not able to make enough to complete the cladding in the first phase, but eventually the entire building was mirror-glazed. The skin consists of 6,800 glass panes, each 3′ by 6′ 6″, in neoprene gaskets. The facade is 700 feet long and 70 feet high, around the six-story interior volume.

54. "The Telephone Company Dials the Moon," *Architectural Forum* 117 (October 1962): 95.

55. An example of such translation is given in International Business Machines Corp., "IBM: The Thomas J. Watson Research Center," 16–17.

Epilogue: Hallucinations

1. Norbert Wiener, *The Human Use of Human Beings: Cybernetics and Society,* 2nd ed. (Garden City, N.Y.: Doubleday, 1954), 21.

2. Warren Weaver uses the expression "freedom of choice" to describe the wider range of messages possible in a highly entropic context. The consumerist overtones of this expression also mark its simultaneous proximity to organizational imperatives, however, and thus its ethicopolitical liminality. See Weaver, "Recent Contributions to the Mathematical Theory of Communication," in Claude E. Shannon and Warren Weaver, *The Mathematical Theory of Communication* (Chicago: University of Illinois Press, 1949), 13. On the information content of messages, see Shannon, "The Mathematical Theory of Communication" (31–35). Shannon's essay was originally published in the *Bell System Technical Journal* (July and October 1948).

3. Max Horkheimer and Theodor W. Adorno, *Dialectic of Enlightenment,* trans. John Cumming (New York: Herder and Herder, 1972), 146.

4. All of the quotations of Cage, Kepes, and Lynch in this section are from "Urban Form Seminar 12/10/54," box 2, Gyorgy Kepes Papers, Archives of American Art, Washington, D.C.

5. See Reinhold Martin, "Organicism's Other," *Grey Room,* no. 4 (summer 2001): 34–51.

6. Robert Smithson, "Entropy and the New Monuments," *Artforum* 4, no. 10 (June 1966): 26.

7. Sigfried Giedion, "The Need for a New Monumentality," first published in *New Architecture and City Planning,* ed. Paul Zucker (New York: Philosophical Library, 1944), and José Luis Sert, Fernand Léger, and Giedion, "Nine Points on Monumentality," originally written as a position paper in 1943. The two texts are included in Giedion, *Architecture, You and Me: The Diary of a Development* (Cambridge, Mass.: Harvard University Press, 1958), 25–39, 48–51.

8. Smithson, "Entropy and the New Monuments," 27.

9. Ibid.

10. Robert Smithson, "The Monuments of Passaic," *Artforum* 6, no. 4 (December 1967): 51.

11. Smithson, "Entropy and the New Monuments," 29.

12. Mildred Hall and Edward Hall, *The Fourth Dimension in Architecture: The Impact of Building on Man's Behavior, Eero Saarinen's Administrative Center for Deere and Co., Moline, Illinois* (Santa Fe: Sunstone Press, 1975), 8.

13. W. Ross Ashby, *An Introduction to Cybernetics* (New York: John Wiley and Sons, 1956), 86.

14. Forrest Wilson, "Pavilion in an Industrial Xanadu," *Contract Interiors* 124, no. 6 (January 1965): 80.

15. See ibid., 85.

16. Eero Saarinen to Frank Stanton, 31 March 1961, excerpted in "Eero Saarinen on the CBS Building," Eero Saarinen Papers, group 593, Sterling Memorial Library (SML), Manuscripts and Archives, Yale University.

17. Columbia Broadcasting System, Inc., "CBS Skyscraper Plans Announced," press release, 18 February 1962, Eero Saarinen Papers, SML.

18. Mildred F. Schmertz, "Distinguished Interior Architecture for CBS," *Architectural Record* 139, no. 7 (June 1966): 129–134.

19. Peter Blake, "Slaughter on Sixth Avenue," *Architectural Forum,* 122, no. 3 (June 1965): 13–19.

20. Gilles Deleuze, *Cinema 2: The Time-Image,* trans. Hugh Tomlinson and Robert Galeta (Minneapolis: University of Minnesota Press, 1989), 205–206.

21. Ibid., 1–24.

22. Ibid., 207.

23. Ibid., 211–215.

24. John Baxter, *Stanley Kubrick: A Biography* (New York: Carroll and Graf, 1997), 222–223.

25. Douglas Trumbull is quoted in Gene Youngblood, *Expanded Cinema* (New York: E. P. Dutton, 1970), 151–153.

26. Friedrich A. Kittler, "Media and Drugs in Pynchon's Second World War," in his *Literature, Media, Information Systems,* ed. John Johnston (Amsterdam: G and B Arts, 1997), 106.

27. Ibid., 105.

28. Thomas Pynchon, *Gravity's Rainbow* (New York: Viking Press, 1973), 258; quoted in Kittler, "Media and Drugs in Pynchon's Second World War," 103.

29. Kittler, "Media and Drugs in Pynchon's Second World War," 106.

30. Pynchon, *Gravity's Rainbow,* 434.

31. Kittler, "Media and Drugs in Pynchon's Second World War," 108.

32. Ibid., 108; the quotations are from Pynchon's *Gravity's Rainbow,* 139.

33. Deleuze, *Cinema 2,* 216.

34. See Gilles Deleuze and Félix Guattari, *Kafka: Toward a Minor Literature,* trans. Dana Polan (Minneapolis: University of Minnesota Press, 1986).

35. Deleuze, *Cinema 2,* xi.

36. Ibid., 221.

37. Kittler, "Media and Drugs in Pynchon's Second World War," 105.

38. Friedrich A. Kittler, *Gramophone, Film, Typewriter,* trans. Geoffrey Winthrop-Young and Michael Wutz (Stanford: Stanford University Press, 1999), 2.

Time Inc. © 1950, reprinted by permission: figures 1.1, 1.2, 1.3, 1.4, 1.5

Reprinted by permission of *The Bulletin of the Atomic Scientists*, © 2002 by the Educational Foundation for Nuclear Science, Chicago, Illinois: figure 1.6

Courtesy Julie Kepes Stone: figures 1.10, 2.1, 2.7, 2.8, 2.9, 2.10, 2.14, 2.15, 2.16, 2.17, 2.18, 5.1, 5.2

Property of AT&T. Reprinted with permission of AT&T: figure 1.11

Hattula Moholy-Nagy: figures 2.2, 2.3, 2.4, 2.5, 2.6

© Harold and Esther Edgerton Foundation, 2003; courtesy of Palm Press, Inc.: figure 2.9

Cranbrook Archives: figure 3.2

© *Architectural Record*, a publication of the McGraw-Hill Companies, Inc.: figures 3.6, 3.7

Ezra Stoller © Esto: figures 3.8, 3.13, 3.14, 3.26, 3.27, 3.28, 3.29, 3.30, 4.14, 4.19, 4.20, 4.21, 4.22, 4.23, 4.24, 5.13, 7.2, 7.3

Library of Congress, Prints and Photographs Division, Gottscho-Schleisner Collection (LC-G613-T-56725): figure 3.9

© Skidmore, Owings and Merrill, LLP: figures 3.15, 3.25

Lucia Eames dba Eames Office: figures 3.19, 3.20

Photograph by Erich Locker: figure 3.24

© Balthazar Korab, Ltd.: figures 4.2, 5.4, 5.5, 5.7

Courtesy General Motors Corporation: figures 4.3, 4.4, 4.7, 4.8

Reprinted with the permission of Cambridge University Press: figure 4.5

From *Industrial Design* by Raymond Loewy. © 1979 by Raymond Loewy. Published by the Overlook Press, Peter Mayer Publishers, Inc., Woodstock, New York: figure 4.9

The Papers of Eero Saarinen, Manuscripts and Archives, Yale University Library: figures 4.10, 4.11, 4.12, 4.13, 4.18, 4.25, 5.6, 5.16, 5.17, 6.6, 6.10, 6.11, 6.13, 6.19, 7.5

Chicago Historical Society, Hedrich-Blessing Collection: figure 4.26

Courtesy IBM Archives: figures 5.3, 5.8, 5.9, 5.10, 5.12, 5.14, 5.15

© Yousuf Karsh: figure 5.8

IEEE Computer Society © 1983 IEEE: figures 6.1, 6.3, 6.4

Courtesy Estate of R. Buckminster Fuller: figure 6.2

© Cervin Robinson: figures 6.12, 6.22

Photograph by George Cserna: figures 6.16, 6.18, 6.19, 6.22

Photograph by Yukio Futagawa: figure 6.21

Photograph by J. Alex Langley: figure 7.4

Photograph by Scott Hyde: figure 7.6

© Turner Entertainment Co., an AOL Time Warner Company: figures 7.7, 7.8

Every reasonable attempt has been made to identify owners of copyright. Errors or omissions brought to the author's attention will be corrected in subsequent reprints.

Office buildings (general), 5, 6–7, 82, 114
Office of Naval Research (ONR), 185, 187
Office of Scientific Research and
  Development (OSRD), 185
Office of Strategic Services (U.S. War
  Department), 143
Office planning, 87, 90–91, 93–97, 254n15
  Chase Manhattan Bank, 116
  Inland Steel, 104–105
  RCA Building, 88–90, 93–94
  Union Carbide Building, 117, 120
Ogilvy, David, 148
Olivetti, Adriano, 166, 273n14
Olivetti Corporation, 166, 172, 273–274n14
  showroom, New York (BBPR), 166,
  273–274n14
Organic architecture, 84
Organic design, 58
Organicism, 4, 8–9
  aesthetic, 71
  and architecture, 82–84
  biological, 17, 19, 23, 52, 243n20
  and capitalism, 90, 115–116
  and entropy, 220–221
  and functionalism, 82–84, 92–93, 134–135
  Gropius and, 46
  and images, 139, 143, 155
  and marketing, 139, 143
  Mies and, 266n29
  military-industrial complex, 43, 155, 186
  Morris and, 53
  optical, 47–48, 59–61
  and organic form, 223, 244n25
  and organization, 8, 17–19, 51–52, 206, 214
  and real estate, 84
  Rockefeller Center and, 88
  and scientific knowledge, 186, 196, 206
  social, 18–19, 23, 92, 111
  and streamlined design, 132–135
  and time, 220–221
  and urbanism, 115–116, 135–138, 143, 227
Organism
  corporation as, 140, 168
  cybernetic notion of, 24
  family as, 111
Organization, 8–9, 10

and architecture, 8–9, 75, 78–79, 214–215
  of Bell Laboratories, 207
  biological models, 17–19, 27
  corporate, 103–104, 121, 140–141, 164–167
  and corporate image, 164–167, 181
  and curtain wall, 7
  cybernetics and, 21, 27
  and entropy, 213–214, 231
  feedback and, 21, 37
  of General Motors, 140–141, 263–264n17
  of IBM, 164–167, 206–207, 272–273n10
  and images, 9, 121, 155
  and language, 61–63
  managerial, 70
  versus mechanization, 70
  as message, 24, 62–63, 79, 213
  modular, 151, 152–153
  and moralism, 221
  and organicism, 8, 17–19, 51–52, 206, 214
  and pattern, 24–25, 37, 40, 59
  of scientific research, 184–186, 187,
  206–207
  self-, 7
  social, 23–24, 27, 35–36, 65, 92–93, 121
  and subjectivity, 214
  visual, 59–61, 64–65, 152–153, 155
Organizational complex, 3–4, 15, 40, 45, 62,
  183, 214, 215–216
  and architecture, 206
  and corporate image, 211
  and disciplinarity, 206–207
  and entropy, 221
  Kepes and, 67
  and media, 216, 231
  and modularity, 5
  and organic integration, 206
  and paranoia, 230
  and space, 197
Organizational cybernetics, 264n17
Organization man, 5, 12, 121, 168, 195–196,
  202, 211, 223, 229, 261n74, 262n78
Owings, Nathaniel, 114–115

Paepcke, Elizabeth, 58
Paepcke, Walter, 58, 63, 247nn42–43
Panofsky, Erwin, 66

Stored program computer, 175, 178, 278n55

Streamlined design, 58, 129–131, 142, 264n20, 265n23

Styling. *See* Automobile styling

Subjectivity
and cold war, 70
and communication, 174
and computing, 159
construction of, 4–5, 7, 9–10
consumer, 4–5, 155
corporate, 160, 167–169, 178, 202, 214
cybernetics and, 26, 214
and environment, 223
and pattern, 10, 12
posthuman, 12, 229
postindustrial, 12
scientific, 195–197, 202
and Turing test, 172–173

Sullivan, Louis, 66, 82, 85, 87, 92, 103, 111, 223, 253n7

Sundberg-Ferar, 170, 275n34

Swanson, Robert, 142

Sypher, Wylie, 220

System, social, 92

Systems theory, 92, 239n54, 243–244n21

Tafuri, Manfredo, 85, 87, 115, 143, 233n9, 252n86

Taut, Bruno, 46

Taylor, Frederick Winslow, 92

Teague, Walter Dorwin, 129, 271n71

Team X, 10

Television, 6–7

Temko, Allan, 269n57

Teyssot, Georges, 274n14, 279n3

Theoretical Biology Club, 52, 71, 243n20

Thompson, D'Arcy Wentworth, 57, 131, 155, 265n25
On Growth and Form, 66, 71, 130, *131*, 265n23

Time, 237n38, 269n57

Topology, 191, 195, 197–199, 208, 227–229

Total war, 185

Touraine, Alain, 234n3

Trans-World Airlines (TWA) terminal (Eero Saarinen), 223, 271n71

Truman, Harry S., 185

Trumbull, Douglas, 229–230

Turing, Alan, 172–173, 181, 278n56

Turing test, 172–174, 223

2001: A Space Odyssey, 7, 227–230, *227*, *229*

Union Carbide Building, New York (SOM), 102, 117–120, *117–119*, 121, 214, 219, 220

Union Carbide Corporation, 102, 117

United Nations Secretariat, New York (Harrison et al.), 95, *96–97*, 102

United States Air Force, 184

United States Air Force Academy, Colorado Springs, Colo. (SOM), *154*, 155, 184, 271n71

United States Gypsum Corporation, 111, *113*

United States Steel Corporation, 103

Unity of Science movement, 52–53, 245n28

Universal Automatic Computer (UNIVAC), 174

University of Chicago, 52, 55, 192, 245n28

University of Pennsylvania, 276nn45–46

U.S. Rubber Building, New York (Harrison & Abramowitz), 257n34

Van der Vlugt and Brinkman, 257n31

Van Nelle factory (Van der Vlugt and Brinkman), 49, *50*, 257n31

Vidler, Anthony, 199, 282n39

Viollet-le-Duc, Eugène-Emmanuel, 266n29

Vision
automobile and, 139
and evolution, 47, 54, 57
and hallucination, 230
and motion, 59
and organization, 59, 64–65
retraining of, 47, 242n10

Von Neumann, John, 38, 175, 276nn45–46

Von Neumann architecture, 175, 277n46

Voorhees, Walker, Foley & Smith, 193, 279n1

Waddington, Conrad, 51–52, 71, 244n24

Wainwright Building (Sullivan), 85

War Department, 185